Assessing
the Quality
of Survey Data

Research Methods for Social Scientists_____

This new series, edited by four leading members of the International Sociological Association (ISA) research committee RC33 on Logic and Methodology, aims to provide students and researchers with the tools they need to do rigorous research. The series, like RC33, is interdisciplinary and has been designed to meet the needs of students and researchers across the social sciences. The series will include books for qualitative, quantitative and mixed methods researchers written by leading methodologists from around the world.

Editors: Simona Balbi (University of Naples, Italy), Jörg Blasius (University of Bonn, Germany), Anne Ryen (University of Agder, Norway), Cor van Dijkum (University of Utrecht, The Netherlands).

Forthcoming Title

Web Survey Methodology
Katja Lozar Manfreda, Mario Callegaro, Vasja Vehhovar

Assessing
the Quality
of Survey Data

JÖRG BLASIUS & VICTOR THIESSEN

Los Angeles | London | New Delhi
Singapore | Washington DC

SAGE Publications Ltd
1 Oliver's Yard
55 City Road
London EC1Y 1SP

SAGE Publications Inc.
2455 Teller Road
Thousand Oaks, California 91320

SAGE Publications India Pvt Ltd
B 1/I 1 Mohan Cooperative Industrial Area
Mathura Road
New Delhi 110 044

SAGE Publications Asia-Pacific Pte Ltd
3 Church Street
#10-04 Samsung Hub
Singapore 049483

Library of Congress Control Number: 2011932180

British Library Cataloguing in Publication data

A catalogue record for this book is available from the British Library

ISBN 978-1-84920-331-9
ISBN 978-1-84920-332-6

Typeset by C&M Digitals (P) Ltd, India, Chennai
Printed and bound by CPI Group (UK) Ltd, Croydon, CR0 4YY
Printed on paper from sustainable resources

CONTENTS

ABOUT THE AUTHORS

Jörg Blasius is a Professor of Sociology at the Institute for Political Science and Sociology, University of Bonn, Germany. His research interests are mainly in explorative data analysis, especially correspondence analysis and related methods, data collection methods, sociology of lifestyles and urban sociology. From 2006 to 2010, he was the president of RC33 (research committee of logic and methodology in sociology) at ISA (International Sociological Association). Together with Michael Greenacre he edited three books on Correspondence Analysis, both are the founders of CARME (Correspondence Analysis and Related MEthods Network). He wrote several articles for international journals, together with Simona Balbi (Naples), Anne Ryen (Kristiansand) and Cor van Dijkum (Utrecht) he is editor of the Sage Series Research Methods for Social Scientists.

Victor Thiessen is Professor Emeritus and Academic Director of the Atlantic Research Data Centre, a facility for accessing and analysing confidential Statistics Canada census and survey data. He received his PhD in Sociology from the University of Wisconsin (Madison) and is currently Professor Emeritus at Dalhousie University in Halifax, Canada. Thiessen has a broad range of skills in complex quantitative analyses, having published a book, *Arguing with Numbers*, as well as articles in methodological journals. He has studied youth transitions and their relationships to school, family, and labour market preparation for most of his professional life. In his research he has conducted analyses of a number of longitudinal surveys of youth, some of which involved primary data gathering and extensive analyses of existing Statistics Canada and international survey data sets.

LIST OF ACRONYMS AND SOURCES OF DATA

AAPOR   American Association of Public Opinion Research

ARS   Acquiescent response style

CatPCA   Categorical principal component analysis

CFA   Confirmatory factor analysis

CNES   Canadian National Election Study; for documentation and the 1984 data, see http://www.icpsr.umich.edu/icpsrweb/ICPSR/studies/8544?q=Canadian+National+Election+Study

DK   Don't know

ERS   Extreme response style

ESS   European Social Survey; for documentation and various data sets see http://www.europeansocialsurvey.org/

FA   Factor analysis

IRD   Index of response differentiation

ISSP   International Social Survey Program; for documentation and various data sets see http://www.issp.org

LRD   Limited response differentiation

MCA   Multiple correspondence analysis

MPR   Mid-point responding

MVS   Material Values Scale

NN   Neither agree nor disagree

NO   No opinion

NSR   Non-substantive responses

PCA   Principal component analysis

PISA   Programme for International Student Assessment; for documentation and various data sets see: http://pisa2000.acer.edu.au/downloads.php

SEM   Structural equation modelling

SMCA   Subset multiple correspondence analysis

WVS   World Value Survey; for documentation and the 2005–2008 data see: http://www.worldvaluessurvey.org/

PREFACE

Calculating a reliability coefficient is simple; assessing the quality and comparability of data is a Herculean task. It is well known that survey data are plagued with non-substantive variation arising from myriad sources such as response styles, socially desirable responses, failure to understand questions, and even fabricated interviews. For these reasons all data contain both substantive and non-substantive variation. Modifying Box's (1987) quote that 'all models are wrong, but some are useful', we suggest that 'all data are dirty, but some are informative'. But what are 'dirty' or 'poor' data?

Our guiding rule is that the lower the amount of substantive variation, the poorer is the quality of the data. We exemplify various strategies for assessing the quality of the data – that is, for detecting non-substantive sources of variation. This book focuses on screening procedures that should be conducted prior to assessing substantive relationships. Screening survey data means searching for variation in observed responses that do not correspond with actual differences between respondents. It also means the reverse: isolating identical response patterns that are not due to respondents holding identical viewpoints. This is especially problematic in cross-national research in which a response such as 'strongly agree' may represent different levels of agreement in various countries.

The stimulus for this book was our increasing awareness that poor data are not limited to poorly designed and suspect studies; we discovered that poor data also characterize well-known data sets that form the empirical bases for a large number of publications in leading international journals. This convinced us that it is essential to screen all survey data prior to attempting any substantive analysis, whether it is in the social or political sciences, marketing, psychology, or medicine. In contrast to numerous important books that deal with recommendations on how to avoid poor data (e.g., how to train interviewers, how to draw an appropriate sample, or how to formulate good questions), we start with assessing data that have already been collected (or are in the process of being collected; faked interviews, for example, can be identified using our screening technique shortly after interviewers have submitted their first set of interviews to the research institute).

In this book we will demonstrate a variety of data screening processes that reveal distinctly different sources of poor data quality. In our analyses we will provide examples of how to detect non-substantive variation that is produced by:

- response styles such as acquiescence, extreme response styles, and mid-point responding;
- misunderstanding of questions due to poor item construction;
- heterogeneous understanding of questions arising from cultural differences;
- different field work standards in cross-national surveys;
- inadequate institutional standards;
- missing data (item non-response);
- respondent fatigue;
- faked and partly faked interviews.

The aim of this book is to give the reader a deeper understanding of survey data, and our findings should caution researchers against applying sophisticated statistical methods before screening the data. If the quality of the data is not sufficient for substantive analysis, then it is meaningless to use them to model the phenomenon of interest. While establishing the extent to which non-substantive variation damages particular substantive conclusions is crucially important, it is beyond the scope of this book; instead, we search for manifestations of 'dirty data'. For example, we found faked interviews for some countries in the well-known World Values Survey. The impact of these fakes on substantive solutions might be negligible since fabricated interviews tend to be more consistent than real interviews. Using traditional measures for the quality of data such as the reliability coefficient or the number of missing responses would be highly misleading, since they would suggest that such data are of a 'better quality'.

Examining the empirical literature on data quality revealed that many analyses relied on data sets that were not publicly available and whose study design features were not well documented. Some were based on small samples, low response rates, or captive non-representative samples. Additionally, insufficient information was given to permit one to assess the given findings and possible alternative interpretations. In contrast to these papers, we based our analyses on well-known and publicly available data sets such as the World Value Survey, the International Social Survey Program, and the Programme for International Student Assessment. However, the techniques described in this book can easily be applied to any survey data at any point in time. The advantage of the data sets we use is that they are publically available via the internet, and our computations can easily be proofed and replicated. Most of them are performed in SPSS and in R (using the ca module – see Greenacre and Nenadić, 2006; Nenadić and Greenacre, 2007). We give the syntax of all relevant computations on the web page of this book: www.sage.com.uk/blasius. In the one instance in which we use our own data, we provide them on the same web page.

Having spent countless hours on the computer searching for illuminating examples, and having presented parts of this book at international conferences, we are happy to provide the reader with a set of screening techniques which we hope they will find useful in judging the quality of their data. We discussed our approach and analyses with many colleagues and friends and would like to thank them for their contributions. Among them are Margaret Dechman, Ralf

Dorau, Yasemin El Menouar, Jürgen Friedrichs, Simon Gabriel, Michael Greenacre, Patrick Groenen, Gesine Güllner, Heather Hobson, Tor Korneliussen, Dianne Looker, Andreas Mühlichen, Howard Ramos, Maria Rohlinger, Tobias Schmies, Miriam Schütte and Yoko Yoshida. Special thanks are due to Michael Greenacre, who read parts of the book and discussed with us on several occasions our measures of data quality, and to Jürgen Friedrichs, who agreed to let us use unpublished data that he collected with Jörg Blasius. We further thank the participants of the 2011 Cologne Spring Seminar where we presented parts of our book in the context of scaling techniques and data quality. We also thank Patrick Brindle and Katie Metzler, from Sage, for their help and understanding while writing this book. Finally, we thank our patient partners Barbara Cottrell and Beate Blasius for giving us the freedom to travel across continents and for graciously smiling when the dinner conversation turned to such dear topics as 'Just what do respondents mean when they say "I don't know"?'.

Bonn and Halifax
April 2011

1

Conceptualizing data quality: Respondent attributes, study architecture and institutional practices

Assessing the quality of data is a major endeavour in empirical social research. From our perspective, data quality is characterized by an absence of artefactual variation in observed measures. Screening survey data means searching for variation in observed responses that do not correspond with actual differences between respondents. We agree with Holbrook, Cho and Johnson (2006: 569) who argue that screening techniques are essential because survey researchers are 'far from being able to predict a priori when and for whom' comprehension or response mapping difficulties will occur; and these are only two of many sources of poor data quality.

We think of data quality as an umbrella concept that covers three main sources affecting the trustworthiness of any survey data: the study architecture, the institutional practices of the data collection agencies, and the respondent behaviours. Study architecture concerns elements in the survey design, such as the mode of data collection (e.g., computer-assisted telephone interviews, mailed questionnaires, internet surveys), the number of questions and the order in which they are asked, the number and format of the response options, and the complexity of the language employed. Institutional practices cover sources of error that are due to the research organization, such as the adequacy of inter-viewer training, appropriateness of the sampling design, and data entry moni-toring procedures. Data quality is obviously also affected by respondent attributes, such as their verbal skills or their ability to retrieve the information requested. While we discuss these three sources of data quality separately, in practice they interact with each other in myriad ways. Thus, self-presentation issues on the part of the respondent, for example, play a larger role in face-to-face interviews than in internet surveys.

While quality of data is a ubiquitous research concern, we focus on assessing survey data quality. Our concern is with all aspects of data quality that jeopardize the validity of comparative statistics. Group comparisons are compromised when the quality of data differs for the groups being compared or when the survey questions have different meanings for the groups being compared. If females are more meticulous than males in their survey responses, then gender differences that may emerge in subsequent analyses are suspect. If university-educated respondents can cope with double negative sentences better than those with less education, then educational differences on the distribution of such items are substantively ambiguous. In short, it is the *inequality* of data quality that matters most, since the logic of survey analysis is inherently comparative. If the quality of the data differs between the groups being compared, then the comparison is compromised.

We further restrict our attention to the underlying structure of responses to a set of statements on a particular topic or domain. This topic can be a concrete object such as the self, contentious issues such as national pride or regional identity, or nebulous concepts such as democracy. Respondents are typically asked to indicate the extent of their acceptance or rejection of each of the statements. Their responses are expected to mirror their viewpoints (or cognitive maps as they will be called here) on that topic or issue. Excluded from consideration in this book is the quality of socio-demographic and other factual information such as a person's age, income, education, or employment status.

In this chapter we first discuss the three sources of data quality, namely those attributable to the respondent, those arising from the study architecture, and those that emerge from inadequate quality control procedures of data collection agencies, including unethical practices. This is followed by a description of the nature and logic of our screening approach, which is anchored in scaling methods, especially multiple correspondence analysis and categorical principal component analysis. We conclude with a sketch of the key content of each of the subsequent chapters.

Conceptualizing response quality_____

1.1 We refer to sources of data quality that are due to respondents' characteristics, such as their response styles and impression management skills, as response quality. Response quality is embedded in the dynamics common to all human interactions as well as the specific ones that arise out of the peculiar features of survey protocol. Common features, as recognized by the medical field, for example, emerge from the fact that a survey 'is a social phenomenon that involves elaborate cognitive work by respondents' and 'is governed by social rules and norms' (McHorney and Fleishman, 2006: S206).

The act of obtaining survey data imposes a particular stylized form of human interaction, which gives rise to its specific dynamics. The parameters that govern the survey form of interaction are as follows:

- The contact and subsequent interaction is initiated by the interviewer, typically without the express desire of the respondent.
- It occurs between strangers, with one of the members not even physically present when the survey is conducted via mail, telephone, or the web.
- The interaction is a singular event with no anticipation of continuity, except in longitudinal and/or other panel surveys where the interaction is limited to a finite series of discrete events.
- Interactional reciprocity is violated; specifically, the interviewers are expected to ask questions while the respondents are expected to provide answers.
- The researcher selects the complexity level of the language and its grammatical style, which typically is a formal one.
- The response vocabulary through which the respondents must provide their responses is extremely sparse.

In short, surveys typically consist of short pulses of verbal interaction conducted between strangers on a topic of unknown relevance or interest to the respondent, often in an alien vocabulary and with control of the structure of the interaction vested in the researcher. What the respondent gets out of this unequal exchange is assurances of making a contribution to our knowledge base and a promise of confidentiality and anonymity, which may or may not be believed. Is it any wonder, then, that one meta-analysis of survey data estimated that over half the variance in social science measures is due to a combination of random (32%) and systematic (26%) measurement error, with even more error for abstract concepts such as attitudes (Cote and Buckley, 1987: 316)? Clearly, these stylistic survey features are consequential for response quality. Such disheartening findings nevertheless form the underpinnings and the rationale for this book, since data quality cannot be taken for granted and therefore we need tools by which it can be assessed.

Given the features of a survey described above, it is wisest to assume that responses will be of suboptimal quality. Simon (1957) introduced the term 'satisficing' to situations where humans do not strive to optimize outcomes. Krosnick (1991, 1999) recognized that the survey setting typically induces satisficing. His application is based on Tourangeau and his associates' (Tourangeau and Rasinski, 1988; Tourangeau, Rips and Rasinski, 2000) four-step cognitive process model for producing high-quality information: the respondent must (1) understand the question, (2) retrieve the relevant information, (3) synthesize the retrieved information into a summary judgement, and (4) choose a response option that most closely corresponds with the summary judgement. Satisficing can take place at any of these stages and simply means a less careful or thorough discharge of these tasks. Satisficing manifests itself in a variety of ways, such as choosing the first reasonable response offered, or employing only a subset of the response options provided. What all forms of satisficing have in common is that shortcuts are taken that permit the task to be discharged more quickly while still fulfilling the obligation to complete the task.

The task of responding to survey questions shares features with those of other literacy tasks that people face in their daily lives. The most important feature is that responding to survey items may be cognitively challenging for some respondents. In particular, responding to lengthy items and those containing a negation may prove to be too demanding for many respondents – issues that Edwards (1957) noted more than half a century ago. Our guiding assumption is that the task of answering survey questions will be discharged quite differently among those who find this task daunting compared to those who find it to be relatively easy.

Faced with a difficult task, people often use one of three response strategies: (1) decline the task, (2) simplify the task, and (3) discharge the task, however poorly. All three strategies compromise the response quality. The first strategy, declining the task, manifests itself directly in outright refusal to participate in the study (unit non-response) or failing to respond to particular items by giving non-substantive responses such as 'don't know' or 'no opinion' (item non-response). Respondents who simplify the task frequently do this by favouring a subset of the available response options, such as the end-points of Likert-type response options, resulting in what is known as 'extreme response style'. Finally, those who accept the demanding task may just muddle their way through the survey questions, perhaps by agreeing with survey items regardless of the content, a pattern that is known as an acquiescent response tendency. Such respondents are also more likely to be susceptible to trivial aspects of the survey architecture, such as the order in which response options are presented. We concur with Krosnick (1991) that response quality depends on the difficulty of the task, the respondent's cognitive skill, and their motivation to participate in the survey. The elements of each of these are presented next.

Task difficulty, cognitive skills, and topic salience

The rigid structure of the interview protocol, in conjunction with the often alien vocabulary and restrictive response options, transforms the survey interaction into a task that can be cognitively challenging. Our guiding assumption is that the greater the task difficulty for a given respondent, the lower will be the quality of the responses given. Task characteristics that increase its difficulty are:

- numerous, polysyllabic, and/or infrequently used words;
- negative constructions (especially when containing the word 'not');
- retrospective questions;
- double-barrelled formulations (containing two referents but permitting only a single response);
- abstract referents.

Despite being well-known elements of task difficulty, it is surprising how often they are violated – even in well-known surveys such as the International Social Survey Program and the World Values Survey.

Attributes of the response options, such as their number and whether they are labelled, also contribute to task difficulty. Response options that are labelled can act to simplify the choices. Likewise, response burden increases with the number of response options. While minimizing the number of response options may simplify the task of answering a given question, it also diminishes the amount of the information obtained, compromising the quality of the data again. Formats that provide an odd number of response options are generally considered superior to even-numbered ones. This may be because an odd number of response options, such as a five- or 11-point scale, provides a mid-point that acts as a simplifying anchor for some respondents.

Whether the survey task is difficult is also a matter of task familiarity. The format of survey questions is similar to that of multiple choice questions on tests and to application forms for a variety of services. Respondents in non-manual occupations (and those with higher educational qualifications) are more exposed to such forms than their counterparts in manual occupations (and/or with less formal education). Public opinion surveys are also more common in economically developed countries, and so the response quality is likely to be higher in these countries than in developing countries.

Van de Vijver and Poortinga (1997: 33) point out that 'almost without exception the effects of bias will systematically favor the cultural group from where the instrument originates'. From this we formulate the cultural distance bias hypothesis: the greater the cultural distance between the origin of a survey instrument and the groups being investigated, the more compromised the data quality and comparability is likely to be. One source of such bias is the increased mismatch between the respondent's and researcher's 'grammar' (Holbrook, Cho and Johnson, 2006: 569). Task difficulty provides another possible rationale for the cultural distance bias hypothesis, namely that the greater the cultural distance, the more difficult is the task of responding to surveys. The solution for such respondents is to simplify the task, perhaps in ways incongruent with the researcher's assumptions.

Whether a task is difficult depends not only on the attributes of the task but also on the cognitive competencies and knowledge of the respondent, to which we turn next. Cognitive skills are closely tied to education (Ceci, 1991). For example, the research of Smith et al. (2003) suggests that elementary school children do not have the cognitive sophistication to handle either a zero-to-ten or a thermometer response format – formats that generally have solid measurement properties among adults (Alwin, 1997). Likewise, understanding that disagreement with a negative assertion is equivalent to agreement with a positively formulated one remains problematic even for some high school students (Marsh, 1986; Thiessen, 2010).

Finally, we assume that respondents pay greater heed to tasks on topics that interest them. Generally these are also the ones on which they possess more information and consequently also the issues for which providing a valid response is easier. Our approach to response quality shares certain features with that of Krosnick's (1991, 1999) satisficing theory, which emphasizes the cognitive demands required to provide high-quality responses. For Krosnick, the probability of taking shortcuts in any of the four cognitive steps discussed previously decreases with cognitive ability and motivation, but increases with task difficulty. We agree that response optimizing is least prevalent among those with least interest or motivation to participate in a survey.

Normative demands and impression management

Surveys share additional features with other forms of verbal communication. First, the form of survey interaction is prototypically dyadic: an interviewer/ researcher and a respondent in real or virtual interaction with each other. In all dyadic interactions, the members hold at least three images of each other that can profoundly affect the content of the viewpoints the respondent expresses: the image of oneself, the image of the other, and the image one would like the other to have of oneself. It is especially the latter image that can jeopardize data quality. Skilful interactions require one to be cognizant not only about oneself and the other, but also about how one appears to the other. Hence, the responses given are best conceived of as an amalgam of what respondents believe to be true, what they believe to be acceptable to the researcher or interviewer, and what respondents believe will make a good impression of themselves. Such impression management dynamics are conceptualized in the methodological literature as social desirability.

Second, we ordinarily present ourselves as being more consistent than we actually are. This is exemplified by comparing the determinants of actual voting in elections with those of reported voting. Typically the associations between various civic attitudes and self-reported voting behaviour are stronger than with actual (validated) voting behaviour (Silver, Anderson and Abramson, 1986). That is, our reported behaviours are more consistent with our beliefs than are our actual behaviours. If respondents initially report that they intended to vote, then they subsequently will be more likely to report that they voted even when they did not. Likewise, respondents who report that it is one's civic duty to vote are more likely to report that they voted when they did not compared to those who did not think it was one's civic duty.

Third, the normative structure places demands on the participants, the salience and extent of which depend on one's social location in society. The social location of some respondents may place particular pressure on them to vote, or not to smoke, for example. These demand characteristics result in tendencies to provide responses that are incongruent with the positions actually held. The existing methodological literature also treats these pressures primarily under the rubric of social desirability, but we prefer the broader term of 'impression management'. Van de Vijver and Poortinga (1997: 34) remind us that '[n]orms about appropriate conduct differ across cultural groups and the social desirability expressed in assessment will vary accordingly'.

It is precisely the existence of normative demands that required modifications to classical measurement theory. This theory provided a rather simple measurement model, whereby any individual's observed score (y_i) is decomposed into two parts: true (τ_i) and error (ε_i); that is, $y_i = \tau_i + \varepsilon_i$. While this formulation is enticingly simple, the problem emerges with the usual assumptions made when applied to a distribution. If one assumes that the error is uncorrelated with the true score, then the observed (total) variance can be decomposed into true and error variance: $\mathrm{Var}_y = \mathrm{Var}_\tau + \mathrm{Var}_\varepsilon$.

This decomposition is at the heart of reliability coefficients, which express reliability as the ratio of the true variance to the total variance. Of course, frequently the uncorrelated error assumption is untenable. One example should suffice: virtually all voting measurement error consists of over-reporting (Bernstein, Chadha and Montjoy, 2001; Silver, Anderson and Abramson, 1986). That is, if a person voted, then there is virtually no error, but if a person did not vote, then there is a high likelihood of (systematic) measurement error. The reason for this is that voting is not normatively neutral. Simply stated, the stronger the normative pressure, the greater is the systematic measurement error. Since societal norms surround most of the issues that typically form the content of survey questionnaires, it follows that the assumption of random measurement error is seldom justified.

Normative pressures are unequally socially distributed, having greater force for some. Returning to the voting example, Bernstein, Chadha and Montjoy (2001) argue that the normative pressure to vote is greater for the more educated and politically engaged. For this reason, these respondents are more likely to claim to have voted when they did not than their counterparts, casting considerable doubt on the estimated strengths of the relationships between education and political interest on the one hand, and voting on the other. Likewise, younger children are under greater pressure not to smoke than older ones. Hence, younger children who smoke are more likely to deny smoking than older ones (Griesler et al., 2008).

Normative demands are not the only source of systematic bias. Podsakoff et al. (2003) summarize 20 potential sources just of systematic bias. While not all the biases they list are relevant to all survey research, their literature review sensitizes us to the complex array of factors that can result in systematic biases. The authors conclude that 'methods biases are likely to be particularly powerful in studies in which the data for both the predictor and criterion variable are obtained from the same person in the same measurement context using the same item context and similar item characteristics' (Podsakoff et al., 2003: 885). That, unfortunately, describes the typical survey.

Campbell and Fiske's (1959) documentation of high proportions of common method variance led to a revision of classical measurement theory to incorporate the likelihood of reliable but invalid method variance. In structural equation modelling language (Alwin, 1997), an observed score can be decomposed into three unobserved components: $y_{ij} = \lambda_i \tau_i + \lambda_j \eta_j + \varepsilon_{ij}$, where y_{ij} measures the ith trait by the jth method, τ_i is the ith trait, and η_j the jth method factor. The λ_i can be considered the validity coefficients, the λ_j as the invalidity coefficients, and ε_{ij} is the random error. This formulation makes explicit that some of the reliable variance is actually invalid, that is, induced by the method of obtaining the information.

Systematic error is crucially important since it provides an omnipresent alternative explanation to any substantive interpretation of a documented relationship. When a substantive and an artefactual interpretation collide, by the principle of parsimony (Occam's razor) the artefactual one must win, since it is the simpler one. As a direct consequence of this, solid research should first assess whether any of the findings are artefactual. A variety of individual response tendencies, defined collectively as the tendency to disproportionately favour certain responses, has been the subject of much methodological research, since they could be a major source of artefactual findings. Response tendencies emerge out of the response options that are provided, which is part of the questionnaire architecture, to which we turn next.

Study architecture

1.2 Data quality is compromised when the responses selected are not in agreement with the cognitions held. One reason for such disparities has to do with the response options provided. Most frequently, the respondent's task in a survey is to select one response from a set of response options. The set of response options is collectively referred to as the response format. These formats range from simple yes–no choices to 0–100 thermometer analogues and, more recently, visual analogue scales in web surveys (Reips and Funke, 2008). One of the most popular response formats is some variant of the Likert scale, where response options typically vary from 'strongly agree' at one end to 'strongly disagree' at the other. Some response formats explicitly provide for a non-substantive response, such as 'don't know', 'no opinion' or 'uncertain'.

Data comparability is compromised whenever respondents with identical viewpoints employ different response options to express them. The survey literature makes two conclusions about response options abundantly clear. The first is that some responses are more popular than others. For example, a response of 'true' is more likely to be selected than a response of 'false' (Cronbach, 1950). Likewise, in the thermometer response format, responses divisible by 10 are far more favoured than other responses (Kroh, 2007). Second, respondents themselves differ in the response options they favour. Some respondents eschew extreme responses; others favour non-substantive responses such as 'don't know'.

Response tendencies represent reproducible or systematic variation that remains after the variation due to item content has been removed. For example, Oskamp (1977: 37) defines response sets as 'systematic ways of answering which are not directly related to the question content, but which represent typical behavioural characteristics of the respondents'. Generally, response style produces systematic measurement error rather than random measurement error. Being partial to certain response options has spawned a huge literature under the rubric of response styles and response sets. Four of them are considered to be particularly consequential. These are:

Acquiescence response style (ARS) is the tendency to provide a positive response, such as *yes* or *agree*, to any statement, regardless of its content. ARS is premised on the observation that endorsing survey items is more common than rejecting them. That is, responses of 'yes', 'true', and various shades of 'agree' are more common than their counterparts of 'no', 'false', and levels of 'disagree'. Although its logical opposite, the tendency to disagree, has also been identified as a possible response style, it has received little empirical attention. One reason is that disagreement is less common than agreement. A further reason is that empirically these two response tendencies are so strongly inversely related that it has not been fruitful to differentiate between them (Baumgartner and Steenkamp, 2001). Finally, as will be detailed in the next chapter, the theoretical underpinnings for ARS are more solid than for its opposite.

It is easiest to differentiate ARS from genuine substantive agreement when an issue is paired with its semantic opposite. Respondents who agree with a statement and its semantic opposite present themselves as logically inconsistent and this inconsistency is generally attributed to either ARS or a failure to pay attention to the content of the question – that is, to a failure to optimize. This is the only response tendency that can materialize with dichotomous response options.

Extreme response style (ERS) refers to the tendency to choose the most extreme response options available (such as 'strongly agree' and 'strongly disagree'). This response tendency can manifest itself only on response formats that have at least four available response options that distinguish intensity of viewpoints. Examples could be the choice of 'always' and 'never' in frequency assessments, or 'strongly agree' and 'strongly disagree' in Likert formats.

Mid-point responding (MPR) consists of selecting a neutral response such as 'neither agree nor disagree' or 'uncertain'. Not much research has been conducted on this response tendency, compared to ARS and ERS. Theoretically, its importance is related to the fact that it is a safe response, requiring little justification. It shares this aspect with non-substantive responses such as 'don't know' and 'no opinion' without the disadvantages of having to admit lack of knowledge or appearing uncooperative. Sometimes the use of the neutral response constitutes a 'safe' form of impression management whereby one can seem to offer an opinion when one fails to have one (Blasius and Thiessen, 2001b; Thiessen and Blasius, 1998).

Limited response differentiation (LRD) arises when respondents tend to select a narrower range of responses out of those provided to them. Typically it is measured by the individual's standard deviation across a battery of items. LRD differs from the other response tendencies in that it is less specific, that is, it does not focus attention on a specific response, but rather on a more global lack of discrimination in responses across items. Like the other response tendencies, it can be viewed as a respondent's strategy to simplify the task at hand.

Other response styles have been identified, such as random or arbitrary response style (Baumgartner and Steenkamp, 2001; Watkins and Cheung, 1995). To the extent that they are actually response styles, what they have in common is either an effort to simplify the task or impression management.

Institutional quality control practices

1.3 Collecting quality survey data requires inordinate financial, technical, and human resources. For this reason such data gathering is usually conducted by public and private institutions specializing in the implementation of survey designs. All of the publicly available data sets we analyse in subsequent chapters were commonly designed by groups of experts but contracted out for implementation to different national data collection organizations. Hence, national variation in the quality of the data is to be expected.

However, data collection agencies operate under financial constraints: private agencies must make a profit to survive and public agencies must operate within their given budgets. This means that a tension between quality and cost arises in all aspects of the production of survey data. This tension leads us to postulate that the satisficing principle applies to data collection agencies and interviewers as much as it does to individual respondents. That is, organizations may collect 'good enough' data rather than data of optimal quality. But what is good enough? To give an example from face-to-face interviews, several methods can be used to draw a sample. The best – and most expensive – is to draw a random sample from a list provided by the statistical office of a country (city) that contains the names and addresses of all people in the relevant population. The survey organization then sends an official letter to the randomly selected target persons to explain the purpose of the survey and its importance, and to allay fears the respondents may have about the legitimacy of the survey. Interviewers are subsequently given the addresses and required to conduct the interviews specifically with the target persons. If the target person is unavailable at that time, they are not permitted to substitute another member of that household (or a neighbouring one). A much worse data collection method – but a relatively cheap one – is known as the random route: interviewers must first select a household according to a fixed rule, for example, every fifth household. Then they must select a target person from the previously selected household, such as the person whose birthday was most recent. In this design, refusals are likely to be high, since there was no prior contact explaining the study's purpose, importance, or legitimacy. Further, the random route method is difficult (and therefore costly) for the survey institute to monitor: which is the fifth household, and whose birthday really was the most recent? If the interviewer made a counting error, but the interview is well done, there is no strong reason to exclude the interview.

As Fowler (2002) notes, evidence shows that when interviews are not tape-recorded, interviewers are less likely to follow the prescribed protocol, and actually tend to become less careful over time. But since monitoring is expensive rather than productive, it ultimately becomes more important to the institute that an interview was successfully completed than that it was completed by the right respondent or with the correct protocol.

Data screening methodology

1.4 The screening methods we favour, namely multiple correspondence analysis (MCA) and categorical principal component analysis (CatPCA), are part of a family of techniques known as scaling methods that are described in Chapter 3. However, our use of these scaling techniques is decidedly not for the purpose of developing scales. Rather, it is to visualize the response structure within what we call the respondents' cognitive maps of the items in the domain of interest. Typically, these visualizations are represented in a two-dimensional space (or a series of two-dimensional representations of higher-order dimensions). Each distinct response to every item included in the analysis is represented geometrically in these maps. As will be illustrated in our substantive analyses, the location of each response category relative to that of all other response categories from all items provides a rich set of clues about the quality of the data being analysed.

MCA and CatPCA make relatively few assumptions, compared to principal component analysis (PCA) and structural equation modelling (SEM). They do not assume that the data is metric, and MCA does not even assume that the responses are ordinal. Additionally, there is no need to start with a theoretical model of the structure of the data and its substantive and non-substantive components. Rather, attention is focused on the geometric location of both responses and respondents in a low-dimensional map. Screening the data consists of scrutinizing these maps for unexpected or puzzling locations of each response to every item in that map. Since there are no prior models, there is no need for fit indices and there is no trial-and-error procedure to come up with the best-fitting model. We are engaged simply in a search for anomalies, and in each of our chapters we discovered different anomalies. We need no model to predict these, and indeed some of them (such as the ones uncovered in Chapter 4 on institutional practices) rather surprised us.

To minimize nonsensical conclusions, standard practice should include data screening techniques of the types that we exemplify in subsequent chapters. What we do in our book can be thought of as the step prior to assessing configural invariance. Scholarly research using survey data is typically comparative: responses to one or more items on a given domain of interest by one group are compared to those given by another group. Comparative research should start with establishing the equivalence of the response structures to a set of items. The minimum necessary condition for obtaining construct equivalence is to show that the cognitive maps produced by the item battery have a similar underlying structure in each group. Issues of response bias are not the same as either reliability or validity. In response bias, the issue is whether the identical response to a survey item by different respondents has the same meaning. In our work, the meaning is inferred from the cognitive maps of groups of respondents who differ in some systematic way (such as cognitive ability, culture, educational attainment and race). If the cognitive maps are not similar, then the identical response is assumed to differ in meaning between the groups.

We apply MCA and CatPCA to the series of statements as a way to describe the structure underlying the overt responses. Analogous to PCA, these techniques locate each of the responses (as well as each of the respondents) in a lower-dimensional space, where the first dimension accounts for the greatest amount of the variation in the responses and each successive dimension accounts for decreasing proportions of such variation. Our guiding assumption is that if the data are of high quality, then the dimensions that reflect coherent substantive patterns of endorsement or rejection are also the ones that account for the greatest proportion of variance. If, on the other hand, the primary dimensions reflect methodological artefacts, or are not interpretable substantively, then we conclude that the data are of low quality.

Our assessment of data quality is stronger when the data have the following characteristics. First, the data set includes multiple statements on the focal domain. Generally, the more statements there are, the easier it is to assess their quality. Second, some of the statements should be formulated in reverse polarity to that of the others, which will allow one to assess whether respondents are cognizant of the direction of the items. Third, the item set should be somewhat heterogeneous; not all items need be manifestations of a single substantive concept.

Chapter outline

1.5 In this chapter we have provided an overview of the sources of data quality. Chapter 2 gives an overview of the empirical literature that documents the existence and determinants of data quality, with a heavy emphasis on factors affecting response quality. A variety of methods have been employed to detect and control for these sources of response quality, each with its own set of advantages and limitations. The empirical review reinforces our view that what response styles have in common is that they represent task simplification mechanisms. There is little evidence that different response styles are basically distinct methodological artefacts. It also shows that cognitive competencies and their manifestations such as educational attainment have particularly pervasive effects on all aspects of response quality. Finally, it highlights some special problems in conducting cross-national (and especially cross-cultural) research.

Chapter 3 gives a brief overview of the methodological and statistical features of MCA and CatPCA, and their relationship to PCA, which helps to explain why these are our preferred methods for screening data. To exemplify the similarities and differences of the methods, we use the Australian data from the 2003 International Social Survey Program (ISSP) on national identity and pride. This overview assumes readers have some familiarity with both matrix algebra and the logic of multivariate statistical procedures. However, the subsequent chapters should be comprehensible to readers who have a basic knowledge of statistical analyses.

Our first exercise in data screening is given in Chapter 4 in which three different data sets are analysed and in which a different source of dirty data was implicated. The examples show how the anomalies first presented themselves and how we eventually found the source of the anomalies. In all three data sets, the problem was not the respondent but the survey organization and its staff. The 2005–2008 World Values Survey (WVS) was employed for two of the analyses in this chapter. The first shows a high probability that some interviewers were prompting the respondents in different ways to produce very simple and often-repeated response combinations that differed by country. The second analysis shows that the survey organizations in some countries engaged in unethical behaviours by manufacturing some of their data. Specifically, we document that some of the data in some countries were obtained through the simple expedient of basically a copy-and-paste procedure. To mask this practice, a few fields were altered here and there so that automated record comparison software would fail to detect the presence of duplicated data. Secondly, we show how to detect (partly) faked interviews using data from our own survey based on sociological knowledge of stereotypes. The last example, using data from the 2002 European Social Survey (ESS), shows that even fairly small errors in data entry (in the sense that they represented only a tiny proportion of all the data) were nevertheless detectable by applying MCA.

We use the ESS 2006 in Chapter 5 to provide an example of data we consider to be of sufficiently high quality in each of the participating countries to warrant cross-national comparisons. We conclude that the relatively high quality and comparability of the data used in this chapter is due to the low cognitive demands made on respondents. The construction of the questions was extremely simple on a topic for which it is reasonable to assume that respondents had direct knowledge, since the questions involved how often they had various feelings. However, the example also shows that reliance on traditional criteria for determining the number of interpretable factors and the reliability of the scale can be quite misleading. Furthermore, we show that the common practice of rotating the PCA solutions that contain both negatively and positively formulated items can lead to unwarranted conclusions. Specifically, it suggests that the rotation capitalizes on distributional features to create two unipolar factors where one bipolar factor arguably is more parsimonious and theoretically more defensible. An additional purpose of this chapter was to show the similarities and differences between the PCA, MCA, and CatPCA solutions. It shows that when the data are of high quality, essentially similar solutions are obtained by all three methods.

The purpose of Chapter 6 is to show the adverse effect on response quality of complicated item construction in measures of political efficacy and trust. On the basis of the 1984 Canadian National Election Study (CNES), we show that the location of response options to complex questions is theoretically more ambiguous than for questions that were simply constructed. By obtaining separate cognitive maps for respondents with above- and below-average political interest, we document that question complexity had a substantially greater impact on the less interested respondents.

Chapter 7 uses the same data to exemplify respondent fatigue effects, capitalizing on the feature that in the early part of the interview respondents were asked about their views of federal politics and politicians, while in the latter part of the interview the same questions were asked regarding provincial politics and politicians. In this chapter we also develop the dirty data index (DDI), which is a standardized measure for the quality of a set of ordered categorical data. The DDI clearly establishes that the data quality is markedly higher for the federal than the provincial items. Since interest in provincial politics was only moderately lower than that for federal politics, we conclude that the lower data quality is due to respondent fatigue.

The links between cognitive competency (and its inherent connection to task difficulty) and task simplification dynamics that jeopardize data quality are explored in Chapter 8. For this purpose we use the Programme for International Student Assessment (PISA) data, which focused on reading and mathematics achievement in 2000 and 2003, respectively. Our analyses show consistent patterns in both data sets documenting that the lower the achievement level, (1) the higher the likelihood of item non-response, (2) the higher the probability of limited response differentiation, and (3) the lower the likelihood of making distinctions between logically distinct study habits. The results suggest that the cognitive maps become more complex as cognitive competence increases.

2

Empirical findings on quality and comparability of survey data

This chapter reviews the empirical literature relevant to our focus on data quality and comparability. We start with a review of the findings on response quality, followed by an evaluation of previous approaches assessing such quality. We then turn our attention to the effects of the survey architecture on data quality and conclude with a discussion of issues in the assessment of cognitive maps in comparative contexts.

Response quality

Sources of response tendencies

2.1 Response tendencies have been conceptualized as systematic response variation that is the result of one of four factors: (a) simplification of the tasks required to respond to survey questionnaire items, (b) personality traits, (c) impression management, and (d) cultural (including subcultural) normative rules governing self-presentation.

Task simplification
Since comprehension of survey tasks and response mapping difficulties are likely to decrease with education, one would expect a variety of response simplification strategies, such as favouring a particular subset of response options, to also decrease with educational attainment. The empirical literature provides ample evidence that all forms of response tendencies such as non-substantive responses (NSRs), ERS, ARS, and LRD are associated with cognitive competence and its manifestations such as educational attainment, achievement test scores and academic performance (Bachman and O'Malley, 1984; Belli, Herzog and Van Hoewyk, 1999; Billiet and McClendon, 2000; Greenleaf, 1992b; Krosnick, 1991; Krosnick et al., 2002; Watkins and Cheung, 1995; Weijters, Geuens and Schillenwaert, 2010). Although these findings are relatively consistent, they are

often modest, typically accounting for less than 5% of the variance – for notable exceptions, see Watkins and Cheung (1995) and Wilkinson (1970).

When tasks are simplified, the effect of education on the quality of data should become smaller. Steinmetz, Schmidt and Schwartz (2009) provided simple one-sentence vignettes describing a person's characteristics and asked respondents to indicate their similarity to that person on a four-point scale from 'very similar' to 'very dissimilar'. This simplified procedure to measure values could account for the fact that there was little difference by education in the amount of random measurement error.

Arce-Ferrer (2006) argued that rural students have had less prior experience with standardized rating scales than their urban counterparts. One manifestation of this was a substantially lower concordance between rural students' subjective response categories and the researcher-assumed meanings. Respondents were given a seven-point rating scale with the end-points labelled as 'totally agree' and 'totally disagree' and asked to provide labels for the five unlabelled responses. Researchers coded the congruity between the subjective response categories and the typically assumed ordinal meaning (e.g., that the middle category should reflect neutrality rather than 'no opinion' or 'don't care'). Additionally, rural students appeared to simplify the task by choosing responses close to the labelled end-points. The interpretation that the underlying dynamic was simplification of the task was strengthened by the fact that the correlation between subjective response congruity and choosing a response close to the labelled end-points was –0.27 (Arce-Ferrer, 2006: 385).

Personality

Like many other scholars, Couch and Keniston (1960: 151) argued that response tendencies reflect a 'deep-seated personality syndrome' rather than a 'statistical nuisance that must be controlled or suppressed by appropriate mathematical techniques'. This implies that response tendencies are not 'superficial and ephemeral' phenomena, but rather stable ones that are psychologically determined. Their research is frequently cited as providing compelling evidence for a personality interpretation, since they obtained a correlation of 0.73 between the sum of 120 heterogeneous items obtained in the first two weeks of testing and the sum of 240 additional heterogeneous items given in the third week of testing. While the size of their correlation is impressive, the nature of the sample is not: 61 paid second-year male university students. Bachman and O'Malley (1984: 505) found impressive annual stability rates ($r \approx 0.9$) for ARS and ERS among high school students. However, the reliabilities of these measures were in the vicinity of 0.6 to 0.7. In a four-year longitudinal study, Billiet and Davidov (2008) successfully modelled a latent acquiescence style factor. With a correlation (stability) of ARS across the four years of 0.56, the authors conclude that acquiescence is part of a personality expression. Alessandri et al. (2010) came to the same conclusion on the basis of their evidence suggesting a modest heritability of ARS. Weijters, Geuens and Schillenwaert (2010) document a stable component of response style over a one-year period. However, only 604 follow-up responses were obtained out of an initial pool of 3,000 members of an internet marketing research firm.

Impression management

Goffman (1959) popularized the notion that individuals constantly attempt to manage the impressions they make on others. Some response tendencies might be due to forms of impression management that are due to the survey context. Lenski and Leggett (1960) pointed out that when the interviewer has higher status than the respondent, a deference or acquiescent strategy might be invoked. They showed that blacks were more likely than whites of similar education to agree to mutually contradictory statements. Carr (1971) found that the race of the interviewer appeared to be more important than the item content for his sample of 151 blacks of lower occupation, education, and income: when the interviewer was white, four out of every five respondents agreed with at least four of five Srole's anomie items, while only three in five did so when the interviewer was black. Similarly, Bachman and O'Malley (1984) attempted to explain their finding of a greater tendency to agree among black than white high school students. The only robust finding was that this tendency was consistently higher in the rural South, where deference was more entrenched.

Ross and Mirowsky (1984: 190) argued that both acquiescence and giving socially desirable responses are forms of adaptive deferential behaviour: 'Acquiescence may be thought of as the deferential response to neutral questions, and the tendency to give the socially-desirable response may be thought of as the deferential response when the question has a normatively-correct answer.' Their guiding hypothesis is that both of these forms of impression management are more prevalent among the less powerful and more excluded groups such as the elderly, visible minorities, and the less educated. Such a formulation is enticing in that it gives both a theoretical rationale for several response tendencies as well as being parsimonious. Their own research as well as six studies they reviewed documented that socio-economically advantaged and younger respondents were less likely to acquiesce or to give socially desirable responses than their less advantaged and older counterparts.

Progress on understanding social desirability effects has been hampered by assuming that a given issue is equally desirable to all respondents. To address this limitation, Gove and Geerken (1977) asked more than 2,000 respondents from a national survey to rate the desirability of some self-esteem items. They found that the better-educated respondents rated the self-esteem items as being more desirable than did those with less education. Simultaneously, and this is where the problem resides, they also found education to be positively related to self-esteem, creating the possibility that this relationship is an artefact of social desirability.

Kuncel and Tellegen (2009) attempted to assess how desirable an item is, and whether extreme endorsement (such as 'strongly agree') of a (presumably) socially desirable item corresponds to greater socially desirable responding than does a less extreme response such as 'mildly agree'. For some items they found a monotonic relationship between the amount of a trait and its social desirability, as is assumed for all items in social desirability scales. Of some importance is that the monotonic relationship held particularly for negative traits. That is, one can never have too little of a negative trait, such as being mean and cruel. Second, some traits, such as caution and circumspection, had a pronounced inverted U-curve distribution. For such items, there was an optimal amount or an ideal point, with deviations at either end being judged as less socially desirable.

Kreuter, Presser and Tourangeau (2008) obtained information from both self-reports and university records on several negative events (such as dropping a class) as well as on several desirable ones (e.g., achieving academic honours). As expected, failing to report a negative behaviour was consistently more likely than failing to report a positive one. Groves, Presser and Dipko (2004) had interviewers provide different introductions to potential respondents. The particular topic the interviewer mentioned in the introduction appeared to act as a cue to the respondent about the social desirability of certain answers. For example, respondents given the 'voting and elections' introductions were more likely to have claimed to make a campaign contribution than did respondents in the other conditions.

Studies with independent estimates of normatively desirable or undesirable behaviours are particularly useful for assessing the role of normative demand pressures. Griesler et al. (2008) had separate estimates of adolescent smoking behaviour from a school-based survey and a home interview. Adolescents who smoke coming from households with high normative pressures not to smoke were most likely to falsely report not smoking in the household context. The normative pressure not to smoke arguably decreases with age, is less when parents or peers smoke, and is less for those who are engaged in other more serious delinquent activities. Griesler et al. (2008) found that the patterns of under-reporting of smoking in the home interview are consistent with each of these expectations.

Ethnicity and cultural differences

Several researchers have investigated ethnic and racial differences in response styles. Hispanics (Weech-Maldonado et al., 2008) and blacks (Bachman and O'Malley, 1984) are generally more likely to select extreme responses than whites. The evidence for ARS is more mixed. Bachman and O'Malley (1984) found that blacks were more likely to exhibit ARS than whites. Gove and Geerken (1977), on the other hand, failed to find such differences. Hui and Triandis (1989: 298) found that Hispanics were substantially more likely than non-Hispanics to use the extreme categories when the five-point response format was used but no statistically significant difference when the 10-point format was used. They suggest that the reason for this is that Hispanics make finer distinctions than non-Hispanics at the extreme ends of judgement continua. However, a closer scrutiny of the distribution of the responses does not support their argument. It shows that Hispanics were more likely than non-Hispanics to utilize three response options: the two extremes and the mid-point, regardless of whether a five-point or 10-point response format was used. Hence, Hispanics are actually less likely than non-Hispanics to require fine distinctions at the extreme ends. We think these patterns are better interpreted as task simplification: Hispanic respondents were more likely than non-Hispanics to simplify the cognitive demands by focusing on just three responses – the two ends and the middle, regardless of whether the response format consisted of five or 10 alternatives.

Non-response and non-substantive responses

We argued in the previous chapter that both unit and item non-response are partly a function of task difficulty. The consistent finding that the response rate to surveys increases with educational attainment (Krosnick, 1991; Krysan, 1998) and with standardized achievement tests (Blasius and Thiessen, 2009) testifies to that dynamic with respect to unit non-response. Our focus here, however, is on item non-response and its relationship to task difficulty and cognitive competency. Converse (1976) classified over 300 items taken from several opinion polls on whether the referent was one on which respondents can be assumed to have direct personal experience or involvement. On such topics she found only trivial differences by educational attainment, while on more abstract issues the more educated were consistently more likely (three to seven percentage points) to provide a substantive response. Indeed, education is one of the best predictors of NSRs, whether in the form of selecting 'don't know' (DK) or 'no opinion (NO) (Converse, 1976; Faulkenberry and Mason, 1978; Ferber, 1966; Francis and Busch, 1975; Krosnick et al., 2002).

Judd, Krosnick and Milburn (1981) found significantly more measurement error among respondents with low education, suggesting that the task of placing themselves on various political orientation scales was more difficult for them. Additionally, missing data were especially prevalent on the most abstract orientation (liberal-conservative), particularly for the low-education group. Again, this suggests that task difficulty interacts with cognitive complexity to produce non-response.

We also argued that topic salience would increase substantive responses. Groves, Presser and Dipko (2004) bought four sampling frame lists whose members would be likely to find a particular topic salient: teachers, political contributors, new parents and the elderly. Each of the samples was randomly assigned to an interviewer introduction that either matched their assumed interest (e.g., that teachers would be interested in 'education and schools', the elderly in 'Medicare and health') or did not. As expected, the likelihood of responding was substantially higher (about 40%) when assumed interest in the topic matched the interviewers' introduction.

Crystallized by Converse's (1964) finding of widespread non-attitudes, survey researchers have been divided about whether to include an NO response option. Those who favour its inclusion argue that the resulting quality of the data would be improved. This argument is based on the assumption that in face-to-face interviews, interviewers implicitly pressure respondents to appear to have opinions. Krosnick et al. (2002) argued that if explicitly providing an NSR option increases data quality, this should manifest itself in the following:

- The consistency of substantive responses over time should be greater in panel studies.
- The correlation of a variable with other measures with which it should in principle be related should be stronger.
- The magnitude of method-induced sources of variation (such as response order effects) should be smaller.
- Validity coefficients should be higher and error variances lower.

In a review of the empirical literature, Krosnick et al. (2002) found little support for any of these expectations. Their own analyses of three household surveys that incorporated nine experiments also failed to find that data quality was compromised by not having an NO option. They offer the satisficing dynamic as an alternative explanation. From this perspective, some individuals who actually have an opinion will take shortcuts by choosing the NO option since it is cognitively less demanding. By offering the option, the interviewer inadvertently legitimates this as a satisficing response.

Blais et al. (2000) assessed whether respondents who claim to 'know nothing at all' about a leader of a political party nevertheless had meaningful positive or negative feelings about that leader. The authors argued that if the ratings of the subjectively uninformed are essentially random, there should be no relationship between their ratings of a leader and their vote for that party. In contrast, if the ratings of those who claim to be uninformed are just as meaningful as those who feel informed, then the relationship between ratings and subsequent vote should be just as strong for these two groups. In actuality, the findings were midway, suggesting that the feelings of those who say they know nothing about the leader result in a weaker attitude–behaviour link. As expected, they also found that the less educated, less objectively informed, less exposed to media, and less interested in politics were the most likely to report that they knew nothing at all about the party leaders.

Including an NSR option has on occasion improved the data quality; that is, it produced higher validity coefficients, lower method effects and less residual error (Andrews, 1984). Using a split-ballot design, Sturgis, Allum and Smith (2008) showed that when respondents are given a DK choice, and then subsequently asked to guess, their guesses were only trivially better than chance. Hence, it is not always the case that partial knowledge is masked by the DK choice. Conversely, the likelihood of choosing the DK response option decreases with educational attainment (Sigelman and Niemi, 2001), indicating that the DK response is to some extent realistically chosen when a respondent has insufficient knowledge.

On normatively sensitive issues, respondents may mask their opinion by choosing an NSR (Blasius and Thiessen, 2001b). Berinsky (2002) documented that in the 1990s respondents who chose a DK or NO response represent a mix of those who actually did not have an enunciable opinion on the issue of their attitude towards government ensuring school integration, together with those who did not wish to report their opinion because it was contrary to the current norms. He buttressed this with the finding that three-quarters of those who were asked what response they would give to make the worst possible impression on the interviewer chose that school integration was none of the government's business. Berinsky argued that in 1972 there was much less consensus on this matter, and so respondents could more easily express their opinion regardless of whether it was positive or negative. An indirect measure of the normativeness of the racial issue is that in 1992, 35% of the respondents failed to express an opinion, compared to 18% in 1972.

Consequences of response tendencies

Does acquiescence make a difference? In some instances it apparently does not (Billiet and Davidov, 2008; Gove and Geerken, 1977; Moors, 2004). It is important to keep in mind that the mere existence of response styles on the outcome variable does not imply that they will obfuscate substantive relationships. To have confounding effects, the response style must also be associated with one or more of the independent variables. In a widely cited article, Gove and Geerken (1977: 1314) remark that their results 'lead to an almost unequivocal conclusion: the response bias variables have very little impact on the pattern of relationships'. In a similar vein, Billiet and Davidov (2008) found that the correlation between political distrust and perceived ethnic threat was essentially the same regardless of whether the response style factor was controlled. The correlation should be smaller after controlling for style (removing correlated measurement error that artificially inflates the correlation), but this was only trivially true.

Andrews (1984) performed a meta-analysis of six different surveys that differed widely in data collection mode, constructs to be measured, and response formats. Altogether there were 106 primary measures for 26 different concepts utilizing 14 different response scales or formats. Overall, about two-thirds of the variance was estimated to be valid and only 3% was attributable to method effects (the remainder being random measurement error). Survey characteristics, such as data collection mode, number of response categories and providing an explicit DK, accounted for about two-thirds of the variance in validity, method effects and residual error.

Other researchers have found that response tendencies do make a difference. Lenski and Leggett (1960) document that without adjusting for acquiescence one would come to the conclusion that blacks are more anomic than whites and that the working class are more anomic than the middle class. However, after excluding respondents who gave contradictory responses, both differences became trivial (three percentage points) and statistically insignificant (Lenski and Leggett, 1960: 466). Berinsky (2002: 578) showed that NSRs distorted the prevalence of racially 'liberal' attitudes by an estimated 10 percentage points.

Wolfe and Firth (2002) analysed data from experiments in which participants conversed with other participants on telephone equipment under a series of different conditions (acoustics, echo, signal strength, noise). Respondents were asked to assess the quality of the connection on a five-point scale ranging from 'excellent' to 'bad'. Wolfe and Firth noted distinct individual differences in location and scale that correspond to acquiescence and extreme response style, respectively. They found that adjusting for each response style magnified the treatment differences, which is what one would expect if response styles are essentially measurement noise.

Response styles sometimes resolve patently counterintuitive findings. For example, studies consistently find that better-educated respondents evaluate their health care less positively (Elliott et al., 2009). Yet the better educated objectively receive better health care and are more aware of their health status. Could the negative association between education and health care ratings be a methodological artefact of response bias? Congruent with other research, Elliott et al. (2009) found that ERS was lower among the more educated respondents. After adjusting the data for ERS, most of the findings became less counterintuitive. A similar argument can be made for racial differences in health care. Dayton et al. (2006) found that in two-thirds of clinical quality measures, African-Americans received significantly worse care than whites. At the same time, they were more likely than whites to report that they were 'always' treated appropriately on four subjective measures of health care.

Approaches to detecting systematic response errors

2.2 Three basic approaches to detecting, isolating and correcting for systematic response errors can be identified: (1) constructing independent measures; (2) developing equivalent item pairs of reversed polarity; and (3) modelling a latent response style factor. We next describe each of these approaches, followed by an assessment of their strengths and weaknesses, and culminating in a comparison with our approaches to screening data.

Early studies on systematic response error focused on constructing direct stand-alone measures of specific response tendencies such as ARS, ERS and social desirability. These early efforts soon recognized the difficulty of distinguishing between respondents' actual beliefs and their artefactual response tendencies unless four criteria were met. First, the items should have maximally heterogeneous content so as to minimize contamination of content with response tendencies. Second, to achieve acceptable reliability for items of heterogeneous content, the measures should be based on a large number of items, with some researchers recommending a minimum of 300 (Couch and Keniston, 1960). Third, the polarity of the items should be balanced, containing an equal number of positively and negatively phrased items. The polarity criterion is essential for discriminating between acquiescence and content. Finally, if balanced polarity is crucial for measures of ARS, balanced proportions of extreme responses are important for ERS measures; that is, the distributions should not be markedly skewed. This would decrease the contamination of ERS with social desirability.

In an effort to find acceptable alternatives to these arduous requirements, some researchers emphasized a more careful selection of items. Ross and Mirowsky (1984) used just 20 positively worded items from Rotter's locus of control scale, arguing that since 'the items are positively worded, ambiguous, have no right answer, and are practically clichés about social and interpersonal issues', endorsing them represents acquiescence. Likewise, Bass (1956) developed an ARS scale on the basis of the number of agreements to uncritical generalizations contained in aphorisms. Typical items are '[o]nly a statue's feelings are not easily hurt' and, rather comically, '[t]he feeling of friendship is like that of being comfortably filled with roast beef'.

For Likert items, a count of all responses indicating agreement, regardless of its intensity, constituted the measure of ARS. Measures of ERS typically consisted of the proportion of the two most extreme response options, such as 'all' and 'none' or 'strongly agree' and 'strongly disagree'. Some researchers, such as Couch and Keniston (1960) and Greenleaf (1992a), calculated the individual mean score across all their items as a measure of ARS. From a task simplification perspective, this is not optimal, since identical means can be obtained without any task simplification as well as with a variety of different simplifications, such as choosing only the middle category or only both extremes equally often, for example. Some researchers (e.g., Greenleaf, 1992b) operationalize ERS as the standard deviation of an individual's responses. Elliott et al. (2009) note that with skewed distributions, the individual's standard deviation across items becomes correlated with the mean, thereby confounding ERS with ARS.

An alternative to independent measures of specific response styles is to create sets of paired items for the domain of interest, where each pair consists of an assertion and its logical negation. Gove and Geerken (1977) created four such pairs, with one example being 'I seem to have very little/a lot of control over what happens to me'. Javaras and Ripley (2007) simulated a variety of models to ascertain under what conditions simple summative scoring of Likert items would produce misleading results. They concluded that only when the items are perfectly balanced for polarity will a comparison of group means based on summative scoring lead to appropriate conclusions.

As confirmatory factor analysis (CFA) – or, more generally SEM – became more popular, these techniques were applied to separate method-induced variance from substantive variance. These models simultaneously postulate one or more latent substantive concepts and one or more methods factors. In the simplest application, a single substantive concept and a specific response style is modelled. In such an application, the focal items must be of mixed polarity. Typically CFA is employed when the response style factor is expected to be ARS.

This is the approach Cambré, Welkenhuysen-Gybels and Billiet (2002) used in a comparative analysis of ethnocentrism in nine European countries on the basis of the 1999 Religious and Moral Pluralism data set. Most of the loadings on the style factor were statistically significant, suggesting that acquiescence was prevalent in most of their countries. More convincingly, Billiet and McClendon (2000) modelled two substantive concepts (political trust and attitudes towards immigrants), each of which was measured with a polarity-balanced set of items, with a common methods factor loading equally on all items of both concepts. They obtained a solid-fitting model, but only by permitting correlated error between the two positively worded political trust items. To assess whether the methods factor really tapped ARS, they created an observed measure of acquiescence (the sum of the agreements to the political trust and attitude towards immigrants items plus one additional balanced pair of items on another topic). This independent measure correlated 0.90 with the style factor.

Watson (1992) also utilized both latent and manifest measures of ARS as well as predictor variables. She analysed eight Likert-type variables that were intended to measure the extent of pro-labour or pro-capitalist sentiments, one of which was reverse-keyed. Additionally, she created a summary ARS index by counting the number of 'strongly agree' responses on seven items across two content domains (attitudes towards crime and gender equality) each of which contained at least one pair of items that arguably represent polar opposites. Interestingly, in a model without acquiescence, the reverse-polarity item failed to have a negative loading on class consciousness. When acquiescence is modelled, it has a significant negative loading. One item consistently had the lowest loading on acquiescence, namely the least abstract item. This is consistent with our contention that acquiescence is simply a concrete response to an abstract question. Finally, education was negatively related to acquiescence, supporting a task difficulty interpretation of acquiescence.

While CFA is used to model a latent ARS factor, latent class analysis typically extracts a factor that resembles ERS. Latent class analysis procedures make less stringent distributional assumptions and typically treat Likert-type responses either as ordered or unordered categories.

Moors (2004) developed a three-factor model consisting of two substantive factors and a methods factor that was constrained to be independent of both substantive factors. The betas that linked the response categories of the 10 items to the methods factor showed a consistent pattern: 'strongly agree' and 'strongly disagree' had high positive betas, 'agree' and 'disagree' had high negative betas, and 'rather agree' and 'rather disagree' had weak negative betas. It is the consistency of this pattern that led Moors to conclude that the third factor was indeed an ERS latent response style factor.

Javaras and Ripley (2007) used a multidimensional unfolding model to adjust simultaneously for ARS and ERS response style differences between groups. They took two sets of items (national pride and attitude towards immigrants), one of which (immigrants) was balanced with three negatively and three positively worded items, while the other one had only one of five items negatively keyed. On the assumption that response style represents a consistent pattern of response that is independent of the content of the items, their analysis 'borrows' information from the balanced set of items to adjust the latent scores on the unbalanced items.

Weijters, Schillewaert and Geuens (2008) propose a 'representative indicators response style means and covariance structure' model. This method involves having a separate set of items from which distinct response tendencies can be simultaneously estimated with multiple indicators for each. Of some importance is that the loadings on their substantive factor were inflated substantially by shared response style variance. Including response style in the model reduced the factor loadings. This cautions against thinking of high reliability, as traditionally measured, being synonymous with high data quality, since response style can masquerade as reliability. Van Rosmalen, van Herk and Groenen (2010) developed a 'latent-class bilinear multinomial logit model' to model all forms of response styles simultaneously with substantive relationships.

Advantages and disadvantages of detection methods

Each approach to assessing or controlling for systematic response error has its own strengths and weaknesses. Stand-alone measures are simple to construct and, assuming they are reliable and valid, they permit simple controls for the response errors that they measure. Their main disadvantage is that they drastically increase the length of a questionnaire if they are constructed as recommended. Greenleaf (1992a) based his measures on 224 attitude items; Couch and Keniston (1960) recommended at least 300 items. From a financial point of view this is prohibitive, and from a respondent fatigue perspective (see Chapter 7) the side effects are worse than the problem being addressed.

Constructing equivalent pairs of items of opposite polarity minimizes the main disadvantage associated with the stand-alone measures. However, they are difficult to construct and consequently they are typically composed of just a few pairs of logically opposite statements. Gove and Geerken (1977), for example, created four pairs of items and classified respondents as acquiescent if there were more positive than negative responses. With so few item pairs this measure of acquiescence runs the risk of being confounded with either a lack of ability to perceive patent contradictions or insufficient attention to the task. Consistent with this interpretation, Credé (2010) found that the correlations among substantively related items were weaker for the subset of respondents who gave inconsistent responses to paired items than for those who provided consistent responses. So, while ARS implies a tendency to endorse contradictory statements, we prefer to think of it as one of a number of reasonable task simplification strategies. When contradictions are too close together and too patently obvious, ARS may not constitute a reasonable simplification strategy.

CFA of substantive and methods factors presents an enticing approach to disentangling substance from style. The main advantage is that it offers the promise of both detecting method factors and simultaneously controlling for their effects. However, as a data screening technique it is ill-suited for a variety of reasons. First, CFA already assumes key attributes of the data that need to be tested, for example, that the response categories can be treated as either metric or ordered categorical with little loss of information. Further, it makes a variety of other assumptions such as linear associations and multivariate normal distributions that are not appropriate in most survey data. Second, the modelling approach usually imposes some kind of factor correlations without examining the uncorrelated (and unrotated) solution. As we will demonstrate later, this practice can be hazardous, since method-induced factors are seldom manifest once the solution has been rotated. This rush to rotate in order to produce scales and/or latent structures has, in our opinion, impeded sensitive and sensible social analyses. Greater attention to the uncorrelated and unrotated solution would in many instances have produced less confusion and greater insight. Third, the idea of CFA and SEM is that the theoretical model has to fit the data; if the fit is not sufficient (or if the fit can be improved), the theoretical model will be modified, for example, by adding correlated measurement error. Fourth, the criteria used for assessing whether conceptual, measurement and scalar invariance have been achieved are often fulfilled only through the expedient of making *ad hoc* adjustments. Of course, it is almost always problematic to assess configural invariance, since one is forcing a common base model and the chi-square associated with that base model is typically statistically significant, especially with large sample sizes. Fifth, the factor loadings on the methods factors are typically less than 0.50, which is a problem if the means of methods factors are to be compared across groups.

Questionnaire architecture

2.3 Survey design features can have substantial effects on data quality. For example, because of respondent fatigue, the temptation to provide satisficing responses should be less in the early part of interviews. In line with this expectation, Krosnick et al. (2002) found that NO responses were utilized six percentage points more often on items asked late in the interview. They also found that less educated respondents were particularly likely to choose the NO option on items asked late in the interview, providing evidence for the interaction between ability and motivation.

In his review of the literature, Krosnick (1991) reports that response order effects were more common in longer questions, with more polysyllabic words, and more response alternatives, each of which arguably increases the task difficulty. This pattern is reinforced in Bishop and Smith's (2001) meta-analysis, which found that response order effects were particularly noticeable when the questions and/or the response alternatives were more difficult.

Since ARS takes the form of selecting an agreement response when a Likert response format is used, a possible measure of the magnitude of ARS is the difference in proportion taking a given position when the issue is presented as a Likert format compared to a forced choice format. McClendon (1991) found that a forced choice format produced a higher proportion taking the side corresponding to what would have been the 'disagree' option in the Likert format, documenting that response format influences response behaviours.

Holbrook et al. (2007) performed a meta-analysis of over 500 response order experiments in 149 telephone surveys. Task difficulty (measured as number of letters per word and number of words per sentence) predicted the magnitude of response order effect. The difference between the simplest and most difficult question wording resulted in an 18.5 percentage point greater response order effect. They also documented that questions occurring later in the survey were more susceptible to response order effects than those that occurred earlier. This finding is at odds with that of Bishop and Smith's (2001) meta-analysis of earlier Gallup surveys. The discrepancy in findings is likely due to the fact that the earlier studies were much shorter. When Holbrook et al. replicated their analyses, limiting them to just those with 20 items or fewer (that was the largest in Bishop and Smith's analyses), they also found no waning attention (declining motivation) effect. In his meta-analysis, Andrews (1984) found that data quality was lowest both at the beginning (the first 25 items) and at the end (beyond the 100th item). The finding about data quality at the end fits well with notions of respondent fatigue. Andrews suggests that the initial poor quality is a result of 'warming up' and obtaining rapport. The idea that a response style kicks in after a while is supported by his findings that the longer the battery length within which an item is embedded, the greater the residual error, the lower the validity, and the higher the methods effect.

From a satisficing perspective, the extent of the correlated measurement error should be a function of the item locations. Green (1988) provides evidence that the extent of correlated measurement error is partly a function of the item locations. He found that these errors for the feeling thermometer items were higher among item pairs that were spatially close to each other than for those separated by more items.

In one of several studies that incorporated experimental design features, Krosnick et al. (2002) presented respondents with possible plans that would prevent future oil spills. Respondents were asked to vote on the plan, whose cost per person was randomly assigned to vary between $10 and $120. Respondents were also randomly assigned to voting method, with half dropping their vote in a sealed envelope in a box (anonymous condition) and the other half reporting their vote to the interviewer (accountable condition). If respondents were optimizing (thoughtful), then their responses should be responsive to the cost factor. In the accountable condition, the vote was 40% more responsive to cost than in the anonymous condition, suggesting again that respondents were more likely to satisfice in the anonymous condition.

Educated respondents have greater cognitive skills and are also likely to have had more experience with filling out forms. For this reason one would expect that the responses of the more educated should show less vulnerability to trivial survey characteristics, such as the order in which questions are asked, an expectation that is generally empirically supported (Krosnick, 1991). Holbrook et al. (2007) found evidence that task difficulty interacted with education, with question difficulty (as well as response option difficulty) having more impact among the less educated. Among those with a university education, there was essentially no question order effect associated with task difficulty.

Krosnick and Alwin (1987: 201) employed data from face-to-face interviews where respondents were asked to pick the three most and least important child rearing values out of a list of 13 values. The survey employed a split-ballot design to present the values in reverse order for one-third of the sample. They found that values presented early in the list were disproportionately (up to 17 percentage points) more likely to be endorsed. This is consistent with the satisficing hypothesis that respondents will tend to choose the first reasonable option. More important for our purposes, however, is the finding that the order effect was more prevalent among the cognitively less sophisticated group (measured through a combination of education and a vocabulary test) than among the more sophisticated.

Alwin (1997) found that 11-point feeling items provide higher-quality data (less random error and more valid variance) than the more commonly employed Likert formats. Likewise, Kroh (2007) provided evidence that 11-point scales for left–right orientation of self and political parties in Germany have superior validity (e.g., a sharper relationship with intended vote) and lower method effect coefficients than either 10-point or 101-point scales. Kroh suggests that providing a 101-point scale may induce ambiguity and extra task burden. He bolsters this by noting that 86% of responses to the 101-point scale were multiples of 10. Additionally, the interviews took significantly longer in the 101-point version than in the other two formats. Since it usually takes more time to complete difficult tasks, this finding may be an indirect manifestation of greater task difficulty. Green (1988) also found greater systematic measurement error for the 100-point thermometer format compared to formats with a limited number of labelled response options. Recent research indicates that, if Likert response formats are used, seven-point response options yield optimal criterion validity (Malhotra, Krosnick and Thomas, 2009). At the same time, there is increasing evidence that Likert formats are inferior and should be avoided in favour of other formats (Saris et al., 2010).

Holbrook, Cho and Johnson (2006: 569) designed a study in which they followed up each survey question with a series of probes. Responses to the probes were coded to capture respondent difficulties with either comprehending the question or mapping their judgement onto the response alternatives. They found that mapping difficulties were related to response format, with yes–no giving the least mapping difficulties and open-ended numeric ones giving the greatest. Question length, abstraction and qualified questions were significantly related to comprehension difficulties. Qualified questions also produced greater mapping difficulties, as one would expect. Reading level and age were negatively associated with mapping difficulties.

Data collection context and mode

The survey context and mode have repercussions on matters of accountability. Griesler et al. (2008) reviewed numerous studies documenting consistently lower estimates of adolescent smoking when the interviews take place in the household rather than at school, or when privacy and confidentiality are less secured. In their own study, they first conducted the interviews in schools and then in homes. They found that adolescents were less likely to admit to smoking in the subsequent home interview if the same interviewer interviewed both the adolescent and the parent, even though separately and with confidentiality assurances of not sharing the information with the parent. This suggests that the direct contact of the interviewer with the parent was sufficient to make adolescents falsely report behaving in a fashion that was likely to be congruent with their parents' desires (i.e., by reporting that they do not smoke).

Nederhof (1985) cites several studies to support the conclusion that social desirability effects are weaker in mail questionnaires than in personal interviews. Krysan (1998) also found modest evidence that giving socially desirable responses to questions on racial attitudes was lower in the mail questionnaire than the personal interview mode. Additionally, she noted that five items were cliché-like, and to agree (first response) meant endorsing an unfavourable attitude towards blacks. In the self-administered mode, the least educated were substantially less likely to give prejudicial responses, a finding consistent with Lenski and Leggett's (1960) deference interpretation. Corroborating the general expectation of mode effects, Kreuter, Presser and Tourangeau (2008) calculated the odds of misreporting in a socially desirable direction to be 20% higher for computer-assisted telephone interviews compared to web and interactive voice response modes (see also Heerwegh and Loosveldt, 2011, for similar findings).

Krysan (1998) argued that awareness of what is socially desirable increases with education. She therefore hypothesized that providing socially desirable responses would be especially more likely among educated respondents in a face-to-face mode than in mailed questionnaires. The direction of all interaction effects was consistent with the hypothesis that the better-educated are more prone to give socially desirable responses on racial matters in face-to-face interviews.

Cognitive maps in cross-cultural perspective_____

2.4 Survey research is inherently comparative, and in this context, Van de Vijver and Poortinga (1997) define three types of bias that arise whenever group comparisons are made: construct, method and item. Construct bias exists when the items intended to measure a construct fail to have identical meanings between the groups being compared. Method bias occurs when response styles and social desirability dynamics result in differential use of the available response options. Item bias occurs when a given item in a battery functions differently in the groups being compared. In other words, data are considered to be comparable when three conditions have been met: conceptual invariance, measurement invariance and scalar invariance. These three conditions are often hierarchically assessed via multigroup CFA. In this approach, a series of hierarchically nested equality constraints are imposed. When a given set of equality constraints is not justified, then it is usually inappropriate to proceed to the next level of constraints.

Assessing quality in cross-cultural data is especially difficult. First, the creation of polarity-balanced scales is seldom done in cross-cultural research because translation of negative items is difficult in some languages, is confusing to some respondents, and voicing disagreements is awkward in some countries (Smith, 2004). Wong, Rindfleisch and Burroughs (2003) found that the method effects associated with polarity operate quite differently in Asian countries than in the USA. In the USA, the correlation between the negative and positive items on the Material Values Scale (MVS) is –0.57, whereas in the Asian countries it does not exceed –0.17 and in Japan it is actually positive (0.09).

Second, evidence indicates that response tendencies and cultural values are intricately intertwined. Smith (2004) built a meta-analytic data set from six separate multicultural studies that provided information on cultural values and ARS. His two hypotheses, namely that country-level ARS bias estimates will be consistent (i.e., the same countries will be high on ARS in the different studies), and that ARS will be predicted by the same value profiles, received support. The second hypothesis took the specific form that ARS is predictable from the cultural values of collectivism and uncertainty avoidance. On the basis of these findings, Smith cautions against attempting to remove the bias in cross-cultural studies, since it may represent a genuine cultural communication style.

Few studies have systematically assessed the prevalence and magnitude of Van de Vijver and Poortinga's (1997: 33) cultural distance bias, which states that 'the effects of bias will systematically favor the cultural group from where the instrument originates'. Nevertheless, the pattern of findings in cross-cultural comparative research generally conforms to this hypothesis. Smith's (2004) first hypothesis exemplifies the cultural distance bias, since the countries found to be low on ARS bias were European countries. In a comparative study of four Asian countries together with the USA, Wong, Rindfleisch and Burroughs (2003) found the factor loadings and reliability for the MVS were highest in the USA where this instrument was developed, and lowest in Thailand, which is culturally and economically most different. Watkins and Cheung (1995: 497) report that the reliabilities of the Self Description Questionnaire scales, which were developed in Australia, were highest in Australia (0.86) and lowest in the Philippines (0.75) and Nepal (0.69). Likewise, Murayama, Zhou and Nesbit (2009) found that the reliability of their measures of achievement goals (developed in the USA) were higher in the Canadian sample (between 0.90 and 0.96) than in the Japanese one (between 0.72 and 0.79). Kankaraš and Moors (2009: 558) employed the 1999/2000 EVS to model local, social and global solidarity in 33 countries. The highest residuals in their models were occasioned by Turkey – the country culturally most dissimilar from the others.

The possible confounding of response style with modes of thought requires greater sensitivity in questionnaire construction. Wong, Rindfleisch and Burroughs (2003) made a key improvement in the MVS in that the items were rephrased as questions rather than as statements. An example item is 'How much pleasure do you get from buying things?' with (presumably) seven possible responses with the end ones labelled as 'very little' and 'a great deal'. Additionally, they constructed different response options for each item. As the authors note, 'by being more inquisitive and using response options customized for each question (rather than a uniform disagree–agree scale), this format focuses respondent attention more intently on the content of each question' (Wong, Rindfleisch and Burroughs, 2003: 81; see also Saris et al., 2010, for the data quality advantages of customized response options). They retained the alternating directionality of the possible responses so that polarity could still be operative. In its original form, the psychometric properties of the MVS are rather weak, with the proportion of variance attributable to the substantive scale being less than 20% in all countries, the random error component being as high as 70% (Thailand), and the systematic method variance ranging between 18% and 37%.

Conclusion

2.5 The research reviewed in this chapter has documented an overwhelming array of potential obstacles to obtaining data of sound quality, ranging from the inappropriateness of the study architecture to task simplification behaviours of reluctant respondents – and we did not even consider additional important factors such as the standards of the data collection agencies and the training of the institute staff. The findings reinforce our basic contention that the findings from survey data without meticulous prior data screening are destined to be equivocal.

The research on data quality has increased our understanding of its determinants in several respects. First, it suggests that response tendencies are perhaps best viewed as alternative forms of task simplification behaviours. Since they are alternative forms, they are extremely difficult to separate empirically. Second, poor response quality is primarily a function of the task difficulty relative to the respondent's cognitive competencies and familiarity with the survey topic and process. Overall, we have to pay more attention to what can be done to make the survey task appropriate to the respondents' capabilities and interests.

The literature review has also made it eminently clear that much of the research on social desirability has not been fruitful. Few consistent patterns have been documented, mainly because of an inadequate conceptualization and measurement of the concept. While it is true that social desirability dynamics permeate the research act, we think it is better to conceive of these dynamics as being part of a larger set of impression management techniques. This would make it clear that what is socially desirable is inherently contextual rather than absolute and its success depends on an accurate reading of the societal and group norms and interactional expectations. Chapters 4 and 5 will exemplify some of this diversity.

We have reviewed the methodological and technical advancements that have dramatically expanded the boundaries for detecting and modelling method-induced variation in survey data. Nevertheless, it is hard to disagree with Weijters, Schillewaert and Geuens' (2008: 411) laconic remark that 'a discrepancy exists between our limited understanding of the response process and our advanced models to represent it'. It is precisely the existence of this discrepancy that makes data screening mandatory.

3

Statistical techniques for data screening

The aim of this chapter is to present different methods that enable us to screen data for detecting the presence and magnitude of non-substantive variation. In a series of papers we demonstrated the use of multiple correspondence analysis (Blasius and Thiessen, 2001a, 2001b, 2006a, 2009; Thiessen and Blasius, 1998) and categorical principal component analysis (Blasius and Thiessen, 2006b, 2009; Thiessen and Blasius, 2008) for this task. In this book we would like to expand the toolkit of methods for screening data. What the methods to be discussed have in common is that they can be used to transform a set of observed variables to a smaller set of latent variables (factors, dimensions). That is, they belong to a family of scaling methods where the dependent variables are latent and on continuous scales while the independent variables are the observed ones. The latent variables are normally distributed with mean of zero and standard deviation of one. It is precisely the nature and stringency of the assumptions associated with the different scaling methods that make some of them more suitable for data screening than others.

The most popular scaling methods, principal component analysis (PCA) and factor analysis (FA), also make the severest assumptions and therefore are least adapted to the task of screening data. They assume that the input data have metric properties. When the data consist of ordered categories, such as Likert-type responses, categorical (or nonlinear) principal component analysis (CatPCA) is the better choice. Multiple correspondence analysis (MCA) is particularly suited for the analysis of unordered categorical (i.e., nominal) data. Rasch scaling or the unfolding model are proper choices when the response options are dichotomous (yes–no) with an implicit item-difficulty order, which usually means they have a one-dimensional solution. In the following we concentrate on PCA, CatPCA, MCA, and their further developments.

To illustrate these methods we chose the example of regional identity and national pride, using the Australian data from the ISSP 2003, which were collected within a mail survey. This example was chosen primarily because the quality of the data was sufficiently high that the solutions obtained from the different scaling methods could be readily compared. This should make it easier for readers familiar with PCA to understand the screening methods we prefer, namely CatPCA and MCA. The 14 variables (identified with the abbreviations that will be used in subsequent figures) belong to two different sets of items. The first set contained variables measuring how close the respondent feels to different geographical areas: 'How close do you feel to…

A: Your town or city
B: Your [county]
C: Country [Australia]
D: Continent'.

In a footnote, respondents were informed that 'feel close to' is to be understood as 'emotionally attached to' or 'identifying with', and that 'county' was to be understood as the most relevant administrative unit smaller than the entire country/nation (province, state, …). Four response categories were provided: 'very close', 'close', 'not very close', and 'not close at all'; additionally, respondents could select the 'can't choose' or the 'no answer' option. The second set consisted of 10 variables on national pride: 'How proud are you of Australia in each of the following:

O: The way democracy works
P: Its political influence in the world
Q: Australia's economic achievements
R: Its social security system
S: Its scientific and technological achievements
T: Its achievements in sports
U: Its achievements in arts and literature
V: Australia's armed forces
W: Its history
X: Its fair and equal treatment of all groups in society.

Again, four response options were given: 'very proud', 'somewhat proud', 'not very proud', and 'not proud at all'; and the identical non-substantive responses of 'can't choose' or 'no answer' were provided. All variables are positively formulated; they are all in the same direction. Tables 3.1a and 3.1b show the marginal distribution of the 14 variables, with the two non-substantive responses combined as 'missing value' (MV).

Table 3.1a Marginal distribution, first set of items, Australia (%, N = 2,183)

	Very close	Close	Not very close	Not close at all	MV
How close do you feel to: Your town or city	24.0	54.5	13.8	3.3	4.4
How close do you feel to: Your [county]	20.5	52.5	17.9	3.7	5.4
How close do you feel to Australia	49.4	40.5	5.8	1.2	3.1
How close do you feel to the continent	1.9	12.3	31.2	45.4	9.1

Table 3.1b Marginal distribution, second set of items, Australia (N = 2,183)

	Very proud	Somewhat proud	Not very proud	Not proud at all	MV
How proud: The way democracy works	23.9	51.8	12.7	2.7	9.0
How proud: Its political influence in the world	8.5	44.5	27.5	8.5	11.0
How proud: Australia's economic achievements	20.5	57.2	12.0	2.0	8.3
How proud: Its social security system	11.9	43.2	26.9	10.3	7.7
How proud: Its scientific and technological achievements	46.4	41.9	4.3	0.9	6.6
How proud: Its achievements in sports	55.6	33.8	3.9	1.7	5.0
How proud: Its achievements in arts and literature	30.1	49.3	9.2	1.8	9.5
How proud: Australia's armed forces	39.5	42.5	9.0	2.8	6.2
How proud: Its history	33.6	40.0	14.4	4.9	7.1
How proud: Its fair and equal treatment of all groups in society	17.6	38.6	25.8	10.2	7.7

The marginal distributions of the variables reveal some marked dissimilarities in the two sets of variables. In the first set, the greatest contrast is between feeling close to Australia and the continent. In the second set, feeling proud of the political influence of the country differs especially from such feelings about its achievements in sport. To keep the comparison between the different scaling methods simple, we exclude here any discussion of the treatment of missing data and possible imputation techniques, electing instead to use listwise deletion of cases with missing values. This reduces the sample from 2,183 cases to 1,548 cases.

Principal component analysis

3.1 Let us assume that there are m observed variables with n respondents each. In PCA, these m variables can be re-expressed without any loss of information by m latent variables. That is, when the number of factors retained equals the number of variables, the original observed scores are perfectly recaptured. However, PCA is typically employed to reduce the dimensionality of the data by selecting a substantially smaller number (m^*) of factors. In general, each observed variable (z_j) can be expressed through its association (α_{jk}) with each latent factor (f_k), resulting in the following set of equations:

first variable, $\quad z_1 = f_1\alpha_{11} + f_2\alpha_{12} + \ldots + f_{m^*}\alpha_{1m^*} + \ldots + f_m\alpha_{1m}$

second variable, $\quad z_2 = f_1\alpha_{21} + f_2\alpha_{22} + \ldots + f_{m^*}\alpha_{2m^*} + \ldots + f_m\alpha_{2m}$

any variable j, $\quad z_j = f_1\alpha_{j1} + f_2\alpha_{j2} + \ldots + f_{m^*}\alpha_{jm^*} + \ldots + f_m\alpha_{jm}$

last variable, $\quad z_m = f_1\alpha_{m1} + f_2\alpha_{m2} + \ldots + f_{m^*}\alpha_{mm^*} + \ldots + f_m\alpha_{mm}$

In these equations, z_j is a vector that contains the standardized categories of the jth variable for all n respondents (i.e., all variables have a mean value of zero and a standard deviation of one); α_{jk} is the correlation between the jth observed and the kth latent variable (these are the factor loadings); and f_k contains the values of the kth latent variable of all n respondents (these are the factor scores). With a sufficiently large number of cases, f_k is normally distributed with a mean value of zero and standard deviation of one.

In matrix notation and for the full solution (i.e., where the number of factors is equal to the number of observed variables),

$$Z = FA, \quad \text{with} \quad \frac{1}{n}F^T F = I .$$

I is the identity matrix with m rows and m columns, which by definition has 1s in the main diagonal and 0s in the off-diagonal elements; in other words, the factors are orthogonal (uncorrelated) with each other. Because

$$z_{1i} = \frac{x_i - \bar{x}}{s_x} \quad \text{and} \quad z_{2i} = \frac{y_i - \bar{y}}{s_y}$$

and since

$$r_{12} = \frac{\sum_{i=1}^{n}(x_i - \bar{x})(y_i - \bar{y})}{\sqrt{\sum_{i=1}^{n}(x_i - \bar{x})^2}\sqrt{\sum_{i=1}^{n}(y_i - \bar{y})^2}}$$

it follows that

$$r_{12} = \frac{1}{n}z_1^T z_2$$

or in matrix notation,

$$R = \frac{1}{n}Z^T Z = \frac{1}{n}A^T F^T FA = A^T A$$

The recognition that the correlation matrix can be reproduced by the product of its transposed factor loadings and the factor loadings is known as the fundamental theorem in factor analysis. Since the purpose is to reduce the set of m observed variables to m^* factors, with $m^* < m$, it follows that

$$Z \approx F_{m^*}A \quad \text{and} \quad R \approx A_{m^*}^T A_{m^*}$$

Applying eigenvalue decomposition (also known as canonical decomposition) to the correlation matrix results in

$$R = B\Lambda B^\mathsf{T}$$

where B is the matrix of the eigenvectors and Λ the diagonal matrix of the eigenvalues, with the eigenvalues in descending order $\lambda_1 \geq \lambda_2 \geq \ldots \geq \lambda_{m^*} \geq \ldots \geq \lambda_m$. The eigenvalue decomposition given above can be rewritten as $B\Lambda^{1/2}(B\Lambda^{1/2})^\mathsf{T}$; it follows from this that the matrix of factor loadings can be computed by $A = (B\Lambda^{1/2})^\mathsf{T}$. Further, from $R = A^\mathsf{T}A$ it is clear that the correlations between any two variables (j, l) can be recomputed from the corresponding factor loadings:

$$\sum_{k=1}^{m} \alpha_{jk}\alpha_{kl} = r_{jl}$$

For the reduced set of variables, this yields

$$\sum_{k=1}^{m^*} \alpha_{jk}\alpha_{kl} \approx r_{jl}$$

The factor loadings (α_{jk}), ranging from -1 to $+1$, are the correlations between the latent and observed variables. Because the columns of B are normalized, the sum of squares of the elements in each latent factor over all variables in the matrix A is the corresponding eigenvalue, that is,

$$\lambda_k = \sum_{j=1}^{m} \alpha_{jk}^2$$

The sum of the eigenvalues is equal to the trace of R, which is the number of variables m. Dividing the eigenvalues by m provides the explained variances, which express the explanatory power of individual dimensions. The sum of squares of the elements of each variable over all factors of the matrix A in the complete solution is one:

$$\sum_{k=1}^{m} \alpha_{jk}^2 = 1$$

The communality,

$$h_j^2 = \sum_{k=1}^{m^*} \alpha_{jk}^2$$

describes the proportion of the variance in variable j explained by the m^* factors used to construct the reduced space.

As discussed before, $\mathbf{Z}$ can be written as the product of the factor scores $\mathbf{F}$ (the values of each object on each latent variable) and the factor loadings $\mathbf{A}$ (the correlations between latent and manifest variables), that is, $\mathbf{Z} = \mathbf{FA}$. To compute the factor scores, first multiply both sides of the equation by the inverse matrix of factor loadings $(\mathbf{A}^{-1})$, resulting in $\mathbf{ZA}^{-1} = \mathbf{FAA}^{-1}$. Since the product of a matrix with its inverse yields the identity matrix $(\mathbf{I})$ and since $\mathbf{FI} = \mathbf{F}$, it follows that $\mathbf{F} = \mathbf{ZA}^{-1}$. The factor scores given in $\mathbf{F}$ can be used both to visualize the objects (the respondents) in the latent space and for inclusion as (latent) variables in further analyses, for example, as independent variables in a regression model.

Several approaches exist for deciding on the number of dimensions (m^*) to be considered for substantive interpretation. In survey research, the Kaiser eigenvalue criterion, which considers only eigenvalues greater than 1.0, is the most common. The rationale for this criterion is that each latent variable to be retained should explain more variation in the data than that explained by a single observed variable. Since each observed variable has an explained variance of 1.0 (the correlation of a variable with itself), the eigenvalues of the factors to be considered in the solution should be greater than one, that is, $\lambda_{m^*} > 1$. This is a quite arbitrary criterion since a factor with an eigenvalue of 1.0001 would be considered while one with an eigenvalue of 0.9999 would be excluded.

An alternative criterion for selecting the number of dimensions for interpretation is the so-called 'scree test': the eigenvalues are plotted in successive order; the factor that forms an elbow (i.e., a substantial change in magnitude in the increasing/decreasing list of eigenvalues) will be the first one that is not considered in the solution. Another possibility is to consider just those factors for which one can provide a substantive interpretation. When visualizing the data, a two-dimensional solution is often used, sometimes just for aesthetic reasons.

After choosing the number of factors to be retained in a solution, scholars often rotate the solution to facilitate their interpretation; varimax rotation is the most popular. Applying varimax rotation, the coordinates of variables and cases in the m^*-dimensional latent space are changed in a manner that maximizes the sum of the variances of the squared loadings on each factor. Using this technique, median loadings become either smaller or larger and consequently are more clearly associated with a single factor, making its interpretation more distinct. While varimax rotation keeps the orthogonality of the factors (i.e. the factors remain uncorrelated), other rotation methods such as oblimin allow the factors to be correlated after rotation. We next illustrate varimax rotation with some artificial data. Assume that we have eight variables, four of them phrased positively (p) and the remainder negatively (n). The first (unrotated) dimension of the PCA solution explains a maximum of variance between the variables; the second is orthogonal to the first dimension and explains a maximum of the remaining variation; the first two dimensions and the eight variables are displayed in Figure 3.1.

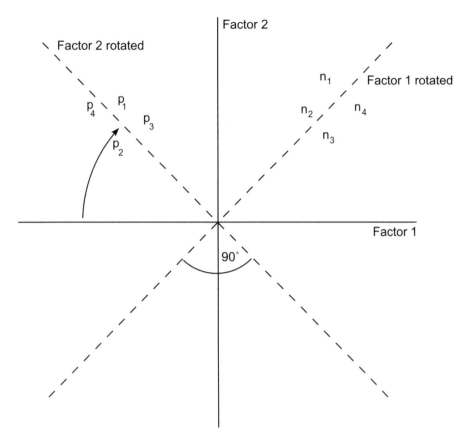

Figure 3.1 Rotated and unrotated solution with eight artificial variables

As one can see, the eight variables divide readily into two groups correspond-ing to whether the items were positively or negatively phrased. In this case, the rotated solution suggests a two-dimensional structure mirroring just the polar-ity of the items: positive-polarity items form dimension 1 and negative-polarity items define dimension 2. Findings such as these have sparked a lively debate about whether the underlying structure consists of two unipolar concepts or one bipolar concept (see Chapter 5). Regardless of which position is taken, it is insufficient to base it just on the rotated solution and the eigenvalue criterion. We will demonstrate later that the unrotated solution is also often meaningful and that in some instances rotation merely highlights the non-substantive variation in the data.

Input for PCA is usually the matrix of product-moment correlation coeffi-cients, which assume metric data. However, categorical variables such as five-point Likert items have often been treated as if they were metric. To show the solution that one would typically find in the literature, we apply PCA to the ISSP data described above. Using the 14 variables on regional identity and

Table 3.2 Factor loadings, PCA, Australia, unrotated and rotated (varimax) solution

	Unrotated solution		Rotated solution	
	D1	D2	D1	D2
How close do you feel to: Your town or city	0.447	0.693	0.121	0.816
How close do you feel to: Your [county]	0.535	0.668	0.212	0.829
How close do you feel to Australia	0.568	0.446	0.333	0.641
How close do you feel to the continent	0.059	0.376	−0.102	0.366
How proud: The way democracy works	0.574	−0.200	0.606	0.055
How proud: Its political influence in the world	0.710	−0.259	0.753	0.057
How proud: Australia's economic achievements	0.673	−0.220	0.704	0.077
How proud: Its social security system	0.405	−0.144	0.428	0.036
How proud: Its scientific and technological achievements	0.533	−0.103	0.528	0.126
How proud: Its achievements in sports	0.580	0.020	0.519	0.258
How proud: Its achievements in arts and literature	0.517	0.008	0.468	0.221
How proud: Australia's armed forces	0.663	−0.177	0.677	0.112
How proud: Its history	0.598	−0.215	0.634	0.051
How proud: Its fair and equal treatment of all groups in society	0.542	−0.281	0.609	−0.032
Eigenvalues	4.240	1.610	3.791	2.058
Explained variances	30.3%	11.5%	27.1%	14.7%

national pride as input data, the first and second eigenvalues are 4.24 and 1.61, respectively (see Table 3.2), accounting jointly for 41.8% of the variation. Both the third and fourth eigenvalues also exceed one ($\lambda_3 = 1.36$, $\lambda_4 = 1.11$), together explaining an additional 17.6% of the total variation (not shown).

By the eigenvalue criterion, the solution is four-dimensional. However, the difference between the first and the second eigenvalues is large, with only small differences between the second and subsequent eigenvalues. Hence, by the scree test criterion, the solution is one-dimensional. With respect to the factor loadings of the unrotated solution (Table 3.2), except for the item 'feeling close to their continent', all variables have substantial positive loadings on the first dimension. Substantively, this factor can be interpreted as the extent to which respondents report feeling regional identity and national pride. The second dimension contrasts the four variables of the first set of items on the positive part of the axis with the second set of items: eight out of the 10 items from this set have slightly negative loadings, while the remaining two items are positive but essentially zero.

For the remainder of the analyses in this chapter, we retain only two dimensions. After varimax rotation of the two-dimensional solution, the respective eigenvalues are 3.79 and 2.06. The rotated solution clearly distinguishes between the two sets of variables: the first rotated dimension is defined by the national pride items; the second dimension is comprised of the items measuring regional identity.

The literature sometimes confuses PCA with factor analysis; in some statistical packages PCA is the default method when running the FA module. The difference between these methods is that PCA does not incorporate any error term; as previously shown, it yields $\mathbf{Z} = \mathbf{FA}$ and $\mathbf{R} = \mathbf{A}^\mathsf{T}\mathbf{A}$. In contrast, FA assumes that each variable has an item-specific error term $(\mathbf{v}_j)$. From this it follows that any variable $\mathbf{z}_j$ can be decomposed as

$$\mathbf{z}_j = \mathbf{f}_1\alpha_{j1} + \mathbf{f}_2\alpha_{j2} + \ldots + \mathbf{f}_{m^*}\alpha_{jm^*} + \ldots + \mathbf{f}_m\alpha_{jm} + \mathbf{v}_j$$

or in matrix notation,

$$\mathbf{Z} = \mathbf{FA} + \mathbf{V}$$

For the decomposition of the correlation matrix as a product of the factor loadings times the transposed factor loading, we obtain

$$\mathbf{R} = \mathbf{A}^\mathsf{T}\mathbf{A} - \mathbf{V}^\mathsf{T}\mathbf{V}$$

If the errors are uncorrelated, only the main diagonal elements of the correlation matrix $\mathbf{R}$ (which are by definition one) have to be reduced iteratively to correct for the item-specific error. The manner of estimating these error terms differentiates the various methods of FA. To allow for correlations between these error terms, as well as for correlations between the latent factors themselves, and to classify observed and latent variables as dependent and independent, is the aim of SEM. While PCA explores the structure of the data, SEM tests whether the data are consistent with the models developed either on the basis of the literature or the assumptions of scholars. Since our interest is on screening the data with a minimum of assumptions about the data, we do not discuss these models in detail, although they too have been used to test for the quality of data (see Chapter 2).

3.2 Categorical principal component analysis

Returning to our example on regional identity and national pride, CatPCA is a more appropriate technique than PCA for analysing ordered categorical variables since the categories are replaced by optimal scores (see Gifi, 1990). The optimal scoring process allows order constraints to be imposed so that ordered categorical variables get increasing, or at least non-decreasing, scores as the category levels become increasingly severe. Responses inconsistent with the implied ordering manifest themselves in tied optimal scores for two or more successive categories. In contrast to PCA, the number of dimensions (m^*) to be considered in the solution must be specified in advance and the solutions for m^* and $m^* + 1$ dimensions are not nested. Once the optimal scores have been calculated, they replace the category codes and the remainder of the analysis can be regarded as (classical) PCA. In short, CatPCA is an appropriate technique to display relationships between cases associated with a set of ordered categorical variables. Like PCA, the method calculates eigenvalues and explained variances, factor loadings, and factor scores with mean zero and unit standard deviation. Furthermore, the solution can be rotated, for example using varimax rotation. Essentially, CatPCA can be regarded as PCA applied to ordered categorical data.

Thus, PCA is commonly understood as a linear technique, since observed variables are approximated by linear combinations of principal components. The aim is to approximate the elements of the matrix $\mathbf{Z}$ by the product of the factor scores and the factor loadings within the m^*-dimensional space, which leads to the well-known equation $\mathbf{Z} \approx \mathbf{FA}$. However, one can also understand PCA as a bilinear technique, since the elements of the data matrix $\mathbf{Z}$ are approximated by inner products that are bilinear functions of factor scores $\mathbf{F}$ and factor loadings $\mathbf{A}$. The degree of approximation can be measured by a least-squares loss function (De Leeuw, 2006; Gifi, 1990):

$$\sigma(\mathbf{F}, \mathbf{A}) = \sum_{i=1}^{n} \sum_{j=1}^{m^*} (z_{ij} - \mathbf{f}_i^\mathsf{T} \mathbf{a}_j)^2$$

As a generalisation of PCA, the nonlinearity in CatPCA can be understood as a nonlinear transformation of the variables that still preserves the (bi)linearity of the technique. It follows that we do not minimize loss merely over the factor scores and factor loadings, but in addition over the admissible transformations of the columns of $\mathbf{Z}$; the loss function becomes

$$\sigma(\mathbf{F}, \mathbf{A}, \mathbf{Z}) = \sum_{i=1}^{n} \sum_{j=1}^{m^*} (z_{ij} - \mathbf{f}_i^\mathsf{T} \mathbf{a}_j)^2$$

For further statistical details and the algorithm, we refer to Gifi (1990) and De Leeuw (2006).

Typically, CatPCA solutions are visualized with the help of biplot axes, which can be interpreted just like other coordinate axes – by projection and reading a value off a scale (Gower and Hand, 1996). The closer two biplot axes are to each other, the stronger the association of the corresponding variables in the m^*-dimensional space (for different forms of visualisation, see Blasius, Eilers and Gower, 2009; for an application, see Blasius and Gower, 2005).

Running CatPCA on the ISSP data described above and restricting the solution to two dimensions, the first factor extracts 30.7% of the variation and the second an additional 11.6%. Comparing the CatPCA with the PCA solution shows a small increase in the explained variation, from 41.8% to 42.3%. This increase in explained variation is always the case since CatPCA does not restrict the items to have constant distances between successive categories as PCA does. As Blasius and

Gower (2005) note, and as discussed in more detail in Chapter 5, the differences in the explained variances can be interpreted as one indication of the quality of the data: the smaller the difference between the solutions, the better the data. Comparing the factor loadings of the unrotated and rotated PCA with the unrotated and rotated CatPCA solution (Table 3.3) reveals only trivial differences.

Table 3.3 Factor loadings, CatPCA, Australia, unrotated and rotated (varimax solution)

	Unrotated Solution		Rotated Solution	
	D1	D2	D1	D2
How close do you feel to: Your town or city	0.452	0.685	0.117	0.813
How close do you feel to: Your [county]	0.528	0.671	0.193	0.832
How close do you feel to Australia	0.565	0.452	0.319	0.650
How close do you feel to the continent	0.064	0.359	−0.095	0.354
How proud: The way democracy works	0.575	−0.238	0.621	0.031
How proud: Its political influence in the world	0.713	−0.270	0.759	0.060
How proud: Australia's economic achievements	0.676	−0.245	0.715	0.067
How proud: Its social security system	0.439	−0.210	0.485	−0.001
How proud: Its scientific and technological achievements	0.543	−0.096	0.533	0.142
How proud: Its achievements in sports	0.573	0.055	0.496	0.291
How proud: Its achievements in arts and literature	0.526	0.031	0.464	0.250
How proud: Australia's armed forces	0.660	−0.148	0.661	0.145
How proud: Its history	0.600	−0.170	0.616	0.100
How proud: Its fair and equal treatment of all groups in society	0.553	−0.274	0.617	−0.011
Eigenvalues	4.295	1.626	3.812	2.109
Explained variances	30.7%	11.6%	27.2%	15.1%

Using the biplot methodology, Figure 3.2 shows the biplot axes of the 14 variables. The labels are affixed to the 'very close'/'very proud' end-point while tick marks represent the category level points. The factorial axes are excluded since they are not useful in the biplot presentation (Gower and Hand, 1996). Two bundles of items can be distinguished, corresponding to the two sets of items. As numerically shown for PCA and CatPCA via varimax rotation, each set of items constitutes its own factor. Inspecting the distances between all successive categories on each item shows that there are no ties (Table 3.4 and Figure 3.2), that is, no two single categories measure the same level of agreement/disagreement to a certain item (for contrasting examples, see Blasius and Gower, 2005; Blasius and Thiessen, 2009). However, the distances between the categories are unequal. Take item O (pride in 'the way democracy works') as an example: the first category (very proud) is relatively far away from the second category (somewhat proud), with respective quantifications of −1.418 and 0.232 (see Table 3.4). The distance between these two categories is 0.232 − (−1.418) = 1.65 (compared to 1.18 between categories 2 and 3, and 0.92 between categories 3 and 4). In fact, the first category is located in the negative

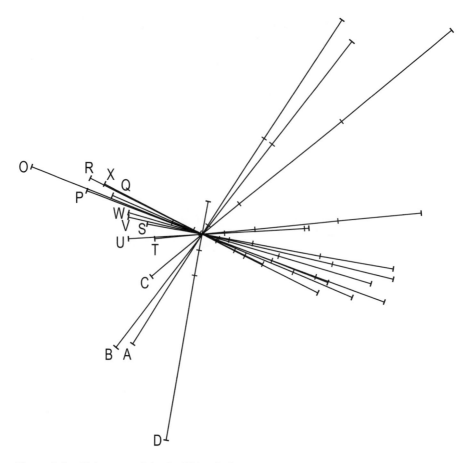

Figure 3.2 Biplot axes of the CatPCA solution

Table 3.4 Quantifications, CatPCA, Australia

	Cat 1	Cat 2	Cat 3	Cat 4
How close do you feel to: Your town or city	−1.403	0.118	1.222	2.750
How close do you feel to: Your [county]	−1.475	0.021	1.176	2.525
How close do you feel to Australia	−0.827	0.592	2.191	3.947
How close do you feel to the continent	−5.028	−1.002	−0.398	0.803
How proud: The way democracy works	−1.418	0.232	1.412	2.332
How proud: Its political influence in the world	−2.170	−0.377	0.867	1.575
How proud: Australia's economic achievements	−1.549	0.191	1.494	2.414
How proud: Its social security system	−2.333	−0.037	0.669	1.240
How proud: Its scientific and technological achievements	−0.925	0.830	1.942	3.159
How proud: Its achievements in sports	−0.756	0.811	2.108	3.426
How proud: Its achievements in arts and literature	−1.278	0.373	1.735	1.805
How proud: Australia's armed forces	−1.007	0.360	1.755	2.595
How proud: Its history	−1.128	0.249	1.126	2.509
How proud: Its fair and equal treatment of all groups in society	−1.612	−0.138	0.680	1.861

part of dimension 1 and in the positive part of dimension 2, while the second category is already located in the opposite parts (i.e., on the other side of the mean, which is the point where the lines for all items cross). In other words, the mean point of the latent concept behind variable O is not between categories 2 and 3; it is between categories 1 and 2.

Inspecting Figure 3.2 in more detail shows that within the first set of items, item D ('closeness to the continent') is somewhat separated from the others. This is easy to explain for Australia: from the geographical point of view the continent Australia is almost the same as the country, differing only by a small number of islands to which Australians feel less close than to their own country. The particular variation of the item is also reflected by the quantifications: the 'very close' is far away from the 'close' category and the mean point of the items is between the third and fourth categories – that is, even a 'not very close' response suggest a level of regional identity with the continent somewhat above average. With respect to the items measuring national pride, the achievements in sports (T) as well as in arts and literature (U) are in somewhat distinct positions; they form their own subcluster within the second set of items.

From Figure 3.2 one can also imagine the concept of rotation: crossing the centre of biplot axes, the principal axes from the unrotated solution are those on horizontal and vertical lines. If one rotates into the centre of the two sets of

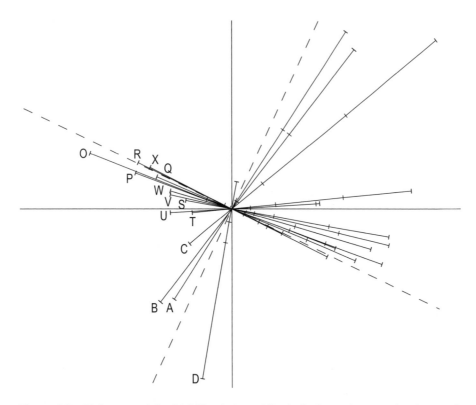

Figure 3.3 Biplot axes of the CatPCA solution, with principal axes (unrotated and rotated)

items by keeping the orthogonality (i.e., the 90-degree angles between the factors), the correlation between unrotated (solid lines) and rotated factors (dashed lines) is 0.905 or 0.425, respectively. In other words, rotating the principal axes clockwise by 25.1 degrees, or by 64.9 degrees anticlockwise, provides the rotated solution (Figure 3.3).

Multiple correspondence analysis_____

3.3 In the next step we perform MCA on the same data. While PCA restricts the data to be metric (i.e., all distances between two successive categories are equal), and while CatPCA keeps the ordinality of the successive categories, MCA makes no assumptions about the measurement level of the variables. In other words, MCA can be regarded as PCA with unordered categorical variables. Although MCA also provides eigenvalues and factor loadings, primary interest usually centres on the visualization of the data.

There are several conceptual and computational approaches to MCA. In the framework in which we discussed CatPCA, MCA is also known under the name 'homogeneity analysis' (Gifi, 1990; Heiser and Meulman, 1994); in Japan it is often discussed under the terms 'dual scaling' (Nishisato, 1980, 2007) and 'quantification of qualitative data III' (Hayashi, 1954). Although the statistical procedures differ, the solutions can easily be converted into each other. We introduce the method from the geometrical point of view, as developed in the 1960s in France by Jean-Paul Benzécri et al. (1973; see also Greenacre, 1984, 2007; Le Roux and Rouanet, 2004; Lebart, Morineau and Warwick, 1984; Rouanet, 2006).

The main objective of MCA is to display objects (respondents) and variables (variable categories) of data tables in low-dimensional spaces, most often in two-dimensional spaces called 'maps'. The philosophy behind MCA can be expressed by the famous quotation of Jean-Paul Benzécri who pointed out that 'The model should follow the data, not the inverse' (see Blasius and Greenacre, 2006: 6). Instead of limiting the data to restrictively (and often subjectively) formulated statistical models, the importance of the data and of the features in the data themselves becomes visualized. Other than excluding negative data, which do not exist in survey research, MCA does not restrict the data. MCA searches for the best 'viewpoint' from which to see the structure of the data, making it an ideal method to screen data and visualize method-induced variance.

To introduce the method, we start with two variables A and B having I rows and J columns. Cross-tabulating them provides the two-way table of frequencies, N. When this table is used as input for the analysis, the method is called simple correspondence analysis (SCA). As will be shown, SCA translates deviations from the independence model of a contingency table into distances in a low-dimensional space. The elements of N (n_{ij}) contain the frequencies of the cross-tabulation of A and B, with $\sum_{ij} n_{ij} = n$. Dividing n_{ij} by the sample size (n)

produces the $(I \times J)$ correspondence matrix $\mathbf{P}$, with elements p_{ij}. The row marginals of $\mathbf{P}$,

$$r_i = \sum_{j=1}^{J} p_{ij} = n_{i+} / n$$

form the vector of the row masses $(\mathbf{r})$, which is also known as the average column profile; the column marginals of $\mathbf{P}$,

$$c_j = \sum_{i=1}^{I} p_{ij} = n_{+j} / n$$

form the vector of column masses $(\mathbf{c})$, also known as average row profile; $\mathbf{D}_r$ and $\mathbf{D}_c$ are the diagonal matrices of the row and column masses, respectively.

As a measure of similarity between two row profiles (or between two column profiles), a weighted Euclidean or chi-square distance is used. For the chi-square calculation, the weighted deviations from independence over all cells of the contingency table are used. For each cell, the unweighted deviation of the observed from the expected value can be calculated by $n_{ij} - \hat{n}_{ij}$, with $\hat{n}_{ij} = (n_{i+} \times n_{+j}) / n$. Dividing $n_{ij} - \hat{n}_{ij}$ by n provides $p_{ij} - r_i c_j$, or, in matrix notation, $\mathbf{P} - \mathbf{rc}^\mathsf{T}$. According to the chi-square statistic, this matrix is weighted by the product of the square root of the row and column masses. This procedure provides the standardized residuals

$$s_{ij} = (p_{ij} - r_i c_j) / \sqrt{r_i c_j}$$

or in matrix notation,

$$\mathbf{S} = \mathbf{D}_r^{-1/2} (\mathbf{P} - \mathbf{rc}^\mathsf{T}) \mathbf{D}_c^{-1/2}$$

The chi-square statistic is defined by the sum of squared deviations from observed and expected values, divided by the expected values:

$$\chi^2 = \sum_{i=1}^{I} \sum_{j=1}^{J} \frac{(n_{ij} - \hat{n}_{ij})^2}{\hat{n}_{ij}}$$

Dividing chi-square by the sample size (n) produces a measure called 'total inertia', whose minimum and maximum values are zero and min $((I, J) - 1)$, respectively. The similarity between chi-square statistics and the standardized residuals becomes apparent by noting that

$$\sum_{i=1}^{I} \sum_{j=1}^{J} s_{ij}^2 = \frac{\chi^2}{n} = \sum_{i=1}^{I} \sum_{j=1}^{J} \frac{(p_{ij} - r_i c_j)^2}{r_i c_j}$$

While in PCA and CatPCA the (symmetric) correlation matrix contains the similarities/dissimilarities between the variables, in SCA (and analogues in MCA) the rectangular matrix $\mathbf{S}$ contains the similarities/dissimilarities between the categories of the variables A and B. Applying singular value decomposition (SVD) to $\mathbf{S}$ results in $\text{SVD}(\mathbf{S}) = \mathbf{U}\Gamma\mathbf{V}^{\mathrm{T}}$, where Γ is a diagonal matrix with singular values in descending order $\gamma_1 \geq \gamma_2 \geq \dots \geq \gamma_S > 0$, with $S = $ rank of $\mathbf{S}$. The columns from $\mathbf{U}$ are the left singular vectors, the columns from $\mathbf{V}$ are the right singular vectors, with $\mathbf{U}^{\mathrm{T}}\mathbf{U} = \mathbf{V}^{\mathrm{T}}\mathbf{V} = \mathbf{I}$. The connection between SVD, as used in correspondence analysis, and canonical decomposition is shown by $\mathbf{S}^{\mathrm{T}}\mathbf{S} = \mathbf{V}\Gamma\mathbf{U}^{\mathrm{T}}\mathbf{U}\Gamma\mathbf{V}^{\mathrm{T}} = \mathbf{V}\Gamma^2\mathbf{V}^{\mathrm{T}} = \mathbf{V}\Lambda\mathbf{V}^{\mathrm{T}}$, with $\mathbf{S}\mathbf{S}^{\mathrm{T}} = \mathbf{U}\Gamma\mathbf{V}^{\mathrm{T}}\mathbf{V}\Gamma\mathbf{U}^{\mathrm{T}} = \mathbf{U}\Gamma^2\mathbf{U}^{\mathrm{T}} = \mathbf{U}\Lambda\mathbf{U}^{\mathrm{T}}$, and $\lambda_1 \geq \lambda_2 \geq \dots \geq \lambda_S > 0$. As in PCA, the first axis explains the maximum variation in the data; the second axis captures the maximum of the remaining variation, and so on. For the graphical representation, $\mathbf{F} = \mathbf{D}_r^{-1/2}\mathbf{U}\Gamma$ provides the principal coordinates of the rows, and $\mathbf{G} = \mathbf{D}_c^{-1/2}\mathbf{V}\Gamma$ provides the principal coordinates of the columns (for further details, see Greenacre, 1984, 2007).

Whereas SCA is applied to a single contingency table or to a stacked table, MCA uses the same algorithm on an indicator or a Burt matrix. Applying the above algorithm to the indicator matrix $\mathbf{H}$, the table of input data has n rows (i.e., the number of objects or respondents) and as many columns as there are response alternatives in all variables included in the analysis. A 1 in a given row indicates a specific response category was chosen; a 0 indicates that it was not chosen. Considering all categories of all variables provides row sums that are all equal to the number of variables (m); the column sums reflect the frequencies of the marginals. An alternative to the indicator matrix as input to MCA is the Burt matrix $\mathbf{B}$ (an example is given in Table 6.2 and in various R files on the web page of this book, see www.xxx). This matrix can be generated by cross-tabulating all variables by all variables, including the cross-tabulations of the variables by themselves, and stacking them row- and columnwise. $\mathbf{B}$ can also be computed by multiplying the transposed indicator matrix by itself, that is, $\mathbf{B} = \mathbf{H}^{\mathrm{T}}\mathbf{H}$. As is true for PCA and CatPCA, MCA contains all first-order interaction effects, and the method can be understood as a generalization of PCA to unordered categorical data.

The solutions from $\mathbf{H}$ can easily be converted to those of $\mathbf{B}$ by rescaling the solution. Therefore, the squared eigenvalues of $\mathbf{H}$ are equal to the eigenvalues of $\mathbf{B}$, and the ratio of the locations of the variable categories, given in the columns of $\mathbf{H}$ and $\mathbf{B}$, is given by

$$\frac{g_{\mathrm{B},jk}}{g_{\mathrm{H},jk}} = \sqrt{\frac{\lambda_{\mathrm{B},k}}{\lambda_{\mathrm{H},k}}}$$

Consequently, $g_{\mathrm{B},jk}$ is the location (the principal coordinate) of variable category j on dimension k in the solution for the Burt table, and $\lambda_{\mathrm{B},k}$ is the corresponding kth eigenvalue for this solution.

With respect to **B**, most of the variation in this matrix is caused by the main diagonal blocks, which contain the cross-tabulations of the variables with themselves. The main diagonal elements contain the marginals of the variables, while their off-diagonal elements equal zero. One straightforward method for excluding at least large parts of this variation has been shown by Greenacre (1988; see also Greenacre, 2007). Assuming that there are Q variables, **B** contains Q^2 cross-tables. Total inertia, which here can be treated as average total inertia of the Q^2 cross-tables, is λ_T. Referring to the (artificial) sum of total inertia for all cross-tables provides $Q^2 \times \lambda_T$. From this value one can subtract the inertia of the main diagonal blocks. Assuming a total of J variable categories, the inertia of the main diagonal blocks sum to $J - Q$. It follows that the inertia of the off-diagonal blocks is $Q^2 \times \lambda_T - (J - Q)$. Dividing this value by the number of off-diagonal blocks $Q(Q - 1)$ provides the corrected value of total inertia. In addition to the rescaling of total inertia one has to rescale the inertia of the single axes (eigenvalues) and of the location parameters (Greenacre, 1988, 2007).

Regardless of the method of rescaling, the concept of inertia is central to MCA: the farther the categories are from the centroid along a given axis (squared distances) and the higher their masses (their marginals), the more the categories determine the geometric orientation of the respective axis. In the graphical solution, the locations of all variable categories can be compared to each other. Specifically, short distances imply strong similarities and long distances strong dissimilarities. Since the manner of rescaling does not affect the graphical interpretation of the solution, which we use to screen the data, we will not go into further details of this discussion. Note that the kind of scaling used depends on the software package; for example, in its current version, SPSS uses the indicator matrix as input data, while SAS uses the Burt matrix; in the ca package of R one can chose between different kinds of scaling (Greenacre and Nenadić, 2006; Nenadić and Greenacre, 2007).

There are several additional types of analyses possible within the MCA framework. One of the most important is the concept of supplementary (or passive) variables that can be included in a given solution. Such variables, or variable categories, have no impact on the geometric orientation of the axes but their location is an aid to understanding the active variables of interest. We will use them to include socio-demographic information in the m^*-dimensional graphical solution of the regional identity and national pride items, for example. With respect to the aim of the book, this feature will help us to assign non-substantive variation to certain demographic subgroups, such as those with low formal education.

A second possibility is the analysis of subsets of response categories. Subset correspondence analysis and subset multiple correspondence analysis (SMCA) concentrate on just some of the response categories, while excluding others from the solution (Greenacre, 2007; Greenacre and Pardo, 2006a, 2006b). For example, with SMCA the structure of the subset of non-substantive responses such as 'don't know' and 'no answer' can be analysed separately, or these responses can be excluded from the solution while concentrating only on the substantive responses, or one can focus on the extreme categories only. Suppose there are five variables with four categories, ranging from 'very proud' to 'not proud at all', with no missing values. Since the row sums of the indicator matrix are 5 in this case, SMCA maintains the equal weighting of all respondents (i.e., the row profile values are 0.2 and 0) when excluding columns (variable categories). If we concentrate on 'very proud', respondents with five answers on 'very proud' will have five profile values of 0.2 (and a row sum of 1.0), respondents with four answers on 'very proud' will have four profile values of 0.2 (and a row sum of 0.8), and respondents with two answers on 'very proud' will have two profile values of 0.2 (and a row sum of 0.4). In the process of screening the data, SMCA will help us, for example, to show the structures of extreme responses and the structure of NSRs, how they interrelate and how they relate to other response categories and to supplementary variables.

One major problem in PCA and in survey research in general is the treatment of missing data. To keep the analysis simple, we applied listwise deletion when running PCA and CatPCA, a procedure that is often the default in statistical packages. The handling of missing cases is – at least in theory – relatively easy within the MCA framework. For example, it is possible to consider them to be just additional response categories. However, missing responses are often highly intercorrelated. In the MCA solution it may turn out that the first dimension just mirrors the substantive versus the non-substantive responses, which is quite meaningless. We will discuss this point later (and how to avoid such a trivial solution). In the following we run MCA (as well as SMCA) on the same subset of respondents as we did in PCA and CatPCA, using listwise deletion; as input we use the indicator matrix based on 1,548 cases. Figure 3.4 shows the MCA map of the 14 variables with its total of 56 categories. To make the figure more legible, we connected the successive categories of the individual variables by trajectories.

Projecting the categories from all variables onto the first dimension shows that all items retain the ordinality of their categories. Therefore, dimension 1 reflects the level of regional identity and national pride: the farther to the left a variable category is located, the stronger is the identity with the region and the greater is the pride in Australia's achievements. The same holds for the respondents (see Figure 3.5): the farther to the left they are located, the closer they feel towards the region and the prouder they feel about the achievements of their country. The second dimension shows the horseshoe (or Guttman) effect, with extreme values in the negative part and moderate values in the positive part. This effect is methodologically induced; it reflects the intercorrelations between the single categories of the variables, that is, the associations within the sets of 'very close'/'very proud', 'close'/'somewhat proud', 'not very close'/'not very proud' and 'not close at all'/'not proud at all' categories (for more details on the horseshoe effect, see Greenacre, 1984; Van Rijckevorsel, 1987). However, it is precisely to exclude methodologically induced variation

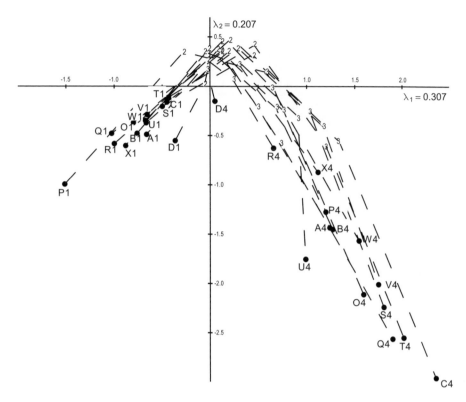

Figure 3.4   MCA map, first and second principal axes, variables

of such kinds in ordinal data that de Leeuw (2006) proposed the use of CatPCA instead of MCA. We will return to this point later.

In addition to the variable categories, it is possible to plot the 1,548 respondents in the map (Figure 3.5). As one can see, their distribution on the two-dimensional map also forms a horseshoe. Using the horizontal axis to aid in the interpretation, the farther the respondents are located in the negative part, the greater their pride in their country's achievements and the closer they feel to the region. Dimension 2 subdivides the respondents by their use of response categories; the negative part is where extreme values are concentrated while the positive part is where the moderate categories have been used above average. Furthermore, a few outlying objects occur on the bottom right. Since the factors are standardized to mean value zero and standard deviation one, there is a high probability that at least one respondent gave some arbitrary answers (or for whom responses were miscoded; see especially Chapter 4). In any case, a few other respondents gave some very negative statements concerning regional identity and national pride. These cases arouse some suspicion and this would be a good reason to examine the corresponding interviews in detail. For example, one can explore whether these items (or the entire interviews) were faked (see Chapter 4).

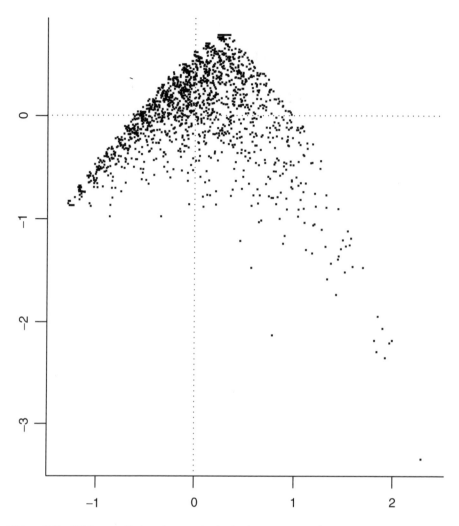

Figure 3.5 MCA map, first and second principal axes, respondents

In the next step we include supplementary information in the given solution. Formal education (with five categories ranging from 'no formal qualification' to 'university degree') and the two categories for gender are entered as passive variables. Since Figure 3.4 is too dense to include additional symbols close to the centroid, Figure 3.6 shows only the seven supplementary variable categories. Note that the scale differs between Figures 3.4 and 3.6; in Figure 3.6 all categories are relatively close to the centroid (compared to the variable categories on regional identity and national pride, shown in Figure 3.4). However, there is a clear relation of educational attainment with the first dimension, namely the level of regional identity and national pride. Specifically, the higher the formal education, the prouder the

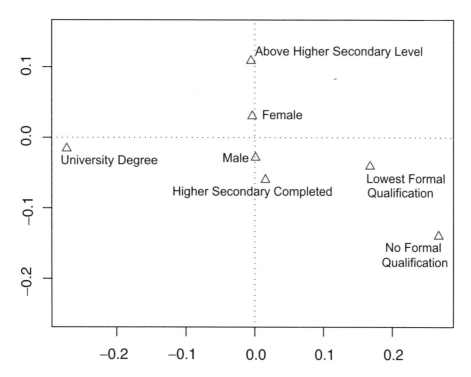

Figure 3.6 MCA map, first and second principal axes, supplementary variables

respondent feels about Australia's achievements and the more they identify with the region in which they live. Sex is not correlated with the first dimension but somewhat with the second: females gave a relatively high number of moderate responses, while males gave a relatively high number of extreme responses.

In the final step, we run a series of SMCAs. To show how the method works, we subdivide the data set on regional identity and national pride in several ways: first, category 1 ('very close', 'very proud') versus the remaining three categories; second, the moderate versus the extreme categories; and third, all categories separately. In the complete solution (using all categories, 'traditional' MCA), we have $J - Q$ dimensions ($56 - 14 = 42$), and total inertia is 3.000 (whenever there are no missing values, the value of the fourth category is determined by the other three; i.e., there are three degrees of freedom for a variable with four categories). In SMCA, in contrast, the number of dimensions is equal to the number of categories since there is at least one remaining category, which belongs to the second subset of variable categories. Table 3.5 shows possible subdivisions of the variable categories within SMCA, given are the respective inertias of dimensions 1 and 2, the explained variances of the two dimensions (without any rescaling), and the degrees of freedom.

Table 3.5 Decomposition of inertia using SMCA

Model	No. of dim.	D1		D2		Total	
		Abs.	(%)	Abs.	(%)	Abs.	(%)
All categories	42	0.307	10.2	0.207	6.9	3.000	100.0
Cat 1 versus 2, 3, 4							
Cat 1	14	0.190	27.0	0.086	12.2	0.703	23.4
Cat 2, 3 and 4	42	0.240	10.5	0.140	6.1	2.297	76.6
Cat 2 and 3 versus 1 and 4							
Cat 1 and 4	28	0.242	14.9	0.149	9.1	1.628	54.3
Cat 2 and 3	28	0.170	12.4	0.099	7.2	1.372	45.7
All categories separate							
Cat 1	14	0.190	27.0	0.086	12.2	0.703	23.4
Cat 2	14	0.092	17.1	0.062	11.6	0.539	18.0
Cat 3	14	0.151	18.1	0.086	10.3	0.832	27.7
Cat 4	14	0.198	21.4	0.102	11.1	0.926	30.9

As shown in the second last column of Table 3.5, the sum of total inertia over the corresponding SMCA is in all cases equal to 3.000; for example, the sum of total inertias of extreme and moderate categories is 1.628 + 1.372 = 3.000. Therefore, when subdividing the data into subsets of variable categories, there is no loss of variation. Furthermore, Table 3.5 shows how much variation belongs to each set of categories. For example, the subset of the categories 'not close at all' and 'not proud at all' (last row) contains 30.9% of the total variation; of this 30.9% (total inertia 0.926), 21.4% is explained by dimension 1 of the SMCA and an additional 11.1% by dimension 2. By contrast, the subset of categories 'close' and 'somewhat proud' contains only 18.0% of the total variation (total inertia 0.539), and the first two dimensions account for low percentages of this variance (17.1% and 11.6%, respectively). As an example for the graphical presentation of the solution, we show the SMCA of the categories 'very close' and 'very proud', with 10 items on national pride and four items on regional identity (Figure 3.7).

Figure 3.7 shows that all categories are located on the negative part of dimension 1. This is due to the MCA solution of the entire data set; in both cases the negative part of dimension 1 mirrors a high level of pride in Australia's achievements as well as a high identity with the country and region. Somewhat outlying on dimension 1 is 'political influence': a high level of pride towards this issue reflects a level of pride in Australia that is above average even within the group of 'proud respondents'. Furthermore, the group of respondents that chose this category is relatively small, as already shown in the table of marginal distributions (Table 3.1). The second dimension reflects the distinction between the two sets of items. Thereby, especially the closeness to the continent is located far away from the centroid, but also the closeness to the town and to the county is clearly separated in the map.

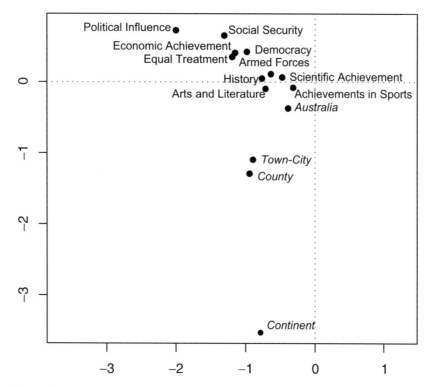

Figure 3.7 SMCA, 14 variables on national pride and regional identity (in italics), with the categories 'very close' and 'very proud' shown

Conclusion _____

3.4 This chapter has shown the mathematical and statistical bases of three scaling methods: MCA (including SMCA), CatPCA, and PCA. MCA and SMCA are the least restrictive: only negative values are not permitted. Since the lowest possible value in a frequency table (including the indicator and the Burt matrix) is zero, this restriction is hardly a limiting one. In these methods, the positions of the variable categories in the latent space are found on the basis of their similarities of co-occurrences. For example, response categories that have been chosen by the same respondents disproportionately often are relatively close to each other, while categories that typically have been chosen by different respondents are relatively distant from each other. When the response categories are best viewed as unordered categorical data, MCA and SMCA are the methods that should be used for data screening purposes.

When the data consist of ordered categorical data (e.g., Likert response formats), the application of MCA and SMCA often produces a horseshoe on the second dimension, although sometimes it occurs in between the first and second dimension and sometimes even on the first dimension. This horseshoe effect is methodologically induced (see Greenacre, 1984; Van Rijckevorsel, 1987). To exclude this kind of variation in ordered categorical data, De Leeuw (2006) proposes the use of CatPCA instead of MCA. In CatPCA, fitting a straight line in a two-dimensional space onto the set of successive categories in a way that minimizes the (weighted) squared distances towards the line produces what is known as a biplot axis (examples are shown in Figures 3.2 and 3.3). Projecting the response categories onto this line shows that the distances between the successive categories are unequal; in some cases they are even interchanged, which would result in tied quantifications.

Finally, PCA essentially forces the unequal CatPCA distances between the successive categories to be treated as though they were equal. For this reason, when the data are close to metric, the differences between CatPCA and PCA are trivial, and the geometric orientations of the axes are (almost) identical (similar eigenvalues, factor loadings and factor scores).

4

Institutional quality control practices

As stated in the previous chapters, the underlying logic of our screening approach rests on detecting unusual patterns in the data. For three reasons, our preferred screening techniques are MCA and CatPCA. First, these techniques make the fewest assumptions about the data; hence they can be safely employed even when the data are far from normally distributed and have poor measurement properties. Second, the numerical solutions are twinned with visual displays of the solutions; graphics facilitate the detection of dirty data. Finally, in MCA there is a simple correspondence between distance and dissimilarity. That is, the closer data points are to each other in the underlying space, the greater their similarity. Puzzles arise when theoretically similar data points happen to be far removed from each other in MCA maps. Conversely, some points may form a cluster for which no convincing theoretical commonality can be found. In CatPCA poor data can be detected in biplots via tied categories. When such unexpected patterns appear in either MCA or CatPCA, the first line of attack is to determine whether this is the result of a methodological artefact pointing to a data quality problem.

This chapter focuses on procedural and institutional factors that can compromise data quality. We use three different data sets to illustrate how we detected anomalous patterns and how we subsequently determined that these unusual patterns were, in all likelihood, artefacts of data collection procedures and the failure of data collection institutions to ensure the authenticity of their survey data. We start with an example from the WVS 2005–2008 where we detect clusters of nation-specific response combinations whose frequency of occurrence defies the odds to such an extent that we conclude that some of them occur because of procedural and/or interviewer deficiencies. Next, on the basis of a more stringent definition of anomalous patterns, we document that some data collection institutions probably obtained their quota of cases through the simple expedient of duplicating cases – that is, the interviews are faked copies, whose existence was masked by making minor changes to the duplicated cases, such as changing the case identifier. This is followed by an example from one of our own primary data collection projects (Blasius, Friedrichs and Klöckner, 2008) during which our screening procedures detected anomalous patterns associated with the interviews collected by a few of the interviewers. Based on the nature of the patterns, we suspected that these interviewers faked or partially faked some of their interviews. Our suspicions were confirmed through the simple expedient of calling the respondents and determining they had not been interviewed. Finally, we give an example from the ESS 2002 of a pattern that we conclude represents inadvertent data entry errors.

Detecting procedural deficiencies

4.1 We initially selected the WVS 2005–2008 for two reasons. First, it contains data from many countries seldom included in any of the other international survey projects together with countries almost always included in these studies. Second, it utilizes a 10-point response format for some items, which allows us to detect misplaced mid-points (i.e., a '5'). As an example we chose the battery of items inquiring about the essential characteristics of democracies, which were assessed through the following:

> Many things may be desirable, but not all of them are essential characteristics of democracy. Please tell me for each of the following things how essential you think it is as a characteristic of democracy. Use this scale where 1 means not at all 'an essential characteristic of democracy' and 10 means it definitely is 'an essential characteristic of democracy':
>
> Governments tax the rich and subsidize the poor.
> Religious authorities interpret the laws.
> People choose their leaders in free elections.
> People receive state aid for unemployment.
> The army takes over when government is incompetent.
> Civil rights protect people's liberty against oppression.
> The economy is prospering.
> Criminals are severely punished.
> People can change the laws in referendums.
> Women have the same rights as men.

Preliminary examination of the intercorrelations of the 10 items separately for each country (not shown) revealed that items 2 ('Religious authorities interpret the laws') and 5 ('The army takes over when government is incompetent') were positively correlated with each other and often negatively correlated with the other possible characteristics of democracy. Additionally, the correlations tended to be weak and variable across countries, suggesting that the underlying structures might not be comparable. Hence, we started our analysis here in our customary manner by examining the response patterns separately for each participating country; that is, we calculated the percentage of times each response option was used for the eight items that typically were positively correlated (see Table 4.1). This simple frequency analysis revealed that in India, only three response options were used, with codes 1, 5, and 10.

The distribution of responses is consistent with a task simplification dynamic in several respects. First, the extreme low end-point (1) was used disproportionately

Table 4.1 Percentage of times each response option was used for the democracy items

Country	1	2	3	4	5	6	7	8	9	10
Andorra	3.2	1.4	1.8	1.6	7.5	4.3	6.5	12.0	8.7	52.0
Argentina	6.6	1.0	1.9	1.6	5.2	3.1	5.1	7.8	5.2	53.8
Australia	4.6	2.0	3.2	3.1	9.7	6.2	8.8	11.7	10.0	38.1
Brazil	9.0	3.0	3.6	4.2	8.9	5.0	6.7	11.9	9.9	31.6
Bulgaria	6.6	3.8	3.4	2.8	5.7	4.4	5.3	10.2	13.5	35.3
Burkina Faso	6.2	3.2	2.3	3.0	7.0	4.9	6.3	7.7	7.4	39.3
Canada	2.6	1.9	2.8	3.3	8.0	6.7	10.4	17.4	13.2	29.1
Chile	4.4	1.6	2.4	3.1	11.4	7.2	7.7	10.5	8.9	35.6
China	2.2	1.1	0.9	1.0	2.7	3.2	4.1	10.0	16.8	36.0
Cyprus	4.6	1.9	2.8	2.4	8.7	5.5	6.7	9.2	10.9	47.0
Egypt	3.6	0.9	2.2	2.5	5.2	4.3	6.3	9.0	6.6	58.5
Ethiopia	1.7	0.6	0.9	0.8	3.4	4.1	10.3	15.4	23.2	35.2
Finland	1.7	1.7	2.8	3.3	7.5	7.4	12.9	20.0	16.9	24.1
Georgia	2.9	0.9	1.2	1.3	3.2	4.4	7.6	9.5	10.0	51.1
Germany	1.9	1.0	1.7	2.4	5.7	5.9	8.2	12.5	10.5	47.8
Ghana	10.2	3.3	3.7	2.9	4.6	6.4	7.9	12.2	15.2	31.2
India	8.8	0.0	0.0	0.0	16.1	0.0	0.0	0.0	0.0	53.5
Indonesia	6.3	2.1	2.3	2.4	6.1	5.0	6.9	9.4	10.1	44.1
Japan	2.1	1.0	1.8	1.8	4.8	13.3	10.7	15.8	10.6	27.1
Jordan	6.0	1.4	1.1	1.2	2.7	4.4	4.8	9.3	7.0	55.3
Malaysia	3.3	2.5	3.3	5.9	16.8	14.4	15.6	14.2	9.9	14.0
Mali	9.0	2.1	1.4	2.0	8.0	5.0	8.5	7.2	7.7	39.7
Mexico	14.4	3.8	3.7	3.4	8.2	5.3	6.5	10.3	8.5	28.2
Moldova	3.1	1.6	2.3	2.9	8.4	6.4	10.2	13.8	17.0	31.0
Morocco	5.7	1.4	1.5	2.3	5.9	3.5	6.3	10.0	10.6	38.2
Norway	5.5	3.4	4.0	3.0	7.8	5.0	9.4	15.4	13.5	31.2
Peru	3.9	2.8	2.9	2.8	7.2	5.7	8.0	13.4	12.5	35.3
Poland	3.0	1.4	2.6	2.6	6.8	4.9	7.6	12.3	10.7	40.9
Romania	1.5	0.8	1.1	1.1	3.6	1.9	4.3	8.7	10.8	57.3
Rwanda	2.6	2.8	4.2	5.1	7.2	7.9	10.2	14.5	17.9	22.4
Serbia	4.4	1.6	2.0	2.2	5.7	4.8	6.8	12.5	13.1	35.7
Slovenia	4.3	2.1	3.2	2.8	7.4	4.9	8.0	13.1	11.3	33.4
South Africa	3.7	2.8	2.5	3.5	8.1	6.7	8.7	11.6	13.3	35.4
South Korea	3.1	1.4	2.3	2.8	8.8	6.0	11.1	17.1	14.7	32.8
Spain	2.3	1.0	1.5	2.6	8.1	6.6	12.1	11.9	10.3	38.3
Sweden	5.3	2.9	3.7	2.3	5.0	3.9	9.6	13.5	11.0	41.6
Switzerland	3.3	1.9	2.1	2.0	5.3	4.7	7.5	16.0	13.5	41.3
Taiwan	1.3	0.6	1.2	1.5	5.5	6.7	9.6	18.1	15.6	39.1
Thailand	3.9	2.8	4.1	5.9	15.5	14.6	17.5	14.1	10.1	11.0
Trinidad and Tobago	6.2	2.4	2.7	3.2	9.2	5.8	6.5	10.2	10.8	41.8
Turkey	2.3	1.0	1.3	2.0	5.6	5.4	10.1	16.5	8.7	44.1
Ukraine	2.1	1.1	2.0	3.1	6.7	7.2	8.1	10.4	14.3	35.9
Uruguay	4.5	1.4	1.9	3.3	12.9	7.9	9.0	11.5	7.3	36.5
USA	5.3	2.4	3.4	3.8	14.5	8.1	9.3	10.0	9.1	30.0
Vietnam	0.9	0.3	0.4	0.9	2.7	4.8	6.3	11.9	13.0	54.3
Zambia	5.6	3.4	4.4	4.5	10.7	8.1	6.5	7.5	8.9	36.4

often; in all countries except Finland and Rwanda, responses of '1' occur more often than those of '2' and except in two additional countries (Canada and Thailand) more often than those of '3'. Second, a response of '5', despite not being exactly at the mid-point of the range between '1' and '10', nevertheless often appears to be used as a convenient mid-point: in 34 of the 46 participating countries, the percentage of '5' responses exceeds that of *both* '4' and '6' responses. Third, in all countries responses of '10' occur more frequently than those of '9', sometimes by as much as ten times (e.g., Argentina). In short, a frequent task simplification strategy for respondents in many countries is to collapse the 10-point scale into a simple three-point scale (see also Belli, Herzog and Van Hoewyk, 1999, for a similar task simplification strategy).

A further feature of the distributions is their consistent negative skew, which sometimes is quite dramatic: in eight countries, more '10' responses were used than all other numbers combined, including the missing responses, which are not shown in Table 4.1. Such a pronounced skew suggests the prevalence of cultural scripts that make it acceptable, indeed desirable, to give extreme endorsement to these eight items as being essential to democracy (despite the introductory caution to the items which stated that not all desirable things should be considered essential). While theoretically there are 10 billion (10^{10}) possible combinations of responses, substantially fewer can be expected because of both the skew and the correlations between the items. Nevertheless, on purely probabilistic grounds, the presence of multiple respondents with identical response patterns should prove to be rather rare. As a quick screening procedure, we applied PCA to the 10 items separately for each country. We saved the factor scores for the first dimension, keeping in mind that identical response combinations will yield identical factor scores. We next obtained the frequency distribution of the factor scores and identified those response combinations that occurred more than once, as well as the ones that occurred most frequently in each country. These results, together with the sample sizes and the percentage of missing cases when listwise deletion is used, are shown in Table 4.2.

Two patterns, identified as pattern 1 and pattern 2 in the table, occur more frequently across the different countries than any others. The first pattern involves giving a response of '1' to the second and fifth items, and giving a response of '10' to the remaining eight items. The second pattern consists of an extreme rejection of the fifth item coupled with an extreme endorsement of all remaining items. In fact, the two patterns differ only with respect to the second item, which is either a strong endorsement or an extreme rejection. Many countries have one or the other of these two patterns disproportionately frequently, while a few contain both of them often. The next column shows the highest share of identical factor scores. For example, Germany has 128 cases (=7.0%) of valid cases giving a pattern 1 response. In contrast, Canada has only 5 instances (=0.3%) in its single most frequent pattern (pattern 1).

A second peculiarity is that a few countries have still different modal response combinations. Ghana, for example, has no cases in patterns 1 and 2, but it has 22

Table 4.2 Response patterns by country

Country	N	Per cent missing	Pattern 1	Pattern 2	Per cent of cases in maximum co-occurrence	Number of duplicate combinations	Per cent duplicate cases	Duplicates–combinations ratio
Andorra	1,003	4.2	51	1	5.3	53	19.3	3.5
Argentina	1,002	31.6	16	23	3.4	41	15.3	2.6
Australia	1,421	6.8	9	4	0.7	29	3.5	1.6
Brazil	1,500	15.7	6	3	0.9	27	5.1	2.4
Bulgaria	1,001	33.3	11	1	2.7	17	7.9	3.1
Burkina Faso	1,534	27.6	12	8	1.5	47	11.7	2.8
Canada	2,164	20.0	5	1	0.3	14	1.3	1.6
Chile	1,000	23.1	13	8	1.7	27	6.5	1.9
China	2,015	62.3	17	1	3.0	20	7.5	2.9
Cyprus	1,050	1.5	36	13	3.5	53	14.8	2.9
Egypt	3,051	6.3	2	33	1.2	151	16.2	3.1
Ethiopia	1,500	18.0	19	25	2.0	220	33.8	1.9
Finland	1,014	6.5	7	0	0.7	4	1.1	2.5
Georgia	1,500	35.2	15	4	2.2	59	16.4	2.7
Germany	2,064	10.9	128	2	7.0	95	15.6	3.0
Ghana	1,534	12.8	0	0	1.6	39	7.1	2.4
India	2,001	48.6	49	2	4.8	132	38.4	3.0
Indonesia	2,050	24.9	3	5	1.5	104	14.7	2.2
Japan	1,096	35.9	15	0	2.1	16	4.4	1.9
Jordan	1,200	20.8	2	9	1.1	43	9.4	2.1
Malaysia	1,201	0.7	0	1	0.5	50	6.3	1.5
Mali	1,534	29.5	4	6	3.7	48	15.5	3.5
Mexico	1,560	16.3	5	1	1.4	28	5.7	2.6
Moldova	1,046	16.0	8	3	0.9	61	9.0	1.3
Morrocco	1,200	32.8	3	0	0.6	17	4.0	1.9
Norway	1,025	4.0	2	1	0.4	13	1.5	1.2
Peru	1,500	18.8	8	6	0.7	19	4.3	2.7
Poland	1,000	22.3	14	4	1.8	19	5.9	2.4
Romania	1,776	24.5	27	10	2.0	72	14.4	2.7
Serbia	1,220	23.6	13	5	1.4	47	8.2	1.6
Slovenia	1,037	23.6	13	3	1.6	16	4.4	2.2
South Africa	2,988	19.8	5	17	0.7	38	4.1	2.6
South Korea	1,200	0.2	22	3	1.8	254	27.0	1.3
Spain	1,200	18.4	48	4	4.9	39	14.0	3.5
Sweden	1,003	6.9	8	0	1.0	29	6.5	2.1
Switzerland	1,241	12.7	17	0	1.6	36	7.0	2.1
Taiwan	1,227	3.1	17	1	1.4	30	5.4	2.1
Thailand	1,534	2.3	3	0	0.7	67	6.7	1.5
Trinidad and Tobago	1,002	8.7	9	2	1.4	19	5.2	2.5
Turkey	1,346	10.9	20	6	1.7	45	11.5	3.1
Ukraine	1,000	32.3	7	6	1.0	15	5.0	2.3
Uruguay	1,000	10.0	21	9	2.3	18	6.2	3.1
USA	1,249	6.2	6	0	0.8	19	3.2	2.0
Vietnam	1,495	23.3	3	51	4.5	49	13.5	3.2
Zambia	1,500	16.0	3	7	0.6	65	8.3	1.6

*Patterns 1 and 2 are defined by the maximum number of occurrences in a single country.
Pattern 1 is 10-1-10-10-1-10-10-10-10 while Pattern 2 is 10-10-10-10-1-10-10-10-10-10

cases (=1.6%) in a pattern of extreme rejection of items 1, 5 and 6, and extreme endorsement of all remaining items. In Mali, 3.7% of the respondents expressed a pattern of extreme rejection of the first two items and extreme endorsement of the remaining items. Finally, in Indonesia, the most commonly occurring pattern consisted of extreme rejection of the fourth and fifth possible elements of democracy combined with extreme endorsement of the remaining elements.

Note also that the number of duplicate combinations (i.e., combinations that appear at least twice) varies markedly between countries, ranging from a low of 4 in Finland up to 254 in South Korea. The second last column contains information on the percentage of duplicate cases. If a combination appears twice, then there is one duplicate. If it appears three times, then there are two duplicates, and so on. Using this algorithm provides the information contained in the column identified as the percentage of duplicate cases. These again show huge country variation from a low of 1.1% in Finland up to 33.8% in Ethiopia (38.4% in India, but on three response alternatives only). The final column provides the ratio of the number of cases that are duplicates to the number of distinct duplicate combinations. Considering only those countries with a large share of duplicate cases, say at least 15%, we again find substantial differences in the ratio of duplicates over combinations. For example, Andorra and Mali with 19.3% and 15.5% of duplicate cases, respectively, have a ratio of 3.5. In contrast, South Korea, with 27.0% duplicates, has a ratio of only 1.3. In other words, South Korea needs approximately three times more combinations than Andorra and Mali to obtain the same number of duplicates. In between these extremes we find, for example, Ethiopia with 33.8% duplicates and a ratio of 1.9. Figure 4.1 shows the pattern of duplicates for these four countries. In addition, as points of contrast, we show the patterns for Malaysia, with 6.3% duplicates, and for Finland, which has only 1.1% duplicates.

In Figure 4.1, the horizontal axis consists of the factor scores while the vertical axis gives the frequency with which each distinct factor score occurs. Factor scores that occur more than once are anomalous from a strictly probabilistic point of view, given the large number of possible patterns. Additionally, the extreme negative skew characterizing the frequency distributions of the individual items should make the incidence of duplicate patterns increase with the value of the factor score. Turning first to Finland, few patterns are duplicated for this country, and in every instance the duplicate pattern is an outlier: only one duplicate pattern is located at the extreme low end of the factor score, while several additional duplicate patterns occur near the extreme top end of the scale. That is, there is nothing puzzling about the distribution of the factor scores in Finland. In contrast, the distribution of the essentials of democracy scale scores for South Korea is perplexing on several counts. First, more than 250 combinations appear at least twice, a number far beyond anything that can be attributed to chance. Second, one (outlying) scale score occurs 22 times, and again such a large number is difficult to attribute to chance. Finally, the cases appearing exactly twice occur about equally across the entire scale. Even

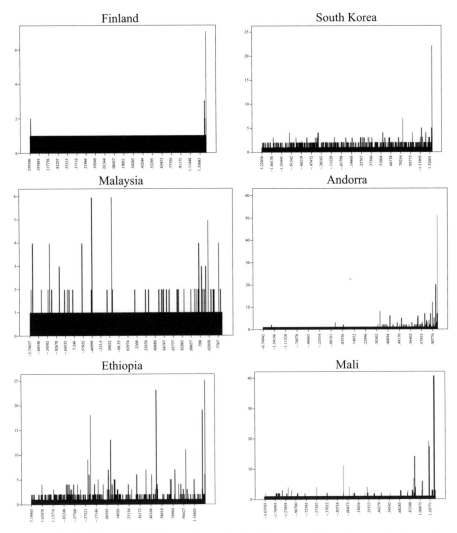

Figure 4.1 Number of duplicate patterns for the democracy items for selected countries

respondents who felt there were next to no essentials of democracy appear twice. It is the fact that infrequently occurring scale positions have just about the same likelihood of having duplicates as the more frequently occurring scale values that is most perplexing. The probability of obtaining duplicate patterns should increase monotonically with the popularity of the points of view. This is clearly not the case in either South Korea or in Ethiopia. Here there are numerous instances of precisely two identical patterns, and again these are nearly equally distributed across the whole scale. A main difference between the two countries is the number of identical factor scores that occur more than 10 times: in Ethiopia, four patterns appear 15 or more times, and another nine patterns appear between 5 and 13 times. The distribution for Malaysia is similar to that of Ethiopia and South Korea, except that there are noticeably fewer duplicate patterns. Mali is similar to Malaysia, except that there are still fewer duplicate patterns; however, there are five spikes in the frequencies, one of which occurs 40 times. The pattern for Andorra conforms to our expectation in one main respect: the duplicate patterns are concentrated in the top third of the essentials of democracy scale scores.

These country differences are peculiar in that they are not derivable from either substantive or stochastic theory. One might have thought that different cultures provide templates for certain response combinations that some respondents have caricaturized (i.e., simplified) by taking them to the extremes of '1' and '10'. But then why would Switzerland and Norway, which are culturally similar to Germany, have so few instances of pattern 1 (17 and 2, respectively), while Germany has so many (128)?

Some researchers consider the percentage of missing cases to be an indicator for overall data quality (Subar et al., 2001). If we accept that the number of duplicate combinations and the number of duplicate cases are alternative indicators of data quality, then there should be a positive relationship between these indicators. Calculating aggregate-level Pearson correlations on the data in the respective columns of Table 4.2 for the 45 countries shows the number of duplicate combinations and the number of duplicate cases to have correlations of –0.12 and 0.17, respectively, with the percentage of missing cases; the correlation between the two indicators of duplicate patterns is 0.82. Further, South Korea has the lowest percentage of missing cases (0.2%), while at the same time also having the highest number of duplicate combinations. These are strong indications that the overall percentage of missing cases can be a misleading indicator of data quality.

Data duplication

4.2 The pattern of identical response combinations in some countries, especially South Korea and Ethiopia, defies both substantive interpretation and the odds, since the duplicates appear across all values of the essentials of democracy scale. Ultimately, the puzzling patterns in these countries made us question their veracity. To assess this possibility more closely, we created even more stringent criteria to reduce the likelihood of obtaining identical factor scores: we generated a new analysis by selecting 36 items that varied widely in content and response format. These variables include eight four-point variables on gender roles, one 10-point satisfaction with financial situation variable, two ranking scales of four choices on national goals, six ranking scales of four choices each on materialism and post-materialism values, 10 six-point self-description variables, and four 10-point variables on technology (v60–v95). We chose to search for duplicates in the data using MCA, which imposes no restrictions on the level of measurement, and we also wanted to include all responses, including missing values within the patterns. With such a large set of heterogeneous and largely uncorrelated items, we did not expect to find any duplicate values. Consistent with our expectation, most of the countries had no duplicate scores. In a few countries (e.g., Jordan and South Africa) exactly one duplicate was found, suggesting a minor data entry error in which a questionnaire was typed in twice. In the USA, 13 duplicates were found, but these were legitimate in that they consisted solely of having missing values for all 36 variables. These cases are trivial and easy to rectify.

However, in some countries an inordinate number of duplicates were uncovered, which implies serious deficiencies in institutional quality control, including the deliberate duplication of data. Figure 4.2 provides the bar charts for some of the countries with particularly implausible distributions of duplicates (South Korea, Thailand, Ethiopia, India, Moldova and Indonesia). The pattern of duplicates in Moldova is perhaps the simplest to explain. Here we find precisely 24 duplicates, that is, 24 distinct instances where precisely the same pattern of responses occurred twice. This could be the result of careless data entry procedures. Specifically, one can imagine a bundle of questionnaires whose data had already been entered being inadvertently placed into the data entry queue. For the remaining countries, the only plausible conclusion is that sample sizes were augmented through copy-and-paste procedures.

One can imagine several variations of such duplicating strategies. In South Korea most duplicate cases were obtained by copying numerous different questionnaires precisely once. India, which has a number of peaks in the distribution, appears to have chosen a different copy-and-paste procedure, which consisted of copying a smaller number of questionnaires numerous times and a larger number of questionnaires precisely once. Ethiopia, in addition to having numerous duplicate cases, has one outlier with 21 copies of the same questionnaire. In the case of South Korea, the effects of the duplicate cases on substantive solutions might not be large: a large number of apparently randomly chosen respondents simply have double the weight they should have. In Ethiopia, the 21 cases might significantly change the entire solution, depending on where in the distribution of the scale scores the 21 cases happen to be.

Table 4.3 shows the duplicates and how often they appear for the countries shown in Figure 4.2. Ethiopia has the highest percentage of copies, with 378 faked interviews (=25.2%), followed by South Korea with 282 (=23.5%), both producing exact sample sizes of 1,500 and 1,200 cases, respectively. For South Korea we inspected the data in greater detail by comparing the entire sequence of responses to the whole survey. This revealed that slight changes here and there were made when the cases were duplicated. The effect of these slight changes is to decrease the likelihood of detecting that they are essentially duplicates. Our procedure identified only those cases that were precisely the same across the 36 variables we entered into the MCA. Had even one variable been changed, we would not have detected the fact that it was a duplicate case. How is it possible for so many instances of data to have been duplicated? We cannot

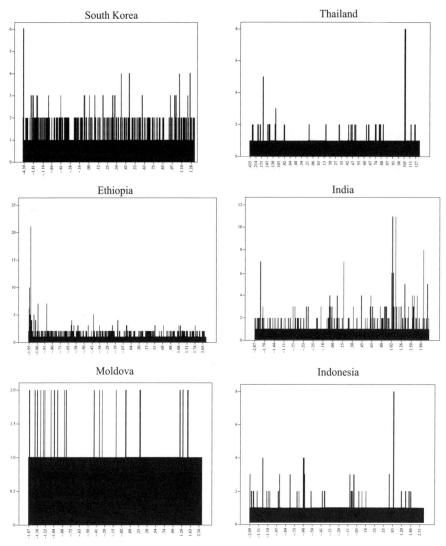

Figure 4.2 Distribution of duplicated interviews for selected countries

answer this question, but obviously it is much cheaper to copy, paste and slightly modify an interview than it is to conduct a genuine interview to achieve the sample size. It could also be that a few interviewers just copied the questionnaires on paper, making a small number of changes so that the institute did not recognize that some of the interviews are fakes. Regardless of who is responsible for the duplicates, our screening procedures detected institutional data quality control problems in some countries that were so serious that the data cannot be repaired. One could of course delete the duplicates that were detected in an attempt to minimize or solve the problem. However, when about one in four cases can be shown to be fakes, it diminishes one's confidence that the remaining three-quarters were obtained in a proper manner.

Table 4.3 Calculation of duplicates for selected countries

k	South Korea		Indonesia		Thailand		India		Moldova		Ethiopia	
	f_1	f_2	f_1	f_2	f_1	f_2	f_1	f_2	f_1	f_2	f_1	f_2
1	671	671	1922	1922	1454	1454	1659	1659	998	998	835	835
2	219	438	26	52	32	64	85	170	24	48	254	508
3	23	69	7	21	1	3	24	73			16	48
4	4	16	3	12			7	28			7	28
5					1	5	3	15			4	20
6	1	6					2	12			1	6
7							2	14			2	14
8			1	8	1	8	1	8				
10											2	20
11							2	22				
21											1	21
N	918	1200	1959	2015	1489	1534	1785	2001	1022	1046	1122	1500
Fakes		282		56		45		216		24		378

Key: k = frequency of occurrence; f_1 = number of instances; f_2 = number of cases represented. The number of duplicates or fakes is obtained by subtracting the N in f_1 from the N in f_2.

Detecting faked and partly faked interviews

4.3 Interviewer cheating is seldom discussed in the field of empirical research. The previous section of this chapter showed that some data collection agencies may manufacture cases by the simple expedient of creating duplicate copies through a copy-and-paste procedure. Similar enticements (maximizing income by faking interviews) operate on interviewers unless stringent quality control procedures are exercised by the research institutes that hire the interviewers. According to the American Association of Public Opinion Research (AAPOR, 2003: 7), interviews should be monitored by the institute by re-contacting 5–15% of all respondents to enquire whether the interview had indeed been conducted. This quality control procedure is probably sufficient to detect completely faked face-to-face interviews and telephone interviews done from a specialized laboratory. It is also possible for interviewers to partially fake the interview. This is done by contacting the respondents but asking them only some of the questionnaire items, filling in the rest of the questionnaire at home by creating response patterns that the interviewer considers to be plausible response combinations. From a rational choice point of view, partially faked interviews could be characterized by the fact that item batteries that take a long time to administer and other questions that are time-consuming are fabricated, while basic and easily verified data such as age and gender are correctly recorded. This strategy can shorten the interview time dramatically, which from a satisficing perspective may please the respondent perhaps as much as the interviewer. The detection of partly faked interviews is significantly more difficult since the interviewers were actually in the household and did ask at least some of the questions.

In this section we use our screening methods to help verify whether sets of items and/or whole interviews are faked. The underlying premise, as discussed in Chapter 1, is that interviewers also have structured images about their respondents, especially if their respondents have distinctive characteristics or the interviews are collected in specific neighbourhoods that have distinctive features. These structured images contain stereotypic elements which result in less variability in responses. That is, interviewers tend to see their 'respondents' as more similar than they are. Schäfer et al. (2005) provide empirical support for this expectation (see also Porras and English, 2004; Turner et al., 2002). A further stereotypical element is that interviewers are apt to see their respondents as being more consistent or predictable than they are. That is, the correlation between elements in their images is likely to exceed the correlation obtained from the genuine respondents. Additionally, since interviewers understand the meaning of the questions, they will not construct any astonishing combination of responses, which respondents sometimes do because they misunderstood the question. This too leads to greater consistency or correlation between related items. A further pattern suggested in the literature is that fakers are more likely to provide a substantive response to every question, thereby minimizing the likelihood of missing data. Finally, interviewers who fake interviews are likely to choose what they consider to be 'safe' responses, which typically means avoiding extreme response options. Taken together, these tendencies will result in the faked interviews being systematically different from the genuine ones.

We demonstrate the screening method using data that Blasius, Friedrichs and Klöckner (2008) collected. In this study a total of 35 interviews done by three interviewers (out of 742 interviews) were identified as fakes. We screened the data on five scales that Blasius, Friedrichs and Klöckner (2008) used in a survey conducted in 2004 of a random sample of German citizens aged 16–85 residing in a disadvantaged neighbourhood in Cologne, Germany. The sample was drawn from the Cologne Population Register. Target persons received a letter from the principal investigators informing them of a forthcoming visit from a member of a Cologne survey research institute who would ask for an interview on behalf of the Universities of Cologne and Bonn. The data collection institute itself was well established, specializing in face-to-face interviews in the area of Cologne, with a large stock of interviewers living in the city.

Five sets of variables were screened. *Perceived neighbourhood disintegration* consisted of 11 four-point Likert items adopted from Ross, Mirowsky and Pribesh (2001). *Collective efficacy* consists of five four-point items and was intended to measure the social capital of a neighbourhood by combining two dimensions: trust and informal control (Sampson and Groves, 1989; Sampson, Morenoff and Gannon-Rowley, 2002). *Intergenerational closure* consisted of five four-point items that measure the amount of supervision or surveillance of children by their parents and neighbours (Sampson and Groves, 1989; Sampson, Raudenbush and Earls, 1997). To measure the *level of deviance* and the *perceived deviance* in the neighbourhood, we used a set of eight four-point items developed by Friedrichs and Blasius (2000, 2003). For both the latter scales, eight scenarios were described, four of them involving violence such as 'a neighbour beats his children', and the other four focusing on non-violent deviant behaviour such as 'an elderly woman steals cheese in the supermarket'. The respondents evaluated the severity of these situations first on four-point scales (running from 'very bad' to 'not at all bad') and then their frequency – whether they 'never', 'seldom', or 'often' observed these kinds of behaviour in their neighbourhood (for the precise wording, see Blasius and Friedrichs, 2007).

Applying CatPCA, we restricted the items describing the eight scenarios to two dimensions. The first dimension, which we call *level of deviance*, can be interpreted as a general factor since all variables are associated with it in the same direction. The second dimension contrasted the four scenarios involving violence with the four non-violent deviant behaviours. For the remaining four sets of items, we restricted the CatPCA solutions to one dimension; the second dimensions can be ignored, since, as Blasius and Friedrichs (2007) previously reported, they had no clear substantive interpretation.

The screening procedure for detecting potentially faked interviews consists of several steps, each of which provides some relevant evidence, yet none of which is conclusive by itself. The first step consists of calculating descriptive statistics on the interviews conducted to that point by each interviewer. More specifically, the percentage of missing values, the relative frequency of 'safe' responses (such as 'agree' or 'disagree' rather than 'strongly agree' and 'strongly disagree') and the individual respondent's variance of responses across the items are calculated. We adopted these potentially identifying features from Schäfer et al. (2005) who used them to detect fakers. In the second step, CatPCA is run separately on each set of domain items. In the third step, ANOVA is employed with interviewer identification as the independent variable and the latent variables (normalized to a mean of zero and a standard deviation of one) obtained from CatPCA as dependent ones. All of these statistics are then examined to check for a tendency for the interviews from some of the interviewers to have (1) relatively few missing values, (2) a high frequency of safe responses, (3) low variance across the different questionnaire items, (4) scores on the latent values that are far removed from the mean of zero and in the direction of prevailing stereotypes, and (5) low standard deviations on the latent variables.

We demonstrate our approach in greatest detail for the *perceived neighbourhood disintegration* items. Table 4.4 shows the CatPCA factor loadings, their eigenvalues, and explained variances. Since all variables are associated in the same direction with dimension 1 (the three reverse-formulated items have a negative sign, all others have a positive sign), we call this latent variable *perceived neighbourhood disintegration*. For this factor, the higher the value, the lower is the perceived neighbourhood disintegration.

Table 4.4 CatPCA factor loadings for perceived neighbourhood disintegration items

Items	Loadings
There is a lot of graffiti in my neighbourhood	0.46
My neighbourhood is noisy	0.61
Vandalism is common in my neighbourhood	0.73
My neighbourhood is clean	−0.23
People in my neighbourhood take good care of their houses	−0.33
There are too many people hanging around on the streets	0.60
There is a lot of crime in my neighbourhood	0.76
There is too much drug abuse in my neighbourhood	0.71
There is too much alcohol abuse in my neighbourhood	0.69
I'm always having trouble with my neighbours	0.35
My neighbourhood is safe	−0.58
Eigenvalue	3.65
Explained variance	33.2%
Cronbach's alpha	0.80

Note: $N = 742$.

Table 4.5 provides the relevant information regarding the five expectations described above for the perceived neighbourhood disintegration domain. Three important conclusions can be made on the basis of this table. First, relatively large differences, as manifested by the magnitude of *eta*, are associated with the interviewers. This suggests strongly that respondents are affected by interviewer characteristics, or that interviewers behave in non-standardized ways to provoke different responses, or that some of the data are fabricated. Second, there is no single statistic that is consistently high (or low) for the same interviewers. For example, for six interviewers there was no missing data, suggesting that on this criterion these may be six cheaters. However, there is no other characteristic where these same six interviewers have the highest/lowest scores. Hence, there is no easy way to differentiate cheaters from non-cheaters. Third, there nevertheless is a discernible tendency for three interviewers to have somewhat outlying features. Interviewers M, U and V have no missing cases, they have the three most deviant means in which their 'respondents' describe their neighbourhood as being particularly disintegrated (latent means of –0.72, –0.53, and –1.24, respectively), two of the three (U and V) have the lowest standard deviations on the latent construct (0.75, and 0.24, respectively) while the third one has a below average standard deviation, and two of the three (M and U) also have the lowest variance across the 11 items (0.59 and 0.50, respectively). Hence, it is likely that these three interviewers fabricated their data. Follow-up telephone calls to the respondents for these three interviewers confirmed that the respondents had not been interviewed.

With the suspicion confirmed that the interviews by M, U and V were fraudulent, we first estimated a two-dimensional CatPCA solution for the neighbourhood disintegration variables and then plotted the object scores from this solution, distinguishing between the faked interviews that came from M, U

Table 4.5 Distribution parameters by interviewers with more than five interviews

Interviewer	N	Criteria, variability method			Screening method	
		MeanMis	Av.Mid.	Variance	Mean	Std.Dev.
A	63	0.81	48.5	1.21	−0.09	1.04
B	64	0.00	47.7	1.25	−0.24	1.02
C	35	1.51	55.5	1.08	0.04	0.90
D	30	0.00	65.2	0.91	0.21	0.90
E	106	0.09	78.7	0.66	0.06	0.76
F	86	0.29	40.4	1.38	0.22	1.13
G	47	0.02	64.1	0.87	0.17	0.96
H	100	0.00	58.3	0.97	0.18	1.01
I	43	0.56	62.5	0.89	0.05	1.20
J	40	0.45	58.2	1.02	0.01	0.93
K	16	1.38	59.4	1.01	−0.10	1.13
L	27	0.48	29.5	1.61	−0.02	1.26
M	15	0.00	63.6	0.59	−0.72	0.84
P	12	0.85	54.5	1.11	−0.24	0.78
Q	20	0.70	63.3	0.87	−0.20	0.95
U	13	0.00	83.9	0.50	−0.55	0.75
V	7	0.00	57.8	0.94	−1.24	0.24
Total	724	0.33	57.7	1.02	0.007	1.007
Statistic		$F = 11.2$ $p < 0.001$ $\eta = 0.45$	$F = 16.7$ $p < 0.001$ $\eta = 0.52$	$F = 19.0$ $p < 0.001$ $\eta = 0.55$	$F = 2.5$ $p < 0.001$ $\eta = 0.23$	

and V with those of the remaining interviews (see Figure 4.3). This figure clearly shows that the faked interviews are located almost exclusively above what would be the major diagonal of the two-dimensional space.

If the confirmation that interviewers M, U and V were manufacturing their data had not been immediately available, evidence from the other domains could have been (and indeed was) used to strengthen the differentiation between genuine and faked interviews. The stereotypical elements in fake interviewers' own cognitive maps should result in noticeably higher concentrations of cases in the negative (or positive) tails of their distribution, in line with the direction of their stereotype. In Table 4.6, the distribution of the faked interviews (combining the faked interviews from M, U and V) is compared to those of the genuine interviews who conducted more than five interviews. Although the remaining interviewers also produced some suspect cases, they have been excluded since we did not cross-validate them and therefore cannot be certain they were faked.

In this table, we subdivided our latent variables into six parts each, consisting of the first 5.0% of the standard normal distribution (values smaller than −1.64), the next 10.8% of the distribution (values between −1.64 and −1.00), via the middle area up to the last 5.0% of the distribution (values higher than 1.64). The outlying values of the three falsifiers in the order M, U and V are given at the bottom of the table.

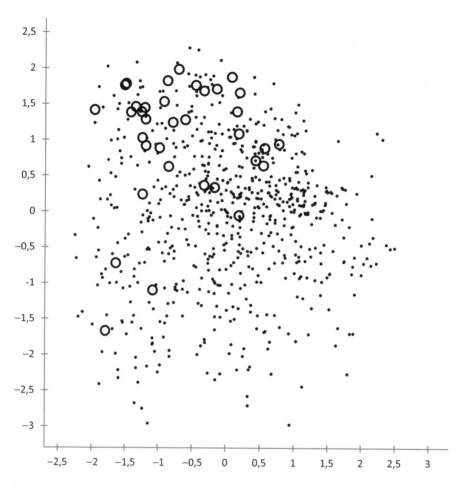

Figure 4.3 Neighbourhood disintegration, CatPCA factor scores for respondents, with faked interviews shown as open circles

Table 4.6 shows that the deviations from observed and expected cases (values derived from the normal distribution; see headers) are also relatively small (compare with rows 'Total', T) for those factors, which are based on relatively few variables. A comparison of the distribution of genuine (G) and faked (F) interviews shows that on most scales the falsifiers clearly fail to produce response patterns that follow the same distribution as obtained from the non-falsifiers; the two response patterns differ significantly. The falsifiers clearly overestimated the levels of deviance, perceived deviance and neighbourhood disintegration, while they underestimated the levels of collective efficacy and intergenerational closure. All these estimations are biased in the direction of 'common knowledge' and stereotypes that people hold about the nature of disadvantaged neighbourhoods: there is a high level of deviance and disorder, residents do not know the children in the neighbourhood and they do not have frequent social interactions. Finally, they substantially overestimated the

Table 4.6 Distribution of genuine (G), faked (F) and total (T) interviews (N = 689, 35 and 724, respectively)

Variable		up to −1.64 (5.0%)	−1.64 to −1.0 (10.8%)	−1.0 to 0.0 (34.1%)	0.0 to 1.00 (34.1%)	1.00 to 1.64 (10.8%)	1.64 plus (5.0%)	Statistic
Collective efficacy (from low to high)	G	4.5	12.1	33.4	27.3	15.6	7.1	$\chi^2 = 11.1$, $p < 0.05$, CV = 0.12
	F	8.6	28.6	25.7	25.7	5.7	5.7	
	T	4.7	12.9	33.1	27.2	15.1	7.1	
Inter-generational closure (from low to high)	G	2.8	12.4	37.7	27.4	10.2	9.5	$\chi^2 = 8.2$, n.s.
	F	2.9	22.9	42.9	28.6	2.9	0.0	
	T	2.8	12.9	37.9	27.5	9.9	9.0	
Level of deviance (from high to low)	G	5.4	7.8	37.7	35.5	9.9	3.8	$\chi^2 = 18.5$, $p < 0.01$, CV = 0.16
	F	20.0	11.4	25.7	20.0	14.3	8.6	
	T	6.1	8.0	37.1	34.8	10.1	4.0	
Perceived deviance (from high to low)	G	6.1	8.6	22.5	40.9	21.9	0.0	$\chi^2 = 93.9$, $p < 0.001$, CV = 0.36
	F	45.7	25.7	22.9	5.7	0.0	0.0	
	T	8.0	9.4	22.5	39.2	20.9	0.0	
Neighbourhood disintegration (from high to low)	G	5.1	12.2	30.6	33.7	13.8	4.6	$\chi^2 = 24.3$, $p < 0.001$, CV = 0.18
	F	5.7	37.1	37.1	20.0	0.0	0.0	
	T	5.1	13.4	30.9	33.0	13.1	4.4	
Acceptance versus violence (from acceptance to violence)	G	0.0	15.8	41.8	27.6	9.1	5.7	$\chi^2 = 20.8$, $p < 0.001$, CV = 0.17
	F	0.0	2.9	25.7	31.4	20.0	20.0	
	T	0.0	15.2	41.0	27.8	9.7	6.4	

Outlier, faked interviews only:
Collective efficacy: −2.33, −2.33/ − / −
Intergenerational closure: −2.25/ − / −
Level of deviance: −2.41/ −2.54/ −4.13, −3.21
Observed deviance:−4.04, −3.79, −3.64, −2.40, −2.01, −1.97/ −4.63, −4.06, −3.94, −3.56, −2.86/ −2.50, −2.49
Observed disorder: −2.35/ − / −
Violence versus tolerance: 2.00, 2.12, 5.46/ − / 2.95, 3.30, 5.38

amount of 'acceptance' of violent deviance: falsifiers failed to appreciate that residents of disadvantaged areas do not condone behaviours such as 'neighbour beats his children' (cf. Friedrichs and Blasius, 2000, 2003). It should be noted that there might be some additional partly faked interviews that we did not recognize in time for cross-validation; the differences between falsifiers and non-falsifiers might be even stronger.

In general, the solutions confirm our expectation that falsifiers produce relatively consistent responses in the direction of everyday knowledge. Compared with the variability method, the screening method is relatively invariant to respondent behaviour (e.g., the use of middle versus end categories); it reflects the latent attitudes of the respondents or their assumed latent attitudes. With respect to a single interview, the number of missing cases and the number of mid-point responses (as well as the variance) are not indicators of a fake; the variability method will not work. In contrast, a value in a latent scale of greater than 2.56 in absolute magnitude has (on average) a less than one chance in 100 of occurring – and should such an occurrence happen on several latent variables, this would be a signal to monitor the interviewer's work.

Data entry errors_____

4.4 There are no universally unusual patterns, since what is unusual in one setting may be quite ordinary in another. It is the characteristics of a set of items that shape our expectations of what the structure underlying the set of items should look like. If the focal domain is a relatively simple one, if the construction of the focal items is also simple and straightforward, and if appropriate response options are provided, then the MCA should be one-dimensional. That is, the first dimension should mirror the successive categories in their correct order on all items, while the second dimension should take the form of the methodologically induced horseshoe in which extreme responses are contrasted with moderate ones. For our example on detecting data entry errors, we chose the European Social Survey (ESS 2002) with the focal domain being personal trust in six institutions (A = parliament, B = legal system, C = police, D = politicians, E = European Parliament, and F = United Nations). The items had a simple construction consisting merely of naming the six institutions and asking the respondent how much they trusted each of them. Additionally, our literature review in Chapter 2 provided evidence that 11-point scales (0–10), which is the response format that was used for this set of items, had measurement properties superior to those of most other response formats such as Likert and the 100-point feeling thermometers. Finally, the Pearson correlations among these items (not shown) were all positive and sufficiently high (ranging between 0.31 and 0.69) to suggest that the underlying structure of the responses to this set of items should be quite simple. Applying MCA, we especially expected that responses of '1' should be located between responses of '0' and '2' of the respective items, responses of '2' in between those of '1' and '3', and so on. This would also imply that responses of '10' would be farthest removed from responses of '0' on the first dimension.

To obtain the underlying response structure, we subjected the six trust items to MCA (using the indicator matrix as input format and listwise deletion), resulting in the two-dimensional map shown in Figure 4.4. The first character in the labels identifies the specific trust items mentioned above, while the numbers in each label identify the 11 response options; thus 'A0' locates the position of lowest possible ('0') trust in the parliament whereas 'B10' refers to highest possible trust in the legal system ('10') in the latent space.

As expected, the overall structure of the responses resembles a horseshoe. Gratifyingly, the first dimension, which by definition is the most important one, reflects the substantive latent concept of amount of trust in the six institutions; the dimension can be labelled as 'level of trust'. This conclusion is formed on the basis of the fact that if one projects the response locations for

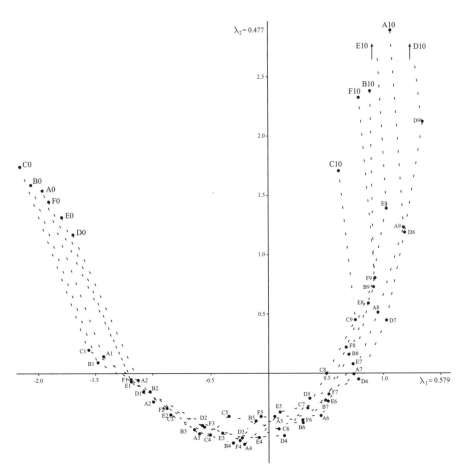

Figure 4.4 ESS 2002, MCA map of trust items, all respondents

each item onto the first dimension, then all responses of '0' are farthest to the left (i.e., the lowest level of trust); all responses of '1' are located somewhat to the right, followed by responses of '2' to '9' being increasingly to the right. Then the anomaly appears: the '10's invariably are located slightly to the left rather than to the right of the '9's. If we do not rotate the solution to obtain a correct order, this nonsensically implies that a response of '10' connotes somewhat less trust than a response of '9'. This counter-intuitive pattern was therefore explored in greater detail using simple descriptive statistics. Table 4.7 provides summary information on response frequencies and some of their co-occurrences. The first column lists the 11 response options, the second provides the total number of times each response option was used: 12,959 times respondents stated they did not trust any institution at all, while 6,627 responses were of complete trust. The third column expresses the occurrences of each response as a percentage of all responses: 3.2% of all responses expressed complete trust. The fourth column provides an index of co-occurrences of each response option whenever a '0' was a response to one of the six items using the following formula:

$$\frac{1}{B}\sum_{i=0}^{6}\sum_{j=0}^{6}a_i \times b_j \times n_{ij}$$

To calculate the relative co-occurrences we multiplied the frequency of the reference category, a_i (the number of times a given respondent chose a '0' for the six items, with a_i running from 0 to 6), by the frequency of the possible response co-occurrences, b_j (with b_j also running from 0 to 6, and $a_i + b_j$ constrained between 0 and 6), by the number of respondents in the respective cell, n_{ij}. Summing over all cells gives the frequencies for all combinations of co-occurrences. In the final step we standardized the values by the total number of possible co-occurrence categories to allow a comparison of the relative

Table 4.7 Occurrences and co-occurrences of response categories

Response category	Absolute number of occurrences	Percentage of occurrences	Relative co-occurrences with '0's	Relative co-occurrence with '1's
0	12,959	6.2	53.0	29.3
1	7,991	3.8	49.2	35.8
2	13,643	6.6	36.1	31.2
3	19,510	9.4	24.1	19.9
4	20,612	9.9	15.2	13.2
5	40,205	19.3	18.0	10.5
6	25,134	12.1	8.5	6.7
7	27,464	13.2	7.9	5.8
8	23,611	11.4	9.6	6.1
9	10,030	4.8	10.3	6.9
10	6,627	3.2	26.1	7.2

occurrence with '1's and '0's. In the case of $a = b$, that is, responding to the items with the same response category several times, we use the simplified equation

$$\frac{1}{A}\sum_{i=0}^{6}(a_i - 1) \times n_i$$

where n_i is the number of respondents choosing i times the same category in the set of items.

To give a reading example and to exemplify the calculation, Table 4.8 shows the cross-tabulation of '0' and '10' responses. Of the 34,631 respondents with no missing data, 25,368 never used a zero–ten combination for any of the items; hence, they do not contribute to the number of zero–ten co-occurrences. Similarly, 68 respondents answered each item with a '10', and they too are irrelevant to the calculation of the number of zero–ten co-occurrences. However, 245 respondents used a '0' exactly once and a '10' once; their share of the sum of co-occurrences is 1 $(a_i) \times 1$ $(b_j) \times 245$ $(n_{ij}) = 245$. Exactly 38 respondents chose a '0' four times and a '10' once; their share is $4 \times 1 \times 38 = 112$. Likewise, five respondents used both categories three times each, resulting in $3 \times 3 \times 5 = 45$ co-occurrences. The sum over all co-occurrences, calculated on the basis of Table 4.8, is 1,727. As shown in Table 4.7, a '10' was chosen 6,627 times; hence, the relative occurrence of the zero–ten combination is $1,727/6,627 = 0.261$, which is the value shown in the last row of the fourth column of Table 4.7.

Given the high intercorrelations of the six trust items, we would expect frequent co-occurrences of identical responses or responses that are numerically close to each other. Most of the co-occurrence proportions given in Table 4.7 conform to this expectation. Looking at the final column, the highest co-occurrence of a '1' is with another '1' (35.8); a somewhat smaller relative proportion of times it co-occurs with a response that is one lower, namely a '0' (29.3) or a response that is one higher, namely a '2' (31.2). As the gap between

Table 4.8 Cross-tabulation of number of '0's by number of '10's across all six institutional trust items

Number of '0's	Number of '10's							Total
	0	1	2	3	4	5	6	
0	25,368	1,858	743	287	129	85	68	28,538
1	2,507	245	82	24	12	9	0	2,879
2	1,216	117	58	9	7	0	0	1,407
3	662	76	18	5	0	0	0	761
4	461	38	11	0	0	0	0	510
5	249	24	0	0	0	0	0	273
6	263	0	0	0	0	0	0	263
Total	30,726	2,358	912	325	148	94	68	34,631

the responses of '1' with that of any other number widens, the relative co-occurrence decreases, with minor fluctuations at the top end of the response options. In any event, the behaviour of the co-occurrences with ones is approximately what one would expect.

Most of the relative co-occurrences of zeros are also in accord with this expectation; that is, the highest relative co-occurrence of zero is with other zeros (53.0), decreasing to 49.2 for a co-occurrence with a one, and so on. However, we note a big spike in co-occurrences of '0's with '10's. The relative co-occurrence of this combination is 26.1, which is larger than all co-occurrences of '0's with '3's to '9's. Additionally, that spike does not occur for the '10'–'1' combination, which has a clearly smaller relative co-occurrence of 7.2. How can this anomalous pattern be explained? One reasonable explanation, and the one we favour, is that in the data capturing process, zeros were sometimes confused with '10's. This example graphically displays the advantage of visualization procedures. The anomaly of the spatial location of '10's relative to '9's is clearly visible in Figure 4.4. Note also that what made the pattern anomalous was the consistency of the dislocations of the '10's. What is noteworthy about this example is that the data entry errors affected relatively few cases, yet our screening techniques clearly revealed the dislocations.

In performing MCA separately for each country (not shown), some countries, such as Poland and Germany, reflect perfect ordinality of responses. Other countries, including Austria and Switzerland, reveal minor violations of ordinality on a few variables. In a few countries, such as Belgium and France, larger anomalous locations appear, especially at the extreme end of the trust scale. In general, though, the results suggest a simple structure similar to that shown in Figure 4.4.

Before concluding this example, two aspects of the distribution given in Table 4.7 should be noted. First, the review of the literature indicated that responses at either extreme and at the mid-point should be disproportionately frequent as a mechanism for task simplification. In line with this expectation, the lowest response occurs more frequently than the second lowest, and the middle response is disproportionately chosen by almost a fifth (19.3%) of the sample. However, the highest response is not disproportionately frequently endorsed, being used less often than any other response option. This suggests an additional response dynamic, namely impression management. From an impression management point of view, respondents may fear that they might appear to be naive if they admit to complete trust in any institution. In contrast, it may be relatively acceptable to express complete cynicism of institutions: As shown in Table 4.7, responses of '0' are about twice as common as those of '10' (12,959 versus 6,627, respectively). Second, the mid-point of the scale ('5') represents the least committal response. This is the response one might expect from a satisficing perspective, and it is indeed the one chosen substantially more often than any other.

Conclusion

4.5 The first step in data screening is to detect anomalous or unusual patterns. Researchers typically screen their data at a cursory level only, in which just the univariate and bivariate distributions are examined. These can point to data quality problems that occur because of undesirable characteristics, such as skewed distributions, lack of variability, and a high incidence of non-substantive responses. A much deeper probe into data quality is afforded with our preferred data screening techniques, which display the multivariate structure of the responses to a set of items on a focal domain.

The analyses conducted for this chapter exemplified data quality problems whose source is not the respondent, but rather the data collection institutions and their personnel. What the four examples have in common is that the starting point of the data screening process was the detection of an unusual pattern. A pattern is unusual if it is unexpected. The location of the '10's relative to the '9's in the last example was unexpected to the point of being theoretically unintelligible. Whenever that occurs, the second step in the data screening process is to conduct a series of additional analyses designed to clarify the reason for the anomalous structure of responses. In the given case, this consisted of calculating a series of co-occurrences of '10's with the other ten possible response options. These showed that in some countries '10's were confused with '0's in the data entry process.

In the first example, the relatively high frequency of certain combinations of responses was puzzling; in this case it was the frequent use of only '1' and '10' responses. If in theory there are 10^{10} combinations of possible responses, one could expect a few duplicate patterns, as was the case for the Scandinavian countries. These may be the result of some respondents and perhaps the occasional interviewer simplifying the survey task by giving caricaturized extreme responses to all of the items. The data may nevertheless be of high quality. A more serious indication of institutional or field process problems occurs in countries where certain patterns occurred clearly more often than one could possibly explain with either stochastic or substantive theory. How can it be that 7% of respondents in Germany gave precisely the same responses to ten items each of which was measured on a 10-point scale, especially in light of the fact that the same pattern hardly ever occurred in Norway?

The detection of data fabrication grew out of the puzzle of the country-specific patterns of duplicate values. The procedure involved subjecting to MCA a different and much larger number of items that had nothing in common. In such an analysis, in which the number of possible response combinations exceeds 10 billion, one should not find duplicate patterns. The fact that in South Korea as many as a quarter of respondents had duplicate patterns cannot be explained in any way other than that copy-and-paste procedures were used. A closer examination of all the responses for some of the duplicate patterns showed that the responses to the entire questionnaire were identical, with just an occasional change to some of the variables, a strategy that ordinarily would make it difficult to detect that the interview was faked. Given that the data that we analysed here came from the WVS, an ongoing cross-national research project used for many scholarly analyses, it is prudent to conclude that data gathering institutions or interviewers are not immune to the profit motive. Faking interviews is clearly an effective cost reduction technique, which unfortunately also reduces the data quality in even greater measure.

It must be kept in mind that faking interviews may be tempting not only to data collection institutes, but also to interviewers. Especially in face-to-face situations in which computers are not used to conduct the interview, the institutes must rely on the integrity of the interviewers – and the interviewers are no more immune to the profit motive than the institutes. As shown and as discussed in the literature, fakers produce relatively coherent interviews with few missing cases, but it would be rather cynical to call this 'high data quality'.

There are additional reasons, already discussed in the mid-1940s, why interviewers may fake or partly fake interviews. Crespi (1945: 431) pointed out that the 'cheater problem is essentially a moral one' but that cheating 'lies as much in the structure of the ballots and the conditions of administration as in the personal integrity of the interviewer'. He discussed several questionnaire design and content features that might demoralize interviewers, for example unreasonable length, too many 'why's' and 'what for's', apparent repetition of questions, lengthy wording, complex, difficult, and antagonizing questions. To minimize faked and partly faked interviews, one can apply our suggested screening method. Using this technique, it is possible to detect single interviews with suspicious sets of items already in the early stages of a project when the first 100 or 200 interviews are machine-readable.

5

Substantive or methodology-induced factors? A comparison of PCA, CatPCA and MCA solutions

This chapter introduces the reader to a comparison of PCA, CatPCA and MCA, and the use(fulness) of rotation. For this purpose we chose a set of 15 four-point items taken from the 2006 European Social Survey (ESS 2006) concerning how respondents felt and behaved during the past week (see Table 5.1 for the list of feelings and their distribution across all participating countries). We will use these items for four reasons: first, the knowledge required to respond should be equally available to all; second, the item formulations are relatively simple; third, personal feelings are universally relevant to all respondents in all countries; and fourth, the items comprise both desirable and undesirable feelings and behaviours. The first two criteria should minimize response differences that are due to task difficulty, since no specialized knowledge and only basic verbal skills are required. This should result in relatively good data quality. The third criterion should increase the likelihood of cross-national comparability of responses, since the items are likely to be of equal relevance. The final criterion was introduced to investigate how items of mixed polarity behave in MCA, CatPCA, and both unrotated and rotated PCA. Since PCA is typically used to empirically validate scholars' measures of theoretical concepts even when the number of ordered categories is limited to four or five, it is vital to assess whether the four approaches would produce mutually reinforcing solutions.

A review of the literature provides abundant evidence that batteries of items of mixed polarity often produce dimensions defined primarily by the polarity of the items. That is, positively worded (or socially desirable) items typically comprise one factor and those of opposite polarity define a second dimension. Schmitt and Stults (1985) showed that the extraction of two factors for bipolar items could be the result of careless respondents. They took three different actual sets of correlation matrices that were calculated on 30 positively worded items. Afterwards the authors used a simulation program to create sets of 400 'respondents' whose response patterns reproduced the correlation matrices.

Schmitt and Stults (1985) then altered the polarity for some of the items, with 5%, 10%, 15% and 20% of their 'respondents' failing to notice the reversed polarity. A PCA of the simulated correlation matrices showed that by the time 10% of the 'respondents' had failed to note the reversal, a separate factor typically emerged on which all or almost all of the reverse-polarity items had their highest loadings. In contrast, when all of the 'respondents' paid attention to the reversals, the reverse polarity items were spread out over the different dimensions rather than forming their own dimension. This strongly suggests that PCA is susceptible to an artefactual dimension when even just a tenth of the respondents fail to take note of reverse polarity.

Barnette (2000) used a split-ballot design to assess the effects of polarity in the stem of items (all positive versus some negative semantic construction). Cronbach's alpha on attitudes towards year-round schooling was substantially higher for the all-positive formulations compared to mixed semantic formulations (the negative formulations took the form of negation of the positive formulation by using and underlining the word 'not'). This is consistent with other research that indicates greater task difficulty for negative formulations. Schriesheim, Eisenbach and Hill (1991) utilized an experimental design in which polarity was manipulated and students randomly assigned to one of the following conditions: standard (positive formulation), polar opposite (term whose meaning is close to the opposite of the positive formulation), negation of standard (through the word 'not') and negation of the polar opposite. The task consisted of the students reading a script describing a hypothetical leader in a particular fashion (as 'always' or 'never' behaving in a certain way). Then the students answered a series of questions about the leader's behaviour (on a five-point scale from 'always' to 'never'). They found that regular items had the best psychometric properties and negated polar opposite items the worst. Clearly, the negation of a negatively formulated item represents the most challenging cognitive task, even for university students.

Consistent with other analyses, DiStefano and Motl (2006) found that a single-factor model for Rosenberg's self-esteem items failed to meet minimum fit standards. The same held true for items intended to measure social physique anxiety. Two unipolar factors met the standards, but a single factor with a response style factor for all negatively formulated items fitted just as well, and sometimes even better than the two-factor models. In the two-factor models, the correlation between the pairs of unipolar factors was high ($r = 0.74$ for self-esteem). The two personality variables that were significantly related to response style suggested greater self-reflective thought. A possible interpretation is that susceptibility to negative response style is less for those who provide careful responses and greater for those whose responses might be superficial. Indeed, in a subsequent analysis based on the same data, the authors hypothesize that 'the presence of method effects due to negative wording is due to careless responses' (DiStefano and Motl, 2009: 312). It could also be a manifestation of cognitive ability, for example, whereby negatively formulated items are intrinsically more difficult to process and therefore respondents who find the task overly difficult simplify their responses in a manner that manifests itself in a response style associated with negative items.

For some phenomena, it is better to conceptualize a respondent as having an ideal point position on a given topic. In such a conceptualization, the greater the distance in either direction that various response options are from that position, the less likely the respondent is to endorse that response option. For such data, van Schuur and Kiers (1994) documented that FA produces a method-induced extra factor. This is especially likely for domains that include items of reversed polarity. The authors point out that the unrotated factor solution can nevertheless often provide a meaningful cognitive map.

Of some importance for cross-national comparative research, Cambré, Welkenhuysen-Gybels and Billiet (2002) found that a single substantive factor plus a methods factor solution resulted in a greater number of countries for which factorial invariance held. This means that where the aim is to do cross-national comparative research, a larger number of countries can be compared.

Countries that have less experience with survey research should find the task of responding to negatively formulated items even more difficult. Data quality should also manifest itself by cultural groups within a given country. In this respect the research by Steenkamp and Burgess (2002) is particularly enlightening. They documented that the two reverse-polarity items on the Change Seeker Index had unacceptably low factor loadings (averaging 0.15) for the three main population groups in South Africa. They report that these negative-polarity items did not create such difficulty in the more developed Western countries. Further, within South Africa, the factor loadings were highest for whites and lowest for blacks. This rank-order corresponds to the aggregate levels of education for whites, so-called coloureds, and blacks. Like many other researchers, their solution to this problem was simply to delete the reverse-keyed items. Wong, Rindfleisch and Burroughs (2003) found poor fit and lack of construct equivalence in a cross-cultural study on the Material Values Scale. Once two methods factors were modelled (one for reverse-worded items and the other for positive-worded items), the fit indices were marginally acceptable. The authors utilized Schwartz's Portrait Values Questionnaire, which was especially designed to be cognitively less challenging. The interesting thing is that, despite this, their analysis showed the least satisfactory solution for the blacks, suggesting that even with a simplified format geared especially to making valid cross-cultural comparisons, the cultural distance bias keeps on showing up.

Mirowsky and Ross (1991: 127) criticize scholars who create subscales of the positive and negative items for making 'contradictory' and 'implausible' arguments. For example, they cite Brewin and Shapiro (1984) as authors who suggest that 'the resources for achieving success are useless for avoiding failure or that people fail to see how the same resources can be used toward both ends' (Mirowsky and Ross, 1991: 127). Mirowsky and Ross (1991) point out that common index-construction practices often are at the root of the problem.

They use Brewin and Shapiro's (1984) logic as an example. First, an exploratory factor analysis is performed in which two factors with eigenvalues greater than 1.0 are extracted. The solution is then rotated, which produces the typical negative–positive dimensions. The problem is compounded by taking the 'purest' items, namely the ones with the highest loadings on a given factor, and discarding the ones with moderate loadings on two or more factors. Mirowsky and Ross state that this increases the likelihood that items that are least affected by response styles are precisely the ones that will be deleted.

Spector et al. (1997) provide additional insight about the conditions under which FA produces an artificial factor. Their main point is that the negation of reverse-polarity items is often not equivalent to affirmation of a regular item if the item distributions are skewed. They showed that both negative- and positive-polarity job satisfaction items that were symmetrically distributed around the mid-point loaded on a single factor. For these items, the reversal of a negative is equivalent to a positive. In contrast, two factors were extracted for items with pronounced positive or negative skew, and a single-factor model did fit poorly. For these items, the negation of a negative is not equivalent to the endorsement of a positive and an 'unfolding' model would be more appropriate. They conclude that 'since the artefact of item wording direction can produce factors, one must provide strong evidence that the factors are substantive' (Spector et al., 1997: 675).

All of the findings on the effects of polarity of items reinforce our concern that screening needs to be done before creating any scales. We agree with Green's (1988: 774) scepticism about the process by which CFA 'magically transforms the weak and uneven' observed correlations to powerful and consistent ones among the latent variables.

Descriptive analysis of personal feelings domain _____

5.1 Polarity of items is intrinsically connected to normative regulation, which in turn almost inevitably produces skewed distributions, with the direction of the skew being a function of the polarity of the item. Readers will agree that items A, B, C, E, G, H, J, K and N in Table 5.1 refer to feelings one would rather not have, with the remaining six being desirable ones. Of course, the classification of items as positive or negative is easier for some feelings than for others. For example, being absorbed in what one is doing can sometimes be a negative attribute, at least to one's spouse if not to oneself. From an impression management point of view, one would expect individuals to more frequently endorse positive than negative feelings. This becomes a partial test for determining the polarity of the items. Table 5.1 shows the distribution of the items over all countries without missing values, which ranged from 0.7% (C and K) up to 4.8% (I). It can be seen that only three items (I, L and O) have a near-symmetrical distribution. For these three items, one would not be able

Table 5.1   Distribution of personal feelings (%; *N*=38,296)

During the past week, how often felt...	None or almost none of the time	Some of the time	Most of the time	All or almost all of the time
A. depressed	60.3	32.3	5.5	1.9
B. everything was an effort	45.5	40.3	10.6	3.6
C. sleep was restless	44.8	38.4	12.0	4.8
D. happy	5.3	25.1	47.2	22.5
E. lonely	66.5	25.0	5.7	2.7
F. enjoyed life	6.0	26.0	43.9	24.0
G. sad	51.4	40.8	5.7	2.0
H. could not get going	52.2	38.3	7.2	2.3
I. had a lot of energy	10.7	34.2	40.9	14.1
J. anxious	50.5	39.4	7.8	2.3
K. tired	21.8	58.1	15.7	4.3
L. absorbed in what you were doing	12.9	33.2	39.7	14.2
M. calm and peaceful	8.3	32.9	44.0	14.8
N. bored	62.9	30.5	5.1	1.5
O. really rested when you woke up in the morning	17.3	32.9	35.1	14.7

to infer the polarity or desirability of the item just from its distribution. Rather, one could classify them on the basis of face validity or on the basis of the sign of the correlation coefficients with all other items. For example, the most ambiguous item (L) is positively correlated with all other items classified as being desirable and negatively correlated with all items classified as being undesirable feelings (not shown). This fact supports our decision to classify it as a positive feeling. For the remaining items, the direction of the skew is determined by the item polarity: positive feelings are discernible by the fact that the majority of respondents report having them all or some of the time, while negative feelings can be recognized in that respondents typically deny having them frequently.

A further important feature about the distributions and their polarity is that the negative skew is not symmetric with the positive skew. More specifically, the absence of negative feelings is more pronounced than the presence of positive feelings. For the data at hand, the average ratio over all items between 'none or almost none of the time' and 'all or almost all of the time' for the negative items is 21.4. In contrast, the ratio of (almost) all to (almost) none of the time for the positive feelings is only 2.7. This asymmetry of the skew is, we believe, a crucially important feature that not only violates the assumption of normality of distribution in PCA, but is the source of some methodological artefacts as documented in the above literature review – a point to which we will return.

As indicated above, we chose these items on the assumption that they would be easy to respond to for most individuals in all the countries. Hence, we expected few instances of NSR. Table 5.2 provides the information on nonresponse for all participating countries, together with their sample size. Overall,

Table 5.2 Sample sizes and distributions of item non-response

Country	N	Non-missing (%)	DK*	Refusals*
Austria	2,405	91.2	74.8	25.2
Belgium	1,798	99.7	95.5	4.5
Bulgaria	1,400	77.1	92.9	0.0
Switzerland	1,804	96.8	83.7	0.0
Cyprus	995	93.9	79.5	0.7
Germany	2,916	96.1	46.7	53.3
Denmark	1,505	95.5	16.2	0.0
Estonia	1,517	85.7	100.0	0.0
Spain	1,876	96.9	53.3	46.7
Finland	1,896	98.4	100.0	0.0
France	1,986	99.2	100.0	0.0
United Kingdom	2,394	98.5	100.0	0.0
Ireland	1,800	91.3	26.4	0.0
Netherlands	1,889	98.8	88.0	12.0
Norway	1,750	99.5	100.0	0.0
Poland	1,721	90.2	79.8	7.7
Portugal	2,222	96.4	66.9	33.1
Russian Federation	2,437	73.2	90.7	0.0
Sweden	1,927	97.0	52.9	8.8
Slovenia	1,476	94.4	90.4	0.0
Slovakia	1,766	91.2	61.8	0.0
Ukraine	2,002	69.6	100.0	0.0
All countries	41,482	92.3	81.3	5.5

*as percentage of all NSRs

92.3% of respondents gave a substantive response to all 15 items. Of 2,773 instances where one or more missing items were encountered, over half (52.4%) involved just a single item (calculation not shown). This is in line with our expectation that there would be few NSRs on these items.

We had also expected that there would be few country differences in the frequency of NSRs. This expectation was not fulfilled. In Belgium and Norway, nearly all respondents (99.7% and 99.5%, respectively) gave a substantive response to all 15 items. In contrast, more than one in every five respondents from the three eastern European countries of Bulgaria, Ukraine, and the Russian Federation provided at least one NSR. A one-way ANOVA indicates that 6.7% of the variance in NSRs is associated with country differences. In all but three of the 22 countries, a response of DK was the main source of NSR. Two countries – Denmark and Ireland – stand out as outliers, with only 16.2% and 26.4% of the NSRs being in the form of a DK. However, these two countries (together with 11 others) did not record any instances of refusals (in the data set these are coded as 'no answer'). Such patterns suggest research institutional differences in how NSRs are recorded and/or coded. To exclude the different forms of NSR in the subsequent analyses, and to simplify the task, we employ listwise deletion. That is, respondents are included in the analyses only if a sub-stantive response was given to all 15 items.

Rotation and structure of data_____

5.2 When data are of high quality, one would ordinarily expect that any conclusions based on MCA or CatPCA would be quite similar to those derived from PCA. However, as noted previously, the items contain both negative and positive attributes, a feature that has proved problematic in many PCA applications in that separate factors typically are extracted for the negative and positive items. We begin the multivariate analyses with a separate PCA for each country, using first the Kaiser eigenvalue criterion for the number of factors to be extracted.

Table 5.3 gives the number of eigenvalues that exceed 1.0 and, after rerunning the analysis with a two-dimensional restriction, the percentage of variance before and after rotation of the axes. The number of factors extracted using the eigenvalue criterion ranges between two and four, with three factors being extracted in 15 of the 22 countries, while two factors were extracted in only Ukraine and Slovenia. In contrast, the scree plot suggests that one factor is sufficient for all countries, since the proportion of variance extracted by the second factor is (with the exception of Cyprus and Slovakia) between a fifth and a

Table 5.3   Number of factors and extracted variances in two-dimensional rotated and unrotated PCA solutions

		Unrotated		Rotated	
Country	$k*$	Dimension 1	Dimension 2	Dimension 1	Dimension 2
Austria	4	34.3	9.4	24.6	19.1
Belgium	4	37.9	8.0	23.5	22.5
Bulgaria	3	41.5	12.5	31.8	22.2
Switzerland	3	31.1	8.7	21.0	18.8
Cyprus	3	30.5	13.9	25.4	19.1
Germany	3	32.2	8.8	21.0	20.0
Denmark	4	31.3	9.2	20.4	20.1
Estonia	3	37.9	9.8	28.3	19.4
Spain	3	39.1	8.6	27.1	20.7
Finland	4	33.7	9.5	23.3	19.9
France	4	36.7	9.0	27.0	18.7
UK	3	37.1	8.3	24.8	20.6
Ireland	3	31.7	9.9	22.5	19.1
Netherlands	3	34.8	8.5	24.0	19.3
Norway	4	31.4	9.0	21.6	18.8
Poland	3	41.3	8.7	29.9	20.1
Portugal	3	39.2	12.9	28.5	23.5
Russia	3	42.8	9.3	30.4	21.7
Sweden	3	37.0	8.5	28.3	17.2
Slovenia	2	37.0	9.8	28.8	17.9
Slovakia	3	31.8	10.7	22.5	19.9
Ukraine	2	37.0	11.2	28.2	20.1
All countries	3	36.2	9.7	27.5	18.4

*Number of dimensions based on Kaiser criterion of eigenvalues greater than 1.0.

third of that extracted by the first factor. Of course, once the axes are rotated, the second dimension becomes much more equal to the first, sometimes almost at par (e.g., Belgium, Germany and Denmark).

The issue is how many dimensions suffice to capture the meaningful substantive variation in the personal feelings domain, and how comparable these factors are. We address this by scrutinizing the factor loadings more closely, starting with the unrotated solutions (data not shown). For all countries, the sign of the loadings on the first dimension on all items corresponds to the polarity of the item; that is, all desirable feelings have one sign, while all undesirable feelings have the opposite sign. Not only that, but in seven countries all 15 items had their highest loading (absolute values) on the first dimension; in an additional four countries all but one item had its highest loading on the first dimension, and in no country did fewer than 12 items have their highest loading on the first dimension. In all countries that had one or more loadings that were higher on the second dimension than on the first, one of the aberrant items was always the most ambiguous one with respect to whether it is a positive or a negative attribute, namely being absorbed in what one was doing. These features, in our judgement, constitute strong evidence that the first dimension can be considered a substantive factor assessing the (reported) extent of positive–negative feelings experienced during the previous week.

It is debatable whether one should even attempt to interpret the second dimension. By the eigenvalue criterion, the second dimension binds sufficient variation to warrant interpretation; by the scree test it does not. In this particular instance, some patterns exist on the second dimension that are suggestive. The most striking pattern (other than the generally low loadings) is the strong tendency for the loadings to be positive. In 11 countries, the loadings of all 15 items are positive, five countries have one negative loading, three countries have two negative loadings and two countries have three negative loadings on the second dimension (not shown). Only in the Netherlands, with eight negative loadings, does this tendency not exist. A pattern of all positive loadings on a set of items that contains both desirable and undesirable attributes is consistent with a response set interpretation. Specifically, it suggests that some respondents tended to give the same response consistently to items whose content is patently inconsistent, for example, to indicate that they were happy and that they were sad all or almost all of the time in the preceding week.

Examining the magnitude of the loadings on the second dimension shows a second pattern: feelings that are desirable tend to have higher loadings than those that are undesirable. Such a pattern is consistent with previous findings of lower data quality for negatively formulated items. Alternatively, the second dimension may represent a statistical artefact reflecting the negative skew in the distribution of these items, a pattern that has also been reported in previous research. If we accept this latter interpretation, it would also account for a large proportion of the instances where a negative loading was found on the second dimension. In eight of the 11 countries in which there was a negative loading on the second dimension, feeling tired was involved. This is also the feeling that is least often rejected outright among the undesirable feelings: only 22% said they never or almost never felt tired the previous week, while the next least frequent rejection is double that (at 45%) for both feeling that everything was an effort and for restless sleep (see Table 5.1). Regardless of whether one favours a methodological artefact (poor data quality due to negative polarity) or a statistical artefact (distributional features) interpretation, only one substantive factor seems to account for the variation in this set of items.

Rotating the PCA solution yields a starkly different picture. In 15 countries, the rotated solution perfectly divides the items into desirable and undesirable sets. Specifically, the nine socially undesirable feelings have their highest loadings on the first factor, while the remaining six desirable feelings have their highest loadings on the second factor. A similar tendency exists in the remaining countries, although with varying numbers of exceptions. In short, the rotated solutions provide the familiar two unipolar factors discussed in the literature review. Should we conclude that we need two substantive unipolar concepts to describe the variation in respondent feelings? The scree test and the parsimony principle argue against concluding that two substantive concepts are needed to adequately describe the variation in this set of items. In the next step we employ CatPCA in the screening process.

As discussed in Chapter 3, even when the quality of data is high, CatPCA is a more appropriate technique for analysing ordered categorical data. To the extent that the data violate the metric assumption, the explained variance in CatPCA will exceed that in PCA. Separate country analyses were performed, imposing a two-dimensional solution on all countries. Poor data quality would be manifested by the presence of tied optimal quantifications, which indicate that the measurement level may not even be ordinal (see Chapter 3). We show the CatPCA biplots for four countries: United Kingdom (Figure 5.1), Finland (Figure 5.2), Spain (Figure 5.3), and Ireland (Figure 5.4).

From the biplots shown in Figures 5.1–5.4 one can depict what happens when rotating the solutions. The biplots for Spain, Ireland, and Finland show two clusters each, one reflecting the desirable, the other one the undesirable feelings. Varimax would rotate the axes to the centre of the clusters, or as close to them as possible, since it constrains the factors to remain uncorrelated (i.e., separated by an angle of 90 degrees); some kind of oblique rotation would fit the data better than varimax. In the UK the two sets of feelings are also well separated along dimension 1, but they measure almost opposite feelings, such as 'felt rested' (O) versus 'felt tired' (K) and 'happy' (D) versus 'lonely' (E).

Confirming our expectation that the feelings data are of relatively good quality, not a single instance of a tied optimal quantification for any of the items in any of the countries was found, although for a few countries (e.g., Ireland), some successive categories were quite close to each other (see Figure 5.4). This is one indicator of the quality of the data, at least with respect to the ordinal measurement

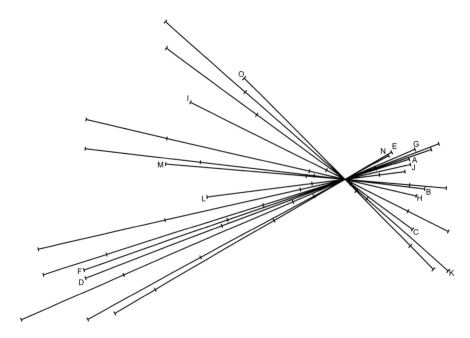

Figure 5.1 CatPCA biplot, United Kingdom

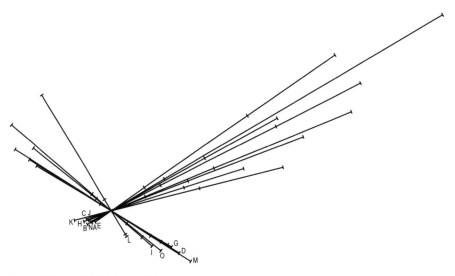

Figure 5.2 CatPCA biplot, Finland

assumption. Another indicator would be small increases in the explained variance between PCA and CatPCA in the two-dimensional solution (Table 5.4).

Finally, we apply MCA to the same set of items. MCA makes no statistical and distributional assumptions; the only requirement is that the data have no negative entries (which in survey data do not exist). MCA can be regarded as

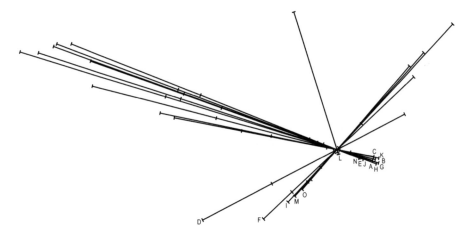

Figure 5.3 CatPCA biplot, Spain

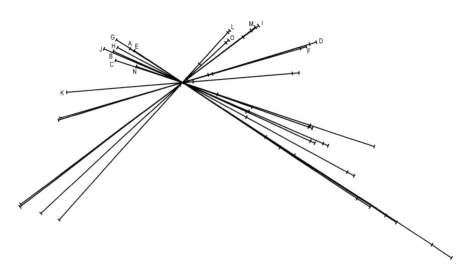

Figure 5.4 CatPCA biplot, Ireland

PCA applied to unordered categorical data. To compare the eigenvalues of MCA that are calculated on the basis of the indicator matrix with those from CatPCA and PCA, we multiply them by the number of variables (as done by SPSS Version 18). Since the maximum value is equal to the number of variables, the amount of explained variance is simply the ratio of the eigenvalue to the number of variables. Since MCA assumes only unordered categorical data, a one-dimensional solution should explain more variation than CatPCA. (Note that comparisons of explained variances using the SPSS adjustments are only meaningful for the first dimension; in the second and higher dimensions they are misleading.)

In MCA, if the input data are unidimensional and of high quality, then the plot of the response categories in the latent space should conform to the following:

- The first (horizontal) dimension permits a substantive interpretation. This means that (almost) all response categories are located in their correct position, reflecting increasing (or decreasing) quantities of the substantive concept as one moves from left to right along the horizontal dimension. In the current application, the location of the response categories when projected onto the horizontal axis should reflect increasing values of positive feelings and decreasing values of negative feelings (or vice versa).
- The response category locations of the negative items should form a mirror image of the positive ones. That is, responses of 'none or almost none of the time' to the negative items should be located in the approximate vicinity of 'all or almost of the time' to the positive items.
- The second (vertical) dimension should form what is referred to as a horseshoe, arch or Guttman effect, with the extreme responses to all items (regardless of whether negative or positive) near the top or near the bottom and with the moderate responses opposite to them. For the 15 feeling items, the location of the response categories of 'none or almost none of the time' and 'all or almost of the time' should be in close proximity near the top (or bottom) when projected onto the vertical axis, with the remaining response categories located in the bottom (or top).

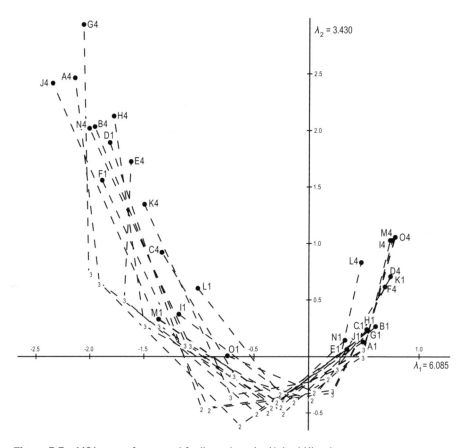

Figure 5.5 MCA map of personal feelings domain, United Kingdom

The data largely conform to these criteria. With respect to all 15 items, the four response categories are in their correct position relative to each other in 11 countries: Belgium, Bulgaria, Estonia, Spain, Finland, France, Poland, Portugal, Russia, Slovenia and Ukraine. Minor dislocations occur in Austria, Switzerland, Germany, UK, the Netherlands and Sweden. For the remaining two countries (Ireland and Slovakia) there are five or more instances of a response location inconsistent with their initial order. We show the MCA maps for the same four countries as used for the CatPCA: the UK (Figure 5.5), Finland (Figure 5.6), Spain (Figure 5.7), and Ireland (Figure 5.8).

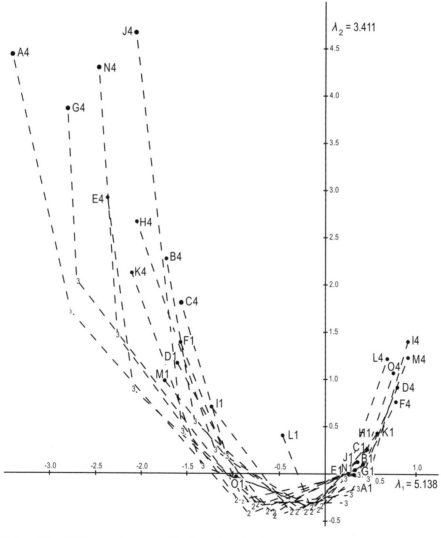

Figure 5.6 MCA map of personal feelings domain, Finland

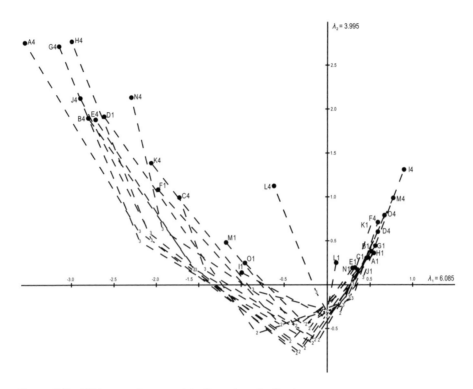

Figure 5.7 MCA map of personal feelings domain, Spain

In all four countries, the negative feelings can be described by the (almost) daily presence of depression (item A), sadness (G), and anxiousness (J), followed by some country-specific undesirable feelings: in Finland and Spain this is boredom (N). Again for all four countries the most positive part of the personal feelings maps can be described by the (almost) daily presence of happiness (D), enjoying life (F), being calm and peaceful (M), being rested when waking up in the morning (O), having a lot of energy (I), and by the absence of being tired (K). The ambiguous item (L), being absorbed in what you were doing, is weakly associated with the other items; it belongs mainly to a higher dimension (not shown). With respect to the first dimension, in Finland, Ireland and the UK this feeling belongs to the desirable ones, while in Spain it has the tendency to be undesirable. With respect to extreme responses, they are stronger among the negative feelings than among the positive ones. From these findings it could be concluded that the presence of undesirable personal feelings contains a stronger response style element than that of desirable ones, and therefore they determine to a larger extent the geometric orientation of the second dimension. However, this is simply a matter of their masses, which are lower than those of their desirable counterparts (cf. Table 5.1). Since the respective categories are highly intercorrelated, they move to an outside position on dimension 2. With increasing distance to the centroid, the inertias of the

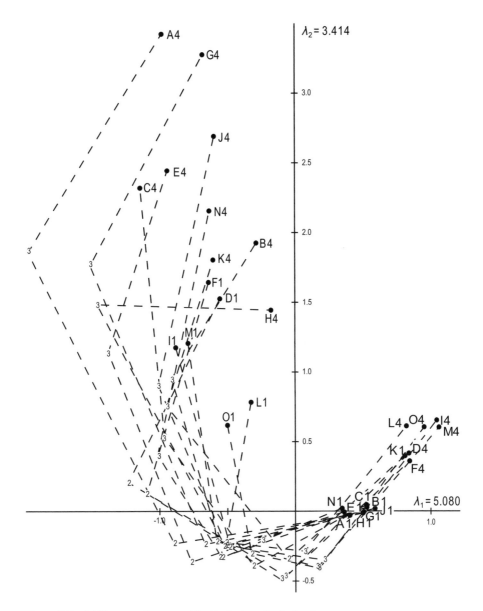

Figure 5.8 MCA map of personal feelings domain, Ireland

item categories belonging to the second dimension increase by the factors of the squared distance (cf. Chapter 3). Hence, they define the geometric orientation of the second dimension to a large degree. But as shown, the resulting horseshoe is simply an artefact of the method; the solutions are one-dimensional. Rotating the solution would just capitalize on the skew of the distributions.

All in all, with the possible exception of the item 'absorbed in what you were doing', the data form a pattern that is similar across all participating countries

Considering the large number of possible dislocations (four response categories for 15 items across 22 countries), the MCA findings confirm that the personal feelings data are of good quality. This makes the data appropriate for cross-national comparative purposes. Furthermore, the MCAs confirm for all countries that a single underlying substantive dimension is sufficient. This dimension reflects the extent of negative/positive feelings, ranging from most undesirable on the far left to most desirable on the far right. Rotating this data set in PCA, CatPCA, or MCA would add a second, method-induced dimension.

So far, MCA, CatPCA and the unrotated PCA solutions point to the identical conclusion that variation in this set of items can be parsimoniously attributed to one underlying substantive concept, namely the prevalence of desirable – and absence of undesirable – feelings in the preceding week. Next, we compare the unrotated PCA, CatPCA and MCA one-dimensional solutions for all countries (Table 5.4).

Table 5.4 supports the previous findings that the personal feelings data are of respectable quality. This is inferred from the fact that for most countries only modest improvements in extracted variances occur as one moves from the most restrictive method (PCA) to the least restrictive (MCA) one. In only two countries (Ireland and Cyprus) does the improvement exceed 5%, but there the explained variance is relatively low. Second, only small country differences exist in the reliabilities of a one-dimensional solution: Cronbach's alpha (computed

Table 5.4 Comparison of variance in the first dimension extracted by PCA, CatPCA, and MCA

Country	PCA	CatPCA	MCA	MCA improv. over PCA (%)	CatPCA improv. over PCA (%)	CatPCA Cronbach's alpha
Austria	34.3	35.0	35.2	2.6	2.0	0.85
Belgium	37.9	38.7	38.7	2.1	2.1	0.88
Bulgaria	41.5	42.6	42.8	3.1	2.7	0.89
Switzerland	31.1	31.6	31.7	1.9	1.6	0.82
Cyprus	30.5	32.0	32.3	5.9	4.9	0.81
Germany	32.2	33.1	33.3	3.4	2.8	0.84
Denmark	31.3	32.3	32.5	3.8	3.2	0.83
Estonia	37.9	39.0	39.1	3.2	2.9	0.88
Spain	39.1	40.4	40.6	3.8	3.3	0.86
Finland	33.7	34.2	34.3	1.8	1.5	0.85
France	36.7	37.9	37.9	3.3	3.3	0.86
UK	37.1	38.0	38.1	2.7	2.4	0.87
Ireland	31.7	33.4	33.9	6.9	5.4	0.84
Netherlands	34.8	35.7	36.1	3.7	2.6	0.86
Norway	31.4	32.2	32.6	3.8	2.5	0.83
Poland	41.3	42.8	42.8	3.6	3.6	0.89
Portugal	39.2	39.6	39.7	1.3	1.0	0.88
Russia	42.8	44.1	44.5	4.0	3.0	0.90
Sweden	37.0	38.4	38.5	4.1	3.8	0.86
Slovenia	37.0	38.3	38.6	4.3	3.5	0.87
Slovakia	31.8	32.8	33.2	4.4	3.1	0.84
Ukraine	37.0	38.3	38.6	4.3	3.5	0.88
All countries	36.2	36.8	36.9	1.9	1.7	0.87

in CatPCA) ranges between 0.81 (Cyprus) and 0.90 (Russia). However, country differences in the adequacy of a one-dimensional cognitive map are substantially greater: The CatPCA extracted variance in that dimension ranges between 32.0% and 44.1% for the same two countries.

If one accepts that a one-dimensional solution suffices to account for the substantive variation, then either the percentage of variance extracted by that dimension or Cronbach's alpha is usually applied as a measure of its adequacy. By these measures, Table 5.4 points to an interesting conclusion, namely that a one-dimensional solution is more adequate in certain eastern European countries than in many western European countries. Specifically, Bulgaria, Poland and Russia have the highest explained variance and the highest reliabilities, while Switzerland, Denmark and Norway (together with Cyprus) have the lowest of both of these quantities. Hence, one would come to the conclusion that Russia, Poland and Bulgaria provide the highest quality of data while Norway and Switzerland have the lowest. This is opposite to the findings we reported for other data (Blasius and Thiessen, 2006a, 2006b).

An alternative interpretation is that the elicited cognitive maps with respect to feelings are less complex in countries that have high extracted variance and high reliabilities. It is not necessarily the case that the quality of the data is lower in the western European countries, but rather that the respondents in these countries perhaps make finer distinctions between their various feelings. A lower reliability, then, does not necessarily indicate greater measurement error, but rather that a one-dimensional map does not capture the complexity of the reported feelings as adequately. We will discuss this point in detail on the basis of the PISA data in Chapter 8, which is concerned with cognitive competencies and response quality.

Conclusion

5.3 When analysing the personal feelings domain with MCA, the first dimension mirrored the feelings on a latent scale ranging from undesirable to desirable, with the second one forming the methodologically induced horseshoe. Applying PCA or CatPCA to these data, in all countries the first dimension contrasted desirable with undesirable feelings, while the second dimension also seemed to be a methodological one; in all countries except one, all or almost all items had small positive loadings. Hence, by the scree test one would conclude that a one-dimensional solution would be adequate, while by the eigenvalue criterion a minimum of two dimensions, and as many as four, would be required. Applying varimax rotation drastically changed the eigenvalues and showed a two-dimensional solution that separated desirable from undesirable feelings. In this particular case, rotation produced nothing more than a methodological artefact: one dimension is sufficient to describe the structure of the feelings data. Therefore, we recommend screening the data, and in particular examining the unrotated solution before applying varimax or any other kind of rotation. However, there will be other cases where the first dimension reflects substantive variation in the focal domain, with the second dimension being clearly methodological, but where there is also a meaningful third dimension. We will give such examples in Chapters 6 and 7, where the focal domain is political efficacy and trust.

This chapter has illustrated several important principles of data analysis:

- When the focal domain is a simple one that is meaningful to respondents (such as one's own feelings) and asked in a simple and straightforward manner, the resulting data are likely to be of solid quality. In such situations, compatible conclusions are reached regardless of whether MCA, CatPCA or PCA is employed. Additionally, the benefits of using MCA or CatPCA under these circumstances are modest: the explained variance of the focal domain items utilizing MCA or CatPCA is likely to be only marginally higher than for PCA. However, four-point scales are by definition not metric. Hence, one should apply CatPCA to assess the ordinality of the data.
- Even with high-quality data, when the distribution of items is skewed, as will be the case in any normatively regulated domain or on topics on which impression management dynamics are aroused, PCA will be especially susceptible to generating a pseudo-factor that is formed primarily on the basis of the frequency distribution of the items.
- In a normatively regulated domain in which the items are of mixed polarity the distributions will be skewed, with the direction of the skew being a function of the polarity of the item. In such instances, rotation of the PCA solution is likely to produce two factors defined solely on the basis of the polarity and the skew. An examination of the graphic displays produced by MCA and CatPCA would caution the researcher against concluding that two unipolar concepts are necessary to adequately describe the cognitive maps of the respondents. The MCA and CatPCA solutions would clearly point to the more parsimonious bipolar one-dimensional conceptualization.
- The traditional eigenvalue criterion for deciding on the number of dimensions needed to adequately describe the cognitive maps of respondents is often unwise. For the personal feelings domain, this criterion indicated that in some countries two dimensions were sufficient while for others up to four dimensions would be necessary. In the given example, the scree test produces more consistent patterns, with a single dimension being sufficient for all countries. However, even with similar one-dimensional solutions for the different countries, the adequacy of the solution will not necessarily be the same. In the case of personal feelings, a single dimension was less adequate for western European countries than for their eastern European counterparts. As will be argued in Chapter 8, we can learn more about group and/or national differences from the relative adequacy of a given low-dimensional solution than from determining how many dimensions meet a specific criterion.

6

Item difficulty and response quality

In Chapter 1 we discussed how the language used in surveys is one component of task difficulty affecting data quality. We also argued that those who find the task difficult will ordinarily either refuse the task or perform it less adequately. As a result, the less educated, who generally find the language used in interviews to be more alien, are expected to give suboptimal responses or fail to respond at all. For similar reasons, respondents interested in a topic should be less likely to exhibit satisficing behaviours or to simplify the task. The 1984 Canadian National Election Study (CNES) contains items on political efficacy and trust that lend themselves well to exploring the connections between political interest and education on the one hand, and data quality on the other. Balch (1974) first introduced these items, spawning voluminous research based on variations of his items, including national election studies, several ISSP surveys, and other cross-national studies. Regardless of the particular operationalization of political efficacy and trust, positive relationships with both education and political interest are generally reported (Blasius and Thiessen, 2001a; Finkel, 1985; Hayes and Bean, 1993; Parry, Moyser and Day, 1992). In this chapter we argue, with supporting evidence, that unequal data quality produced artefactual relations that masqueraded as substantive theoretical ones.

In previous work, we applied MCA to confirm findings that political interest and educational level are linked to the use of NSRs and to show how to visualize such effects (Blasius and Thiessen, 2001a; Thiessen and Blasius, 1998). We documented that the political efficacy and trust items are fraught with numerous methodological difficulties such as assessing ordinality, detecting response sets, and determining whether the middle ('neither agree nor disagree') categories are substantive or non-substantive responses. In this chapter we reanalyse and extend our previous findings to show that large parts of the substantive relationships reported in the literature on political efficacy and trust are better interpreted as method-induced effects.

As in our previous paper (Blasius and Thiessen, 2001a), we analyse the CNES 1984 data, which asks the same nine questions twice, first with respect to the federal government and subsequently about the provincial governments in Canada (see Table 6.1 for the item wordings). The opinions concerning the federal government constitute the focal domain for this chapter, while the next chapter compares the solutions obtained for the two levels of government, as well as question order effects. For both domains, respondents were asked if they 'strongly agree', 'agree somewhat', 'disagree somewhat' or 'strongly disagree' with the given statements. Interviewers were explicitly instructed not to mention a 'neither agree nor disagree' response option. However, if a respondent volunteered this response, it was to be recorded as a separate middle category. In theory, this method of invoking the middle category should guarantee that 'neither agree nor disagree' would not be used to hide non-response – that is, as a safe response that would mask the fact that they have no substantive opinion. In addition, respondents had the opportunity to indicate they had no opinion on the matter. Another advantage of this data set is that it contains eight questions on political interest instead of a single question. Since a main focus in this chapter is a comparison of the response structures of respondents who differ in their level of political interest, it is vital to have a solid indicator of this concept. We will assess whether the amount of method-induced variation differs between two subgroups defined on the basis of their political interest.

Descriptive analysis of political efficacy domain

6.1 Table 6.1 provides the distributions of the political efficacy and trust items of both the federal and the provincial government. The first line in each row provides the values for the federal government ($N = 3,377$), the second gives the comparable figures for the provincial governments ($N = 3,346$; 31 respondents failed to answer the entire set of questions).

Comparing the two sets of items reveals only minor differences in the marginal distributions. The largest are for items D, 'People like me don't have any say about what the Government in Ottawa/Halifax/Edmonton/Vancouver/ … does' and G, 'People in the Federal/Provincial Government waste a lot of money we pay in taxes': in both cases strong agreement is higher with respect to the federal than the provincial government. These findings are not surprising since the federal government is more distant from the population and has more money to waste than any of the provincial governments, just by the fact that their budget is larger. For the remainder of this chapter, the focus is on the federal government.

Detecting patterns with subset multiple correspondence analysis

6.2 We use MCA and SMCA to visualize the underlying structure of responses to the political efficacy and trust items, and especially to detect patterns that suggest method-induced variation in these data. Applying

Table 6.1 Political efficacy items, federal and provincial government

Item	Strongly agree	Agree somewhat	Neither nor	Disagree somewhat	Strongly disagree	No opinion
A. Generally, those elected to Parliament soon lose touch with the people.	26.6 24.2	44.5 42.0	3.5 2.7	16.1 19.8	4.8 6.2	4.5 5.1
B. I don't think the (Federal) Government cares much about what people like me think.	26.9 24.7	32.9 31.7	3.8 2.2	24.2 28.4	9.0 9.3	3.2 3.8
C. Sometimes, (Federal) Politics and Government seem so complicated that a person like me can't really understand what's going on.	30.8 25.9	33.1 36.6	2.5 1.6	19.1 18.5	12.6 14.6	1.9 2.8
D. People like me don't have any say about what the Government in (Ottawa) does.	33.4 25.1	28.3 29.7	2.2 2.0	20.0 25.1	14.0 15.1	2.1 3.0
E. So many other people vote in (Federal) elections that it does not matter very much whether I vote or not.	7.8 6.7	9.9 9.0	1.8 1.6	16.0 17.2	62.8 62.5	1.7 2.9
F. Many people in the (Federal) Government are dishonest.	10.5 8.9	25.1 22.9	10.1 9.3	24.6 26.7	18.2 18.3	11.5 14.0
G. People in the (Federal) Government waste a lot of the money we pay in taxes.	46.3 35.2	33.2 39.3	3.9 3.7	9.0 11.7	3.6 3.8	4.1 6.3
H. Most of the time we can trust people in the (Federal) Government to do what is right.	10.4 11.0	46.0 49.2	6.2 5.7	23.5 18.4	9.7 10.2	4.2 5.4
I. Most of the people running the (Federal) Government are smart people who usually know what they are doing.	15.9 14.1	45.5 49.3	5.9 5.1	21.0 18.2	8.2 7.5	3.6 5.7

In each cell, the first row is for the federal government (N = 3,377) and the second is for the provincial government (N = 3,346).

MCA to the nine items on political efficacy and trust, the first dimension should capture the variation due to the substantive content. Since previous research showed that these items are highly intercorrelated (Blasius and Thiessen, 2001a), all items should be associated with the first dimension. If the data are of high quality, all items should retain their ordinality in the first dimension. If they do not (e.g., the locations of 'strongly agree' and 'agree somewhat' for a certain item are interchanged), one would question the reliability of that item, since in such a case expressing less trust in the federal government on the manifest item implies having more trust in that government on the latent scale. Even worse would be interchanges across more than one category, for example between 'neither agree nor disagree' and 'strongly agree.' Such a result would suggest that a substantial number of respondents failed to comprehend the questions.

When applying SEM or other methods that require metric or at least ordinal data, the 'no opinion' (NO) response option is usually excluded from the analysis via listwise deletion. If the number of missing responses is large, the remaining sample might be biased since less educated (and less politically interested) respondents are more likely to use an NSR. In MCA, the NO responses can be included just like the other item categories. The NSRs should load on a higher dimension and be negatively associated with the substantive responses on the respective dimension. If the 'neither agrees nor disagrees' (NNs) are also NSRs, and if respondents fluctuate between NN and NO responses, then both sets of categories should be located close to each other and opposite to the substantive responses on the respective dimension. In the event that the NNs are non-substantive, but respondents relatively consistently choose either the one or the other NSR option, the two sets of categories should be separated in the latent space, be uncorrelated with each other, and both should be negatively associated with the substantive responses but on different dimensions.

If the NNs are substantive, they should be located between 'agree some-what' and 'disagree somewhat' on the first dimension and be negatively cor-related with the NSRs on the second (or higher) dimension. If the middle categories were used both substantively and non-substantively, they should be in their correct positions between 'agree somewhat' and 'disagree some-what' on the first dimension but be positively correlated with the NOs on the second (or higher) dimension. If a substantial number of respondents failed to notice the item direction (polarity), the responses to the two reversed items will not conform to an ordinal scale on the first dimension. The greater the number of respondents who did not notice the changed direction of the questions, the greater will be the disorder of categories along the first dimension.

We first apply MCA and SMCAs on the total sample to obtain information about the overall structure of the relationships within and between substantive and non-substantive responses. We then repeat these analyses separately for respondents having low and high political interest. Comparing the solutions per-mits us to detect any differences in the quality of the data between the two groups. In the initial step we apply MCA to the total sample on the basis of the 54 × 54 Burt table (nine items by six response categories, without any adjust-ment). The graphical solution for the first two dimensions is given in Figure 6.1; as abbreviations we use the letters that we assigned to the corresponding items in Table 6.1, while the response categories are numbered from 1 (strongly agree) via 3 (neither agree nor disagree) to 5 (strongly disagree); the NO option is symbolized by '9'.

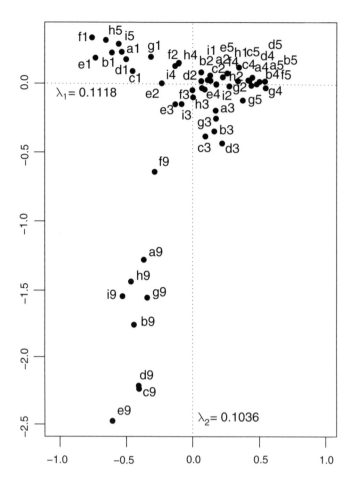

Figure 6.1 MCA map of federal government political efficacy and trust data, first and second dimension.

Figure 6.1 shows that the first dimension mirrors the degree of political effi-cacy and trust in the federal government. Specifically, the left-hand side is populated by 'strongly agree' responses (except items H and I whose polarity is reversed), the right-hand side mainly by 'disagree somewhat' and, somewhat further to the right, 'strongly disagree'. The middle categories of NN are mostly at their ordinally correct locations on the first axis, but they are also situated on the negative part of the second axis. The NO responses are also located on the negative part of dimension 2, but farther removed from the centroid. The prox-imities of the NNs and the NOs on the second axis could indicate some alter-nating use of the two resonse categories.

Overall, the ordering of the categories for all items seems satisfactory, including those with reversed polarity. Consequently, the first dimension can be interpreted as the 'level of political efficacy and trust towards the federal government', with a low level of trust on the left and a high level of trust on the right. The second dimension contrasts NSRs (located on the negative part) with substantive responses (located on the positive part). The NNs are associated with both dimensions, suggesting two overlapping effects: they are used to express real opinions as well as to mask NSRs. In short, the second dimension can be interpreted as 'substantive versus non-substantive' responses; the negative part of the axis reflects a high share of NSRs, the positive part a high share of substantive responses.

In the next step we exclude the categories of NO from the data with help of SMCA to examine the structure of just the substantive responses (including the middle categories); the graphical solution is given in Figure 6.2. The first dimension reflects variation in the amount of efficacy and trust in the federal government, with low trust on the left-hand side and high trust on the right. The second dimension is the methodologically induced horseshoe. If we

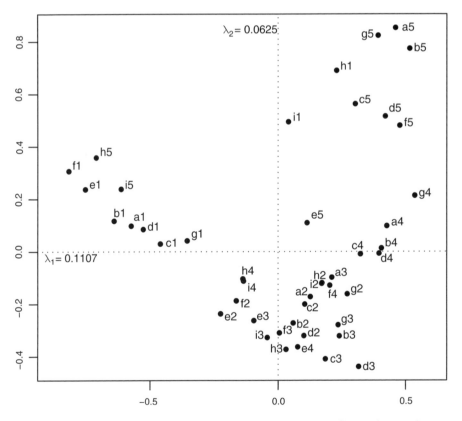

Figure 6.2 SMCA on substantive responses, federal government, first and second dimension (N = 3,377)

project the response categories onto the first dimension, there are only a few reversals; for example, 'strongly agree' and 'agree somewhat' responses are interchanged on the reversed polarity item I. With respect to the distances between the single categories, the 'strongly agree' categories of the first seven items and the two 'strongly disagree' categories of the reverse-formulated items H and I form a well-separated cluster. The same holds for the opposite end of the scale, with the exception of item E where the 'strongly disagree' category ('e5') is somewhat separated from its cluster. The moderate responses are somewhat interspersed, although there are clear proximity patterns (for example, C4, D4, B4, A4, and G4). Farthest away from the 'disagree somewhat' cluster is E4, which is located between two clusters of NNs and very close to D2 and B2.

On a graph of the first and third dimensions (Figure 6.3), the NNs are clearly separated on the negative part of the third dimension. Furthermore, the 'strongly agree' responses, including the 'strongly disagree' responses of items H

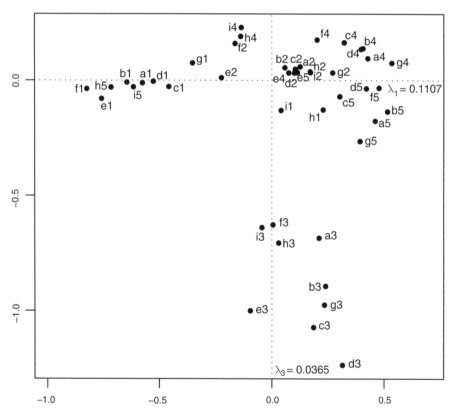

Figure 6.3 SMCA on substantive responses, federal government, first and third dimension (N = 3,377)

and I, form their own cluster. With respect to the opposite side of the scale, E5 is somewhat separated from its cluster of 'strongly disagree' responses and E4 is somewhat removed from its cluster of 'disagree somewhat' responses. Finally, I4, H4, E2, and F2 form their own cluster, which is relatively close to the 'strongly agree' cluster, symbolizing a below-average level of political trust. In contrast, for items A, B, C, D and G, the 'agree somewhat' responses are located on the right-hand part of dimension 1, symbolizing an already above-average level of political efficacy and trust.

Figure 6.1 shows some similarities between the NN and the NO responses. To check for a possible association between these two kinds of responses, we conducted SMCA on only these respective 18 categories (not shown). This

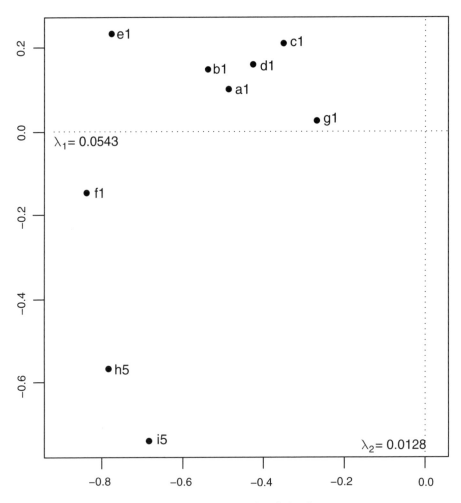

Figures 6.4a SMCAs on single response categories, federal government

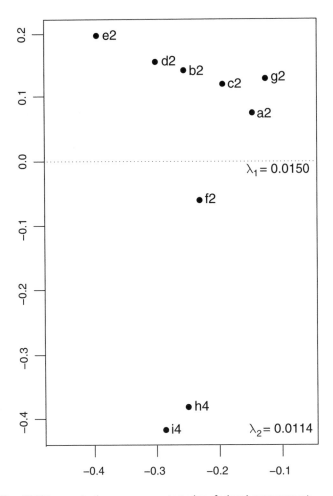

Figures 6.4b SMCAs on single response categories, federal government

analysis revealed that there is no alternating use of these categories: while the NOs are located along the first axis, the NNs are located along the second one; the two sets of categories are uncorrelated in the two-dimensional solution. In other words, respondents who use NN are different from those who use NO.

With SMCA it is also possible to study the structure of responses within a single category, such as 'strongly agree' responses. Since we have two reverse-polarity items, we combined the 'strongly agrees' from items A to G with the 'strongly disagrees' from items H and I into the same subset of response categories; we formed the analogous combinations for the other response categories. Figures 6.4a to 6.4f show the structures of the single response categories.

Figure 6.4a shows the 'strongly agree' responses on the negatively formulated items A to H and the 'strongly disagree' responses on the positively formulated items H and I, that is, the categories that reflect the lowest level of political trust. While on the first dimension all items are located on the negative part of dimension 1, the second dimension distinguishes items H, I and F from the remaining ones, whereby H and I form their own cluster. All three items have in common that they are formulated in a straightforward manner; one can agree or disagree with the respective statements without encountering difficulties occasioned by double negations. A similar structure holds for the 'agree somewhat' responses (Figure 6.4b); here again items H and I form their own cluster, with item F relatively close to it. The patterns for the subsets of 'disagree somewhat' and 'strongly disagree' are not that clear (Figures 6.4d and 6.4e). For the NNs (Figure 6.4c) and the NOs (Figure 6.4f) items H and I are relatively far from items E, D and C. The latter three items have in common that they have quite complicated

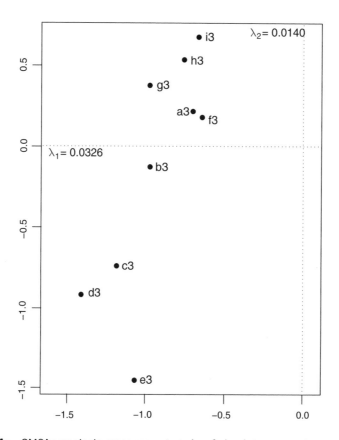

Figures 6.4c SMCAs on single response categories, federal government

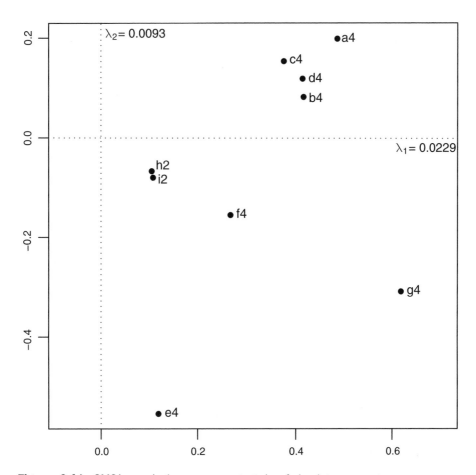

Figures 6.4d SMCAs on single response categories, federal government

formulations, all contain a negation ('can't', 'don't', 'does not') and all of them contain qualifications such as 'sometimes', 'seem so', 'any say' and 'very much'.

Implementing SMCA on the Burt matrix instead of the indicator matrix (see Chapter 3), it must be remembered that all response categories appear in the rows as well as in the columns. When partitioning this matrix, interactions between the subsets have to be considered for the decomposition of the Burt table. Take as an example two subsets of response categories, one containing the substantive responses 'strongly agree', 'agree somewhat', 'disagree somewhat' and 'strongly disagree', the other containing the NNs and the NOs. Since the Burt matrix has a quadratic form, we must consider in total four subsets of tables, with the interactions between the subsets occurring twice (cf. Table 6.2). Although the explained variance of the

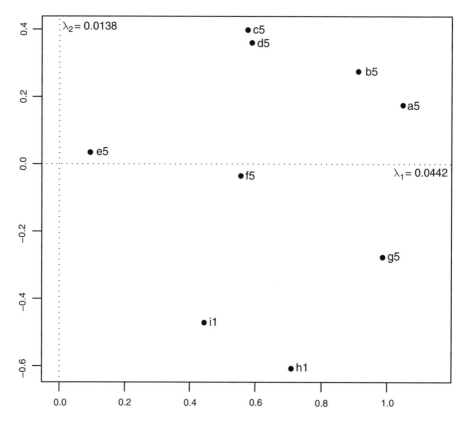

Figures 6.4e SMCAs on single response categories, federal government

interactions between the subsets is usually small, there might be some structure in the data.

Table 6.3 shows the decomposition of inertia obtained through SMCA
from which one can form conclusions about the structure of the single
response categories. The first row consists of the MCA solution for the entire
set of categories of the Burt table. The total inertia is 0.7083, of which the
first and second dimensions explain almost an equal proportion of variance
(15.8% and 14.6%, respectively). The next three rows show the SMCAs for
the substantive versus the non-substantive categories (cf. Figures 6.2, 6.3,
6.4f). When excluding the NOs, the amount of explained variance of the
first dimension increased from 15.8% to 20.3% for the substantive responses
that researchers are usually interested in. In the SMCA, the second dimension forms the horseshoe, which explains less variation than the contrast
between substantive and NSRs in the MCA (14.6% and 11.5%, respectively). Although on average only 4.1% of the respondents used the NO

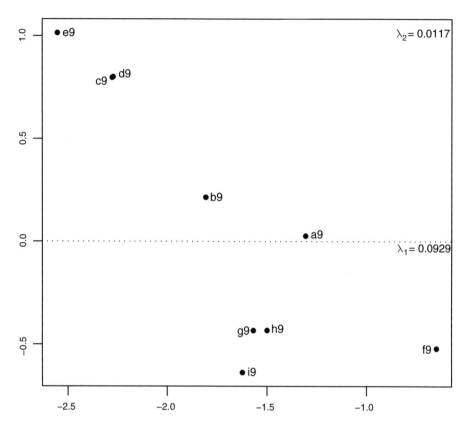

Figures 6.4f SMCAs on single response categories, federal government

Table 6.2 SMCA, Burt table

	a1 a2 a4 a5 b1 b2 ... i1 i2 i4 i5	a3 a9 b3 b9 c3 c9 ... i3 i9
a1		
a2		
a4		
a5		
b1	Subset MCA, Set 1	Interaction, Set 1 × Set 2
b2		
...		
i4		
i5		
a3		
a9		
b3		
b9	Interaction, Set 2 × Set 1	Subset MCA, Set 2
...		
i3		
i9		

option (cf. Table 6.1, average value of the nine items, value not shown), their share of total inertia is more than 20% (last column of Table 6.3). That is, when including the NO option in MCA (or SMCA), their contribution to total inertia is relatively high, which is caused by high intercorrelations between the NOs; that is to say, respondents who failed to express an opinion on one item had high probabilities of not expressing an opinion on the other items.

Out of a total inertia of 0.1481 contained in the NO subset, the first dimension explains 62.7% of the variation. From this finding one can conclude that there is a successive increase in the use of 'no opinion' from item E, the item with the lowest NO percentage (cf. Table 6.1), to item F, which has the highest percentage of NOs. In other words, a large number of respondents giving an NO response to item E gave the same response to items C and D, which have the second and third lowest share of NOs. A large number of the latter group(s) gave the same response to item B, and again a large number of them gave an NO response to item E. This order of responses according to their level of use is almost perfectly reflected by dimension 1 of the respective SMCA (cf. Figure 6.4f). The interaction between non-substantive and substantive responses is very low (not shown). The sum of the total inertias for the four subsets is equal to the total inertia for the entire data set: 0.5441 + 0.1481 + 2 × 0.0080 = 0.7083.

When subdividing the items by NN and NO responses vs. the remaining substantive responses, the latter explain just under 60% of the total variation, reflecting that a large amount of variation is caused by the other responses.

Table 6.3 Decomposition of inertia, SMCA, federal government

Model	K	D1		D2		Total	
		Abs.	(%)	Abs.	(%)	Abs.	(%)
All categories	45	0.1118	15.8	0.1036	14.6	0.7083	100.0
Subset(1,2,3,4,5)	45	0.1107	20.3	0.0625	11.5	0.5441	76.8
Subset(9)	9	0.0929	62.7	0.0117	7.9	0.1481	20.9
Interaction	9	0.0046	57.8	0.0010	12.7	0.0080	1.1
Subset(1,2,4,5)	36	0.1095	25.9	0.0599	14.2	0.4225	59.6
Subset(3,9)	18	0.0934	36.2	0.0327	12.6	0.2583	36.5
Interaction	18	0.0066	47.9	0.0017	12.2	0.0137	1.9
Subset(1)	9	0.0543	56.7	0.0128	13.3	0.0959	13.5
Subset(2)	9	0.0150	24.1	0.0114	18.3	0.0622	8.8
Subset(3)	9	0.0326	30.0	0.0140	12.9	0.1086	15.3
Subset(4)	9	0.0229	32.4	0.0093	13.2	0.0705	10.0
Subset(5)	9	0.0442	45.5	0.0138	14.2	0.0972	13.7
Subset(9)	9	0.0929	62.7	0.0117	7.9	0.1481	20.9

Subset(1): first category variables A to G, last category variables H and I, and so on.

Without taking the interaction effects into account, the variation within the common subset of 4.4% neutral and 4.1% non-substantive responses (in total, 8.5% of the cases; cf. Table 6.1) together explains 36.5% of the total inertia. Analysing each of the six response options separately (the last six rows of Table 6.3) shows that the subset of NOs has the highest amount of total inertia (second last column, last row), followed by the middle category (total inertia 0.1086) and the two extreme categories. From these findings it can be concluded that there are high intercorrelations in the use of the respective categories, which means that some kinds of response styles are present. But this does not mean respondents treated all items identically; there could be two or three clusters within the single categories, as already shown in Figures 6.4a to 6.4i.

With respect to the variance explained by dimension 1, with 62.7% the NOs show the highest homogeneity in answering the nine questions; here we have a successively increasing use of this response option as described above. Further, there is also a large consistent use of 'strongly agree' for items A to G, and 'strongly disagree' for items H and I (subset 1); 56.7% of the variation within these categories is explained by dimension 1. In contrast, for the subset of 'agree somewhat' responses (including the 'disagree somewhat' responses for items H and I) the explained variance of the first dimension is only 24.1% – and with 30.0% of explained variance even the middle categories were not used in a strongly cumulative manner.

Moderator effects

6.3 The next question we address is whether the response pattern itself differs by political interest. The measure of political interest consists of eight variables, with questions such as '[h]ow often do you read about politics in the newspaper and magazines' and '[h]ow often do you attend a political meeting or rally'; response categories were 'often', 'sometimes', seldom', and 'never'. CatPCA was applied to these items to take into account unequal distances between successive response categories, and was restricted to a one-dimensional solution. All items are highly positively associated with the first dimension, which explains 44.9% of the total variation (not shown). Dividing the sample at the mean value of the latent 'political interest' variable results in 1,935 respondents (57.3%) being classified as having 'low political interest' and 1,441 respondents (42.7%) as having 'high political interest'. Table 6.4 compares the two political interest groups on the political efficacy and trust items.

Comparing the two subgroups reveals that respondents with low political interest consistently use the NO as well as the NN categories more often than respondents with high political interest. Substantively, respondents with

Table 6.4 Political efficacy items, federal government, subdivided by political interest

Item	Strongly agree	Agree somewhat	Neither nor	Disagree somewhat	Strongly disagree	No opinion	χ^2
A. Generally, those elected to Parliament soon lose touch with the people.	28.1	44.4	3.9	13.5	3.5	6.6	85.2
	24.6	44.8	3.0	19.5	6.5	1.7	
B. I don't think the Federal Government cares much about what people like me think.	30.0	33.0	4.1	22.2	6.5	4.2	69.5
	22.7	32.8	3.4	26.9	12.3	1.9	
C. Sometimes, Federal Politics and Government seem so complicated that a person like me can't really understand what's going on.	38.4	34.5	2.8	15.1	6.8	2.3	249.7
	20.7	31.4	1.9	24.4	20.3	1.3	
D. People like me don't have any say about what the Government in Ottawa does.	38.0	28.8	2.8	16.8	10.7	2.9	111.1
	27.1	27.8	1.5	24.3	18.5	0.9	
E. So many other people vote in Federal elections that it does not matter very much whether I vote or not.	10.4	12.5	2.2	19.2	53.4	2.4	179.2
	4.3	6.5	1.3	11.8	75.4	0.7	
F. Many people in the Federal Government are dishonest.	11.4	26.0	11.0	23.3	13.4	15.0	118.2
	9.2	23.9	9.0	26.4	24.7	6.8	
G. People in the Federal Government waste a lot of the money we pay in taxes.	46.4	33.3	4.5	7.7	2.5	5.5	54.2
	46.1	33.0	3.0	10.7	5.1	2.0	
H. Most of the time we can trust people in the Federal Government to do what is right.	8.8	47.1	7.4	22.4	8.9	5.4	43.9
	12.6	44.6	4.6	24.8	10.8	2.6	
I. Most of the people running the Federal Government are smart people who usually know what they are doing.	14.5	46.8	7.1	19.1	7.6	4.9	51.5
	17.8	43.7	4.2	23.5	9.0	1.7	

In each cell, the first row is for low political interest (N = 1,935) and the second is for high political interest (N = 1,441). One case is missing because one respondent did not answer any of the political interest items.

low political interest seem to have less trust in the federal government; they are particularly likely to 'strongly agree' with the negatively formulated statements. For example, on item C ('Sometimes, Federal Politics and Government seem so complicated that a person like me can't really understand what's going on'), 38.4% of them agreed strongly, compared to 20.7% of their politically interested counterparts. Both findings are well documented in social science research: persons with little political interest and/or low education express less political efficacy and trust (Blasius and Thiessen, 2001a; Finkel, 1985; Hayes and Bean, 1993; Parry, Moyser and Day, 1992) and they are more likely to give NSRs (Blasius and Thiessen, 2001a; Converse, 1976; Francis and Busch, 1975; Mondak, 1999; Thiessen and Blasius, 1998). If we restrict our attention to the marginal distributions of the seven negatively formulated items (Table 6.4), we would clearly support the previous findings. Although the differences between the two groups are also highly statistically significant for the two positively worded items, they do not reflect that politically less interested people have above average distrust of politics and politicians. Of course, such findings are usually interpreted on the assumption that the respondents comprehended the questions. Invariably, researchers whose findings are similar to those we present in Table 6.4 conclude that politically less interested persons distrust politics and politicians more. However, we think such findings are not a sufficient basis for this conclusion. The data need to be screened to determine if the structures of responses contain certain regularities that argue for an alternative understanding about the meaning of the responses.

As input for the next MCAs and SMCAs we use the data from the two political interest subgroups. Both analyses provide distributions of eigenvalues that are similar to those in the first analysis; we again restrict our attention to the two-dimensional maps. For both solutions, we first show the MCA based on all categories followed by SMCA of just the substantive response categories. Figures 6.5 and 6.6 give the graphical solutions of MCA and SMCA for respondents with high political interest.

The left-hand side of Figure 6.5 contains the 'strongly agree' responses to items A to G and the 'strongly disagree' responses to items H and I; on the right-hand side are the 'strongly disagree' responses to items A to G and the 'strongly agree' responses to items H and I, with the remaining categories in between (detectable from the numerical solution, which is not shown).

Similar to the solution for the total sample, the first dimension mirrors a latent continuous variable that can be interpreted as the level of political efficacy and trust: all 45 Likert-type response alternatives (nine items times five categories) are highly associated with this dimension. Furthermore, the response categories for the two reversed polarity items are appropriately located in the opposite direction along the first axis. Thus, the responses among those with high political interest appear to be consistent with the given ordinal order, regardless of the polarity of the questions.

Furthermore, all NOs except item F are clearly located quite far from the centroid on the second axis. This means that the relatively few politically interested respondents who did not have an opinion (cf. Table 6.4) responded relatively consistently with NO. In addition, only some of the NNs are located slightly in the direction of NO (especially items D, G, and B). From this solution one can conclude that few politically interested respondents used the neutral categories to hide their lack of opinion. Overall, the second dimension distinguishes between substantive (negative part) and non-substantive (positive part)

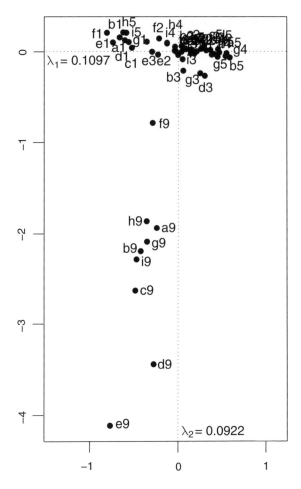

Figure 6.5 MCA map of federal government political efficacy and trust data, high political interest, ($N = 1{,}441$)

responses. With respect to dimension 1, the NOs are closer to the low-trust respondents than to the others. Excluding the NOs by applying SMCA provides a clear picture (Figure 6.6): the first dimension reflects the level of political trust and efficacy, the second the methodologically induced horseshoe.

The pattern differs in some important respects among the politically less interested respondents (Figures 6.7 and 6.8). Note especially that in the MCA solution the first dimension fails to mirror the ordinal order of the substantive categories of the nine items. Instead, it contrasts a 'strongly agree' response to items A to G and a 'strongly disagree' response to items H and I on the left (which was expected), with a mixture of all other categories on the right (which was surprising): Opposite to the respondents with low trust are the NO categories located at the extreme right, as well as the neutral categories of some

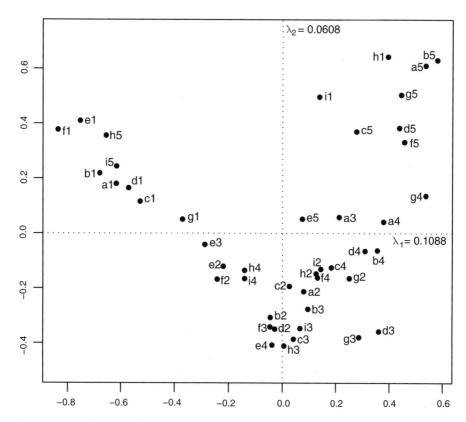

Figure 6.6 SMCA map of federal government political efficacy and trust data, substantive responses only, high political interest, ($N = 1,441$)

of the items (see their projections onto the right-hand part of axis 1). These are strong indications that something is amiss with the indicators. Although the political efficacy and trust items are reasonably valid and reliable instruments for politically interested respondents, it seems that many of the 1,935 politically less interested respondents misunderstood some of the statements, especially if they were likely to disagree with them. Compared to the solutions for the politically interested respondents, there are relatively short distances between the NO and the NN responses (note the different range of the axes in Figures 6.5 and 6.7), which is in an indicator that the NNs have been used relatively often to mask not having an opinion on the issue. Further, projecting the NO and the NN responses onto dimension 1 shows that they are all located on the part of high political trust.

With respect to the MCA solutions, for respondents with high political interest we argued that the first dimension reflects the level of political efficacy and trust in the federal government, with the second axis contrasting substantive and non-substantive responses. For respondents with low political interest, neither interpretation holds. Instead, the first axis mirrors strong agreement with items A to G and strong disagreement with items H and I, together with the NSRs, including some of the NNs. The negative part of the second axis contains a mixture of critical attitudes towards the federal government (project the 'strongly agree' responses onto the second dimension), the NNs and the NOs, while the positive part mainly contains the moderate attitude towards the federal government.

Excluding the NSRs from the data through SMCA provides a map of the substantive responses (Figure 6.8). Again there is a clear horseshoe, but this time not along the second axis, but rather in between the two axes. With respect to dimension 1, the locations of the two reversed items are more disordered than those for the other seven items: the 'strongly agree' responses are located on the same part of the first axis as the 'strongly disagree' responses. From this response pattern it can be inferred that a substantial number of respondents with low political interest did not notice the changed direction of the items. Furthermore,

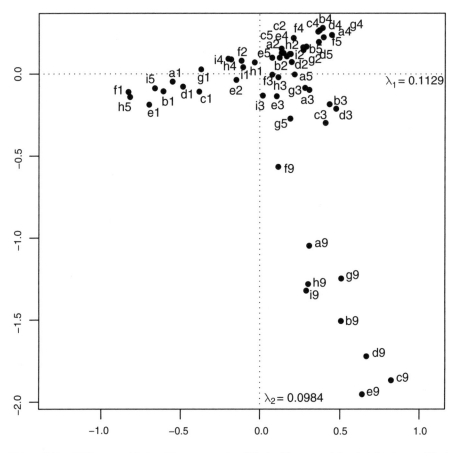

Figure 6.7 MCA map of federal government political efficacy and trust data, low political interest, (*N* = 1,935)

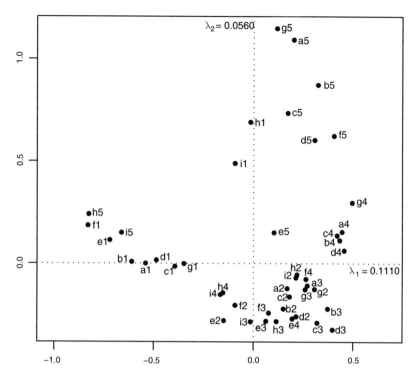

Figure 6.8 SMCA map of federal government political efficacy and trust data, substantive categories only, low political interest, ($N = 1,935$)

on the extreme right are the moderate disagreements, a few NNs and a few strong disagreements. Assuming that the first dimension reflects the 'level of political efficacy and trust', we have to conclude that some respondents had difficulties with the proper handling of the items. The alternative interpretation would be that a 'neither/nor' or a 'disagree somewhat' response to a negative statement reflects more political trust than a 'strongly disagree' response to the same item – this would be meaningless.

To describe the locations of the categories in greater detail and to test each item for ordinality, we show them item by item. In Figure 6.9 we overlap the two-dimensional plots for the two groups of respondents with high and low political interest to save space and to facilitate comparison; solid and dashed lines connect the categories belonging to respondents with high and low political interest, respectively. Note that the distances between the respective variable categories cannot be compared since the axes refer to different data sets whose eigenvalues differ.

Among respondents with high political interest, Figure 6.9 reproduces the ordinal orders of the nine items quite well in the first dimension of the latent space. Only a few small 'errors' (item D, category 4 is slightly dislocated; the same holds for categories E3, G4, and I2) occur and these involve only a few

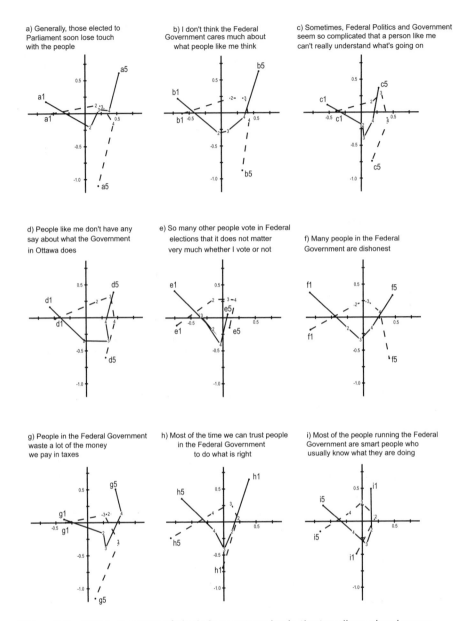

Figure 6.9 SMCA, locations of single item categories in the two-dimensional space

respondents choosing the respective item categories (see the low percentages in Table 6.4). On the second dimension, there are slight deviations from the horseshoe on items A and E; in both cases only two categories are involved.

For the respondents with low political interest only item F mirrors the intended ordinal order of categories along dimension 1. With respect to items A to E and item G, it can be seen that the ordinal scales of the manifest variables are not mirrored on the right-hand side of the first dimension, which are the parts where the respondents have to disagree with the statements. Note that items B, C, D and E have a negation in the text ('I don't think', 'a person like me can't really', 'people like me don't have', 'it does not matter'). Therefore, to agree with the sentiment the respondents would have to disagree with the statement as worded, which would require a double negation. From the maps shown it can be deduced that a substantial number of politically less interested respondents did not pay attention to the direction of the wordings. If they were favourably inclined towards the federal government they often gave any response except the appropriate 'strongly disagree' or 'disagree somewhat'. Furthermore, most of the items include weak qualifiers such as 'soon lose touch', 'cares much about', 'doesn't matter very much', 'seem so complicated' and 'a lot of', which may create further misunderstandings. In effect, although the 'strongly disagree' responses should express the highest trust in the federal government they reflect less trust than 'disagree somewhat' and in some cases even less trust than 'neither agree nor disagree'. Finally, only item F ('Many people in the Federal Government are dishonest') kept its ordinality in the first dimension. In comparison with the other items, F has a quite simple construction, containing just one thought, no negation, and only eight words. From the seven negatively formulated items, this item is constructed most closely to the recommendations of Payne (1951), Edwards (1957) and introductory texts on methods of empirical social research.

The reverse-formulated items H and I also have a straightforward construction without any negation or qualifiers. Nevertheless, for these two items the 'strongly agree' responses are fully misplaced; they are on the same part of the first axis as 'strongly disagree' – that is, both are positively associated with the first dimension. Since both items are phrased in the opposite direction and since they are simply constructed, the conclusion is that the displacements of the 'strongly agree' categories are caused by a response set. In other words, a substantial number of respondents with low political interest did not pay attention to the direction of the questions and simply gave a 'strongly agree' response independent of the content.

We return now to the well-known finding that respondents with low political interest (and/or low education) have relatively little political trust. With respect to Table 6.4, we confirmed these findings by including 'educational level' and 'political interest' as supplementary variables in Figure 6.1 or Figure 6.2 (not shown). However, given that a substantial number of respondents with low political interest seemed to find the task of responding to some of the items difficult, we need to ask what they meant when they consistently gave 'strongly agree' responses. For the last two items we could show that some of them failed to notice the changed direction of the question, but what about the other seven items? Were they even aware of the direction of the questions?

An additional possibility is that a substantial number of politically less interested respondents consistently used the 'strongly agree' response as a socially desirable response to avoid having to admit that they had no opinion on this matter or that they did not understand the question. In other words, could the higher amount of political distrust assigned to the politically less interested be nothing more than a measurement artefact produced by asking complicated questions? If this possibility has merit, it would follow that the simpler the question wording (straightforward sentences, no negations, and no weak expressions), the smaller the differences in political efficacy and trust between politically less and more interested respondents.

Examining the 'strongly agree' column in Table 6.4, the differences between respondents with low and high political interest do indeed vary with the difficulty of the questions. The differences are negligible in relatively simple statements such as item F ('Many people in the Federal Government are dishonest': 9.5% versus 8.1%) and item G ('People in the federal government waste a lot of the money we pay in taxes': 36.3% versus 33.8%). For relatively simply, positively formulated questions, the political efficacy and trust of the respondents with less political interest is even above average (compare the respective 'strongly disagree' responses): item H ('Most of the time we can trust people in the Federal Government to do what is right': 9.5% versus 11.2%) and item I ('Most of the people running the Federal Government are smart people who usually know what they are doing': 6.2% versus 9.2%). In contrast, the largest differences are found in the most complicated question, which is item C (32.3% versus 17.3%). This statement includes a negation combined with two weak formulations ('can't', 'a person like me'), the weak expressions 'sometimes', 'seem so complicated', 'really understand what's going on', and the two stimuli 'politics' and 'government'.

Conclusion

6.4 In this chapter we have applied SMCA to show the structure of subsets of responses. The advantage of SMCA is that one can either exclude single categories from the variables without any missing information (e.g., by excluding the NOs and focusing on the substantive responses), or concentrate on single response categories only (e.g., on the strongly agreements). In the first example, when excluding the NOs, we were able to show the structure of substantive responses. In contrast to listwise deletion, SMCA includes the information also from those respondents who sometimes used the NO option, for example, from respondents who gave substantive answers to seven of the nine items on political efficacy and trust; here the information from these seven (valid) answers was used. When concentrating on single response categories, such as the middle categories, by applying SMCA one can see how strongly these responses are related to each other.

When using 'political interest' as a (dichotomous) moderator variable, it became clear that response quality is highly related to this variable (as well as to education level, not shown here) – respondents with an above average interest in politics handled the questions on political efficacy and trust much better than their less politically interested counterparts, that is, their quality of responses is higher. Interpreting these findings from a task simplification perspective, politically less interested respondents make use of this strategy more often. In the given case, the method-induced variation is so high that it is questionable whether the well-known finding of a negative relation between political interest and political efficacy and trust has any merit.

7

Questionnaire architecture

In this chapter we continue with the example from the previous chapter and show the fatigue effect as well as the effect of the order of questions. Furthermore, based on CatPCA and the assumption that ordered five-point scales also kept their intended order within the latent space, which may or may not hold, we develop a measure to quantify the amount of method-induced variation. The index is standardized between zero and one, with a value close to zero indicating that all respondents understood the questions and were able to comprehend the items and a value close to one indicating that there were systematic and severe violations in the data, while random data produces values around 0.5. This index, which we call the 'dirty data index' (DDI), can be used as a general measure for the quality of ordinal data.

Fatigue effect

7.1 We stated earlier that the fatigue effect is typically defined as the deterioration of the quality of responses near the end of long interviews. One strand of research considers evidence that respondents are less likely to provide substantive responses near the end of interviews to be a manifestation of respondent fatigue, and indeed there is evidence for this (Krosnick et al., 2002). That is, with decreasing respondent motivation there is an increasing tendency to refuse the task. This tendency is also confirmed in the greater use of the NO response for the provincial than for the federal domain (see Table 6.1). Alternatively, the fatigue effect might be tested by showing that the reliability of items located near the end of a questionnaire tends to be lower than those located near the beginning. While this is also a reasonable expectation and one that is empirically supported (Andrews, 1984), we offer yet another interpretation. We hypothesize that near the end of a long interview, respondents and interviewers are more prone to simplify their task in order to complete it more quickly. A common simplification strategy (as we will show in greater detail in Chapter 8) is to disproportionately favour a limited number of the available response options.

The CNES 1984 consists of rather long face-to-face interviews that lasted just over one-and-a-half hours on average. In the first section (A) of the questionnaire, respondents were asked about their attitudes towards the federal government; in the last section (K), just before the demographic items, the same questions were asked about the provincial government. This questionnaire architecture is a felicitous feature for assessing respondent fatigue. Simply stated, the fatigue effect postulates that response quality is a function of the length of the interview, with the response quality decreasing over time, especially near the end of long questionnaires.

A comparison of NN and NO responses (Table 6.1) shows that for all items the federal government has larger percentages of NNs than do the provincial governments; for the NOs, the exact opposite is the case. This is a first hint that there might be a fatigue effect: while in the first case, when the interviews had just started, respondents took more time to answer before finally deciding to volunteer an NN, in the second case, towards the end of the interviews, respondents simply replied with DK. From another point of view the opposite might be expected: during the interviews the respondents learned that there was an NN option which they could use to hide an NSR. Furthermore, there could also be an interviewer effect; at the end of the questionnaire, interviewers might be keen to finish the job as quickly as possible instead of waiting for a substantive answer.

We start by performing the same analyses on the provincial government items as were done for the federal government ones. Again, we use the Burt table without adjustment as input. Figure 7.1 shows the MCA solution for the entire set of questions and all possible responses (including NSRs) towards the provincial governments.

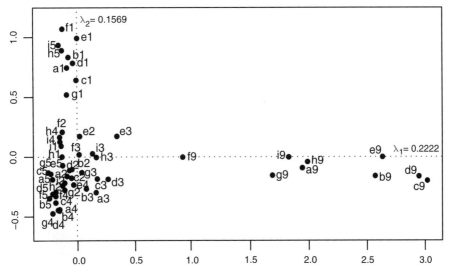

Figure 7.1   MCA map of provincial government political efficacy and trust data

In contrast to the MCA solution for the federal government, the first dimension of the provincial government data differentiates between substantive and non-substantive responses. This might be partly due to the fact that the number of NSRs is higher here than for the federal government; that is, the masses of the NO responses are higher and therefore their corresponding inertias are higher, since inertia is the product of mass and the squared distance to the centroid (see Chapter 3). If the intercorrelations between the NSRs are of approximately the same magnitude for the provincial governments as for the federal government, the difference in inertias could account for the fact that the first axis forms the contrast between substantive and non-substantive responses. In contrast to the findings for the federal government, the second dimension does not reflect the level of political trust and efficacy as clearly. While the top or positive part correctly locates the 'strongly agree' responses (for items H and I the 'strongly disagree' responses), the 'disagree somewhat' responses cluster at the bottom rather than the 'strongly disagree' ones. This is a first indication that methodological effects (apart from the frequency of NSRs) occur in the data. That is, the substantive structure of the responses is not as clean.

For the next analysis, we exclude the effects of the NOs to study the substantive responses by means of SMCA. Figure 7.2 shows some similarities with the corresponding SMCA map for the federal government data (Figure 6.2). Specifically, the negative part of dimension 1 contains the strong agreements for the negatively formulated items (together with the 'strongly disagree' responses for the two reversed items), while the strong disagreements (together with the 'strongly agree' responses for the reversed items) are found on the positive part of dimension 2. If a 45-degree axis from bottom left to upper right were inserted onto the map and the response categories projected orthogonally onto it, most of the items would retain their ordinality in the two-dimensional solution. Further, the horseshoe is formed between the first and second dimension.

However, there is one major difference between the two solutions: for the same set of items, the total inertia for the federal government was 0.7083, while for the provincial government it is 0.8914 – the provincial domain contain more variation. What might account for this difference? One possibility is that it might be caused by response sets. Our argument here is the same as in the previous chapter when discussing the moderator effect of political interest: when respondents answer in a more systematic way (i.e., they have less variation in their use of response categories), total inertia will increase. An even stronger indicator for response sets are the inertias associated with the first dimension: the value for the federal government is 0.1118 (15.8% of explained variation), while the corresponding value for the provincial government is 0.2222 (24.9% of explained variation). Stronger correlations within the response categories will increase the inertia of the first dimension, together with its explained variance.

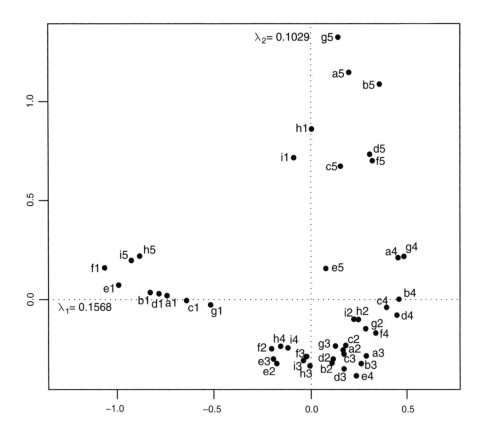

Figure 7.2 SMCA of provincial government political efficacy and trust data, substantive responses only

We have shown the same effect twice, but the reasons were different. In the case of political interest it is a consequence of task simplification due to limited interest. In this case it is task simplification due to increased satisficing because the interview had already lasted more than an hour (on average). It would be understandable if both interviewers and interviewees wished to hasten the end of their formal conversation; in the literature this is the so-called fatigue effect.

Subdividing the provincial government data by the political interest variable introduced in Chapter 6 shows almost the same patterns in the marginal distributions of the two groups as was found for the federal government (not shown). Running MCA separately for the high and low political interest subsamples gives a solution in which the first dimension forms a contrast between substantive and non-substantive responses while the second dimension mirrors the level of political efficacy and trust. While some dislocations occur for the high political interest respondents, even more dislocations occur for politically less interested respondents (figures not shown). Yet again, the total inertia as well as the explained variances of the first dimension are clearly higher when the domain of interest is the provincial rather than the federal government. The SMCAs on just the substantive categories show that the patterns of the two groups do not differ in the two-dimensional space (figure not shown). In both cases the 'strongly agree' responses load on dimension 1, the 'strongly disagree' responses load on dimension 2, while the horseshoe straddles the two dimensions.

With less variation in which responses are used for the different items, some of the profiles of the response categories will become more similar while others become more dissimilar; hence, the first dimension should explain more variance. For the same reason, when respondents use the same response category more frequently, the amount of variation in each item category will increase (i.e., total inertia will increase). Replicating what we did for the federal government domain, we now run the same SMCAs for the provincial government domain in order to compare the solutions (Table 7.1).

Comparing the total inertia for the two solutions shows that the values for the provincial government domain are clearly higher for all subsets. With respect to the single response categories, total inertia for the 'strongly agree' responses (subset 1) are 0.1268 (provincial government) and 0.0959 (federal government); for strong disagreements the respective values are 0.1150 and 0.0972, and for the subset of substantive responses (from 'strongly agree' to

Table 7.1 Decomposition of inertia, Subset MCA, Provincial and Federal Government

Model	K	Provincial Government				Federal Government			
		D1		Total		D1		Total	
		Abs.	(%)	Abs.	(%)	Abs.	(%)	Abs.	(%)
All categories	45	0.2222	24.9	0.8914	100.0	0.1118	15.8	0.7083	100.0
Subset(1,2,3,4,5)	45	0.1568	24.9	0.6309	70.8	0.1107	20.3	0.5441	76.8
Subset(9)	9	0.1972	85.0	0.2320	26.0	0.0929	62.7	0.1481	20.9
Interaction	9	0.0113	79.3	0.0143	1.6	0.0046	57.8	0.0080	1.1
Subset(1,2,4,5)	36	0.1559	31.2	0.4989	56.0	0.1095	25.9	0.4225	59.6
Subset(3,9)	18	0.1976	56.0	0.3531	39.6	0.0934	36.2	0.2583	36.5
Interaction	18	0.0137	69.6	0.0197	2.2	0.0066	47.9	0.0137	1.9
Subset(1)	9	0.0865	68.2	0.1268	14.2	0.0543	56.7	0.0959	13.5
Subset(2)	9	0.0239	34.7	0.0689	7.7	0.0150	24.1	0.0622	8.8
Subset(3)	9	0.0487	40.7	0.1197	13.4	0.0326	30.0	0.1086	15.3
Subset(4)	9	0.0340	46.1	0.0737	8.3	0.0229	32.4	0.0705	10.0
Subset(5)	9	0.0700	60.9	0.1150	12.9	0.0442	45.5	0.0972	13.7
Subset(9)	9	0.1972	85.0	0.2320	26.0	0.0929	62.7	0.1481	20.9

Subset(1): first category variables A to G, last category variables H and I, and so on.

'strongly disagree') the respective values are 0.6309 and 0.5441. This pattern is stable for all subsets shown in Table 7.1; the variation has increased with respect to all subsets since there is less variation in the use of different response categories.

Furthermore, in all cases the inertias referring to dimension 1 are substantially higher for the provincial than the federal government items. In some cases the difference is more than double: 0.1972 versus 0.0929 for the subset on NOs, and 0.1976 versus 0.0934 for the common subset of NOs and NNs. Finally, for all subsets the amount of variance explained by the first dimension is noticeably higher for the provincial than for the federal government data, in some cases by more than 20 percentage points – for example, for the NOs (85.0% vs. 62.7%) as well as for the reported interaction effects. These findings are strong indications that respondents simplified the response task by utilizing a given response option more frequently near the end of the interview than they did at the start.

As shown in the previous chapter, persons interested in politics provide better-quality responses than their politically less interested counterparts. Hence, it is possible that the fatigue effect is confounded with less interest in provincial than federal politics. Respondents were asked about their interest in the different levels of government. Most respondents expressed equal interest in federal and provincial politics, although approximately10% of the respondents stated that they were more interested in federal than in provincial politics.

Question order effects _____

7.2 Another feature of questionnaire architecture is the order of questions within an item battery. The CNES 1984 implemented an experimental design whereby the order of the sets of items concerning political efficacy and trust was varied randomly, either starting with the first question (from 'Generally, those elected to Parliament …' to 'Most of the people running …'; i.e., from A to I) or the last (from I to A). In the A to I order, the seven negatively formulated items preceded the two positively formulated ones; in the I to A order, respondents had to respond first to the two positively formulated items, followed by the seven negative ones. Figures 7.3 and 7.4 show the MCA solution for order A to I and I to A, respectively.

A comparison of Figures 7.3 and 7.4 shows several differences. When the negatively formulated items precede the positive ones (A to I), the first dimension reflects the substantive variation from low to high political efficacy and trust (left to right) while the second one differentiates between substantive and non-substantive responses. In contrast, when the positively formulated items precede the negative ones (I to A), the first dimension reflects the distinction

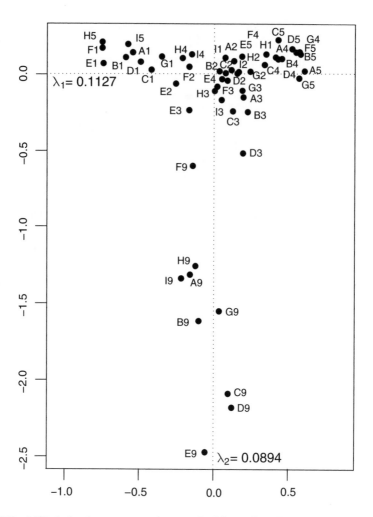

Figure 7.3 MCA, federal government, items asked from 'A' to 'I'

between substantive and non-substantive responses and the second the differences between the substantive responses.

Comparing the substantive solutions on their respective axes, the A to I order results in an almost consistent order of successive categories. When the items are presented in the I to A order, four mid-point categories (for items D, B, C, G, and partly A) are very close to the bottom of the axis. Furthermore, the two 'disagree somewhat' categories of items G and A are close to the extreme of high political trust. From these findings one could conclude that starting with the more complicated negatively formulated items provides a better solution. To examine the substantive solutions in more detail, we ran SMCA for both question order subsamples, excluding the 'no opinion' categories (Figures 7.5 and 7.6).

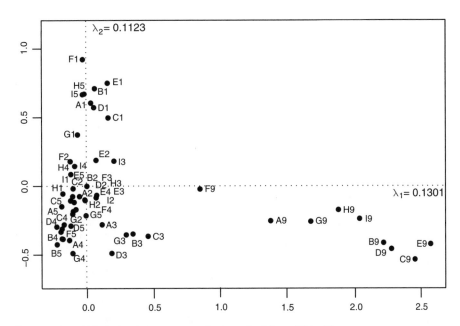

Figure 7.4 MCA, federal government, items asked from 'A' to 'I'

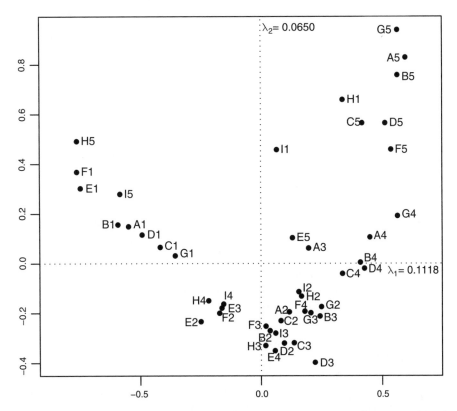

Figure 7.5 SMCA, federal government, items asked from 'A' to 'I', substantive categories only

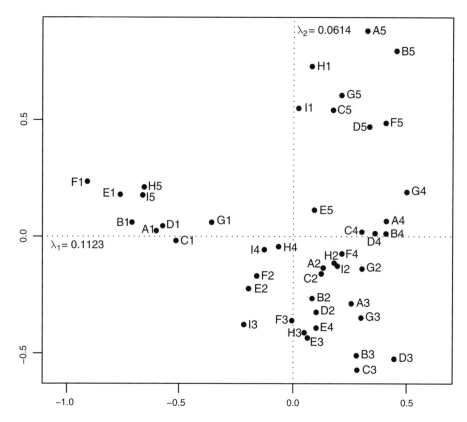

Figure 7.6 SMCA, federal government, items asked from 'A' to 'I', substantive categories only

Comparing Figures 7.5 and 7.6 reveals relatively similar findings. In both solutions there is a clear separation between the extreme categories with the remaining categories located in between them. However, for item order A to I the horseshoe belongs mainly to dimension 2; rotating the axes by approximately 10 degrees, the first dimension almost perfectly reflects the successive order of categories for all items (Figure 7.5). In some contrast, to produce the successive order of categories in version I to A requires a rotation of the solution by approximately 30 degrees (Figure 7.6). Here too, the neutral categories mentioned above have some outlying positions in the lower right-hand part. To provide greater detail, Table 7.2 shows the decomposition of several SMCAs.

As Table 7.2 shows, in the MCA as well as in almost all subsets, the item order I to A produces somewhat more total inertia for the entire solution as well as for the first dimension and a higher amount of explained variance by the first dimension than item order A to I. This is especially true for the NO subset as well as for the common subset of NO and NN.

Table 7.2 Decomposition of inertia, subset MCA, Question order effect, Federal Government

| | | A to I | | | | I to A | | | |
| | | D1 | | Total | | D1 | | Total | |
Model	K	Abs.	(%)	Abs.	(%)	Abs.	(%)	Abs.	(%)
All categories	45	0.1127	16.0	0.7043	100.0	0.1301	17.7	0.7359	100.0
Subset(1,2,3,4,5)	45	0.1118	20.4	0.5494	78.0	0.1123	20.4	0.5502	74.8
Subset(9)	9	0.0793	57.5	0.1380	19.6	0.1149	69.2	0.1659	22.5
Interaction	9	0.0041	48.5	0.0084	1.2	0.0061	61.1	0.0100	1.4
Subset(1,2,4,5)	36	0.1109	26.0	0.4267	60.6	0.1100	25.9	0.4241	57.6
Subset(3,9)	18	0.0799	32.2	0.2481	35.2	0.1162	41.5	0.2798	38.0
Interaction	18	0.0063	42.5	0.0148	2.1	0.0076	47.3	0.0160	2.2
Subset(1)	9	0.0534	56.7	0.0941	13.4	0.0565	56.8	0.0995	13.5
Subset(2)	9	0.0156	24.9	0.0626	8.9	0.0153	24.5	0.0622	8.5
Subset(3)	9	0.0326	30.1	0.1082	15.4	0.0345	31.1	0.1112	15.1
Subset(4)	9	0.0240	33.4	0.0718	10.2	0.0215	31.1	0.0692	9.4
Subset(5)	9	0.0468	47.0	0.0996	14.1	0.0422	44.3	0.0952	12.9
Subset(9)	9	0.0793	57.5	0.1380	19.6	0.1149	69.2	0.1659	22.5

Subset(1): first category variables A to G, last category variables H and I, and so on.

Measuring data quality: The dirty data index

7.3 As discussed previously, both MCA and SMCA are well suited to detecting method-induced variation. These procedures impose no restrictions on the input data other than that negative entries are not allowed. Both methods can be applied to data that are unordered categorical or are treated as such. However, many items contain an implicit order for the successive categories, which one may wish to impose on the data, such as when Likert response formats are used. In such situations one expects a 'strongly agree' response to indicate greater agreement with a given statement than an 'agree somewhat' response, which in turn should reflect stronger agreement than 'neither agree nor disagree' and so on. The lowest agreement or the highest disagreement should be indicated by 'strongly disagree' responses. In contrast to MCA and SMCA, CatPCA permits the assumed order of the successive categories to be tested: violation of ordinality is manifested in tied values for successive categories (cf. Chapter 3).

CatPCA quantification values are standardized to a mean of zero and standard deviation of one (Gifi, 1990; see also Chapter 3). The closer the data are to being metric, the smaller the difference between PCA and CatPCA solutions, and the closer the distribution of the quantification values is to the standard normal distribution. These features suggest that one could create an index measuring the quality of a given item battery that is based on the quantification values. This requires one to compute the respective probability area from the standard normal distribution and then to compare this probability area with the probability area one obtains from the frequencies. If, for example, there are 1,000 cases of which 200 belong to the first category, the left-hand area of the standard normal distribution contains 20% of the cases, with a z-value of -0.842; the mid-point subdivides the cases into two areas of 10% with a respective z-value of -1.282. Going the opposite way (from z-values to proportion of cases), a z-value of -1.0 requires 15.87% of the cases to the left and 84.13% cases to the right, while a value of 0.0 divides the number of cases precisely in half. Comparing the probability areas one gets from the marginals of each item with the probability areas one can compute from the CatPCA quantifications, for each item category a value can be computed that shows how close the quantification value is to the expected value. By performing such calculations for all categories and all items of a given set of questions, counting them and dividing them by the number of items, one obtains a value that indicates the quality of the item battery. In theory, the lower bound of this value is zero, which is empirically not obtainable in survey research since all survey data contain some non-substantive variation. The upper bound of the value is $l/(l-1)$, where l is the number of categories, a value we obtained from simulation studies. Since small values indicate high response quality and high values low quality, we call the index the 'dirty data index' (DDI). A limitation is that missing data must either be excluded through listwise deletion or replaced through imputation techniques, since the DDI can be applied only to ordered categorical data.

The procedure is visualized in Figure 7.7 and we exemplify the calculations with the first political efficacy and trust item from the CNES 1984 federal government data ('Generally, those elected to Parliament soon lose touch with the people'; see Table 6.1). The first category ('strongly agree') contains 736 cases or 28.05% of the 2,624 cases without missing values. The corresponding z-value is -0.58 and the 28.05% area under the standard normal distribution is marked by the leftmost line with short dashes. The z-value for the mid-point of this area (14.025% to the left) is -1.08 and marked with long dashes. The CatPCA quantification value for the first category of the item is -1.5085, (shown as a solid line), and its respective quantification area is 0.0657 (Table 7.3). The difference between the area from the mid-point of the category and the area computed from the CatPCA quantification value is $0.1401 - 0.0657 = 0.0745$; this area is shaded in Figure 7.7. The second category contains 46.65% of the cases, its mid-point is $28.05 + 46.65/2 = 51.37$ (z-value $= 0.03$); the respective CatPCA quantification value is 0.3061 (Table 7.3). The area between the mid-point from the original data and from the quantification area is 0.1065 (second shaded area in Figure 7.7; the three other areas are not highlighted for aesthetic reasons). After computing the areas for all five categories, the differences are summed and standardized by the upper bound. The numerical solution for all categories of the first item is given in Table 7.3.

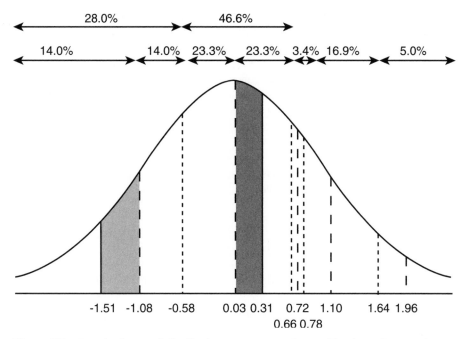

Figure 7.7 Standard normal distribution: category and quantification values, and probability areas

Table 7.3 Computation of probability areas, item A: 'Generally, those elected to Parliament soon lose touch with the people' (federal government)

Category	Frequencies	Quantifications	% of frequencies	Cumulative percentages	Midpoint areas	Quantification area	Differences
SA	736	−1.5085	0.2805	0.2805	0.1402	0.0657	0.0745
A	1224	0.3061	0.4665	0.7470	0.5137	0.6202	0.1065
NN	88	0.7168	0.0335	0.7805	0.7637	0.7632	0.0005
D	444	1.1216	0.1692	0.9597	0.8651	0.8690	0.0039
SD	132	1.3225	0.0503	1.0000	0.9748	0.9070	0.0679
Sum	2624		1.0000				0.2533

Corrected difference: 0.2533 × 0.8 = 0.2026.

In the following we give the computational solution step by step. Here N is the number of cases, K is the number of items, with k the item index, J_K is the number of categories in each item, with j the item category index, f_{jk} is the frequency of category j of item k, m_{jk} is the mass (relative frequency of category j of item k), $c_{(1,j)k}$ represents the cumulative relative frequencies of categories of item k, and q_{jk} is the quantification of category j of item k (provided by CatPCA). The relative frequencies (masses) for each category are given by $m_j = f_j /N$, and for cumulative masses by $c_{(1,j)} = m_j + c_{(1,j-1)}$ (if $j = 1$, $c_{(1,j-1)} = 0$).

1 Compute the mid-points of the item(s). Start with the relative frequency (mass) of the first category and divide its value by 2: $g_1 = m_1 / 2$ (for $j = 1$) → first mid-point of the relative frequencies (first threshold value). Add the mass of the first category (m_1) to half the mass of the second category ($m_2 / 2$): $g_2 = g_1 + m_2 / 2$ → second threshold value. Add the first two masses plus half the mass of the third category, ..., add the first $(J_K - 1)$ masses ($c_{(1,J-1)}$) plus half the mass of the last category. Note that the number of thresholds is the same as the number of categories ($= J_K$): Do: $j = 1$ to J_K (for each item k); $g_j = g_{j-1} + m_j / 2$ (with $g_0 = 0$).

2 Compute the areas to the left of the quantification values (q_{jk}) on the basis of the standard normal distribution).

3 Compute the absolute differences between the thresholds (their respective probability areas) and the quantification (areas) and add them.

4 Standardize the values by the upper bound, which is $I/(I-1)$, with I = number of categories.

Using random data and running simulations on 100,000 cases (nine items, five categories), the DDI fluctuated between 0.5 and 0.7 (corrected values), depending on the given distribution ('normal', 'U-shaped', ...). On the basis of several examples from different data sets we conclude that DDI values smaller than 0.3 indicate relatively good data, and values smaller than 0.15 indicate data of exceptional quality. On the other hand, values greater than 0.5 indicate poor response quality. It is possible to obtain values that exceed 0.7; that is, values that are higher than those generated with random data. One situation in which one may obtain such values occurs when many respondents use the same response option regardless of the content of the questions (e.g., acquiescent response set). In such instances, the data are heavily distorted.

In the next section we use the DDI to evaluate the quality of the political efficacy and trust items from the CNES 1984. Table 7.4 shows the index values for the federal and provincial government domains, Table 7.5 shows the index for the federal government data subdivided by political interest (high versus low; see Chapter 6) and Table 7.6 shows the index again for the federal government data, this time subdivided by the order of items.

Comparing the DDI values for the federal and provincial government domains (Table 7.4) on all items individually as well as for the sum of the items, the DDI indicates that the quality of the federal government items is clearly better than that of the provincial government items; in short, there is a clear fatigue effect. At the start of the interview the respondents seem to be more motivated to provide careful responses and the interviewer more focused on the task; near the end, their concentration and motivation may have waned. Overall, for the provincial government domain the DDI is about 0.47, while for the federal domain it is about 0.34. Since the quantification values are calculated on the basis of the entire scale, we will not use the values of the single items to draw conclusions on the quality of a single item.

Comparing respondents of low and high political interest on the federal government domain (Table 7.5), the DDI for the politically less interested respondents is noticeably higher than for the politically more interested

Table 7.4 DDI for political efficacy items, federal and provincial government, and total

	Federal N=2,624	Provincial N=2,579
A. Generally, those elected to Parliament soon lose touch with the people.	0.2026	0.3481
B. I don't think the (Federal) Government cares much about what people like me think.	0.3002	0.4245
C. Sometimes, (Federal) Politics and Government seem so complicated that a person like me can't really understand what's going on.	0.4194	0.4896
D. People like me don't have any say about what the Government in (Ottawa) does.	0.3959	0.4864
E. So many other people vote in (Federal) elections that it does not matter very much whether I vote or not.	0.4618	0.7136
F. Many people in the (Federal) Government are dishonest.	0.1459	0.2662
G. People in the (Federal) Government waste a lot of the money we pay in taxes.	0.2172	0.3172
H. Most of the time we can trust people in the (Federal) Government to do what is right.	0.3750	0.5432
I. Most of the people running the (Federal) Government are smart people who usually know what they are doing.	0.5504	0.6148
All items, average distance	0.3409	0.4671

Table 7.5 DDI for political efficacy items, federal government, low and high political interest

	Low N=1,381	High N=1,243
A. Generally, those elected to Parliament soon lose touch with the people.	0.2639	0.1993
B. I don't think the (Federal) Government cares much about what people like me think.	0.3854	0.2014
C. Sometimes, (Federal) Politics and Government seem so complicated that a person like me can't really understand what's going on.	0.3368	0.3967
D. People like me don't have any say about what the Government in (Ottawa) does.	0.3965	0.3643
E. So many other people vote in (Federal) elections that it does not matter very much whether I vote or not.	0.6530	0.3581
F. Many people in the (Federal) Government are dishonest.	0.2281	0.1188
G. People in the (Federal) Government waste a lot of the money we pay in taxes.	0.2807	0.2566
H. Most of the time we can trust people in the (Federal) Government to do what is right.	0.5204	0.2219
I. Most of the people running the (Federal) Government are smart people who usually know what they are doing.	0.5194	0.5615
All items, average distance	0.3982	0.2976

Table 7.6 DDI for political efficacy items, federal government, order effects

	A to I N=1,477	I to A N=1,147
A. Generally, those elected to Parliament soon lose touch with the people.	0.1492	0.2215
B. I don't think the (Federal) Government cares much about what people like me think.	0.2211	0.2830
C. Sometimes, (Federal) Politics and Government seem so complicated that a person like me can't really understand what's going on.	0.2049	0.2922
D. People like me don't have any say about what the Government in (Ottawa) does.	0.2530	0.4105
E. So many other people vote in (Federal) elections that it does not matter very much whether I vote or not.	0.3423	0.4295
F. Many people in the (Federal) Government are dishonest.	0.1166	0.1505
G. People in the (Federal) Government waste a lot of the money we pay in taxes.	0.1860	0.2646
H. Most of the time we can trust people in the (Federal) Government to do what is right.	0.2303	0.2535
I. Most of the people running the (Federal) Government are smart people who usually know what they are doing.	0.2948	0.3557
All items, average distance	0.2220	0.2957

respondents. This reinforces the earlier MCA and SMCA findings on the same data (see Chapter 6). Further, the DDI for the entire population is close to the mid-point of the two groups (entire population, 0.3409,; high political interest, 0.2976; low political interest, 0.3982), which suggests that the underlying concept of political efficacy and trust is similar for the two groups.

Finally, again congruent with previous analyses, item order A to I seems to be easier to handle than the reverse item order – the DDI for A to I is lower than for I to A (Table 7.6). In contrast to the subdivision by political interest, the value for the entire population is higher than for both subgroups when dividing the population randomly for an experimental design. As a first interpretation, we assume that the overlapping of the two 'sets of items' provides some additional methodological variation – in the case of A to I the two positively formulated items have been asked for in reversed question order, while in the case of I to A, the seven negatively formulated items have been asked for in reversed order.

Conclusion

7.4 In this chapter we have argued that there is a fatigue effect in the CNES 1984 data and that the order of questions has an impact on the quality of data. Based on two identical sets of questions on political efficacy and trust, one towards the Canadian federal government and one towards the provincial governments, we showed that the set of questions asked roughly an hour later produces more total inertia and a clearly higher amount of explained variance on dimension 1. After a certain duration, the interviewers and/or the interviewees might become tired and wish to finish the task quickly. One strategy to accomplish this is to simplify the task by using a given response category more often. This need not lead to a different marginal distribution since one respondent might use the first category more often while another respondent might use the second category more often. However, the variance in responses for each respondent will decrease while the variation between the respondents will increase. Furthermore, the correlations (absolute values) between the response categories increase (positive values between the same categories, negative values between the opposite categories) while the structure of responses becomes simpler. This simple structure will be captured by the first MCA/SMCA dimension.

Likewise, the question order has an effect on the quality of data. Using the items about the federal government which were asked at an early stage of the interview, it seems to be that it is better first to ask the negatively formulated items, followed by the positive ones. Further, matching the A to I and the I to A increases the variation in the data. The probable reason is that there are two different sources of method-induced variation, both of which are at least partly caused by changing the direction of the questions. Since these changes affect different questions, the total amount of non-substantive variation in the data will increase, the data becoming dirtier as a consequence of the experimental design.

Finally, with the dirty data index we introduced a measure that quantifies the quality of responses in ordered categorical data. The index is based on probabilities and on the assumption that there is an underlying scale that has metric properties. If the questions are meaningful and easy for the respondents to understand, the index will produce low values; otherwise the values will be high – that is, the dirtier the data, the higher the index.

8

Cognitive competencies and response quality

Few publicly available data sets contain direct measures of cognitive competencies, skills or abilities. Yet cognitive skills constitute a major element in our theoretical approach to response quality – the quality of the data that is contingent on the attributes of the respondent. This chapter redresses that omission through a detailed examination of how literacy and numeracy skills systematically shape the structure of survey responses.

The review of the empirical literature revealed that a plethora of response styles have been defined, each of which was assumed to compromise the quality and comparability of the data. The nature and number of response styles have been defined on the basis of which particular response options have been disproportionately used. Thus, ARS is defined by a disproportionate use of 'yes' and 'agree' responses, while disacquiescence is defined as a tendency to respond 'no' or 'disagree'; ERS is the tendency to use the end-points in ordered categorical response formats, while MPR is a proclivity to use the middle or neutral response category. Little research has addressed whether each of these proclivities represents a genuinely distinct response style. Some appear to be virtual opposites, such as acquiescence versus disacquiescence, and extreme versus mid-point responding. While it may not be true that Antonio Salieri criticized Wolfgang Amadeus Mozart for having 'too many notes', we think it is fair to conclude that survey researchers have created too many response styles. An overabundance of concepts is never conducive to parsimonious explanations.

The alternative exemplified in this book is to consider all forms of response tendencies as manifestations of task simplification, either because the task of responding to certain items is cognitively difficult, or because one simply wants to discharge one's felt obligation to provide responses as quickly as possible (satisficing).

Recall from Chapter 1 that our approach to survey data analysis has several distinctive features. First, it treats the act of filling in a questionnaire or responding to an interviewer's questions as similar in many respects to other verbal interactions. From this it follows that providing quality responses to researchers' questions depends on linguistic and other cognitive skills. In particular, responding to some of the questions may prove to be difficult for respondents with limited linguistic and cognitive skills. In such situations we postulated that respondents would either decline the task or simplify it, thereby performing it poorly. One can decline the task completely by refusing to participate in the study (referred to as unit non-response), or one can agree to participate but decline to answer one or more of the questions (known as item non-response). In this chapter we focus on the latter, leading to our first hypothesis: the likelihood of item non-response decreases with increasing cognitive competence. As argued above, we consider all types of response tendencies to be task simplification strategies. That is, they share the feature that the respondent favours a subset of the available responses; the main difference between them is which particular subset is favoured. As a consequence, all forms of response tendencies result in less response differentiation between different items. This leads to the second hypothesis: response differentiation increases with increasing cognitive competencies.

A second form of task simplification consists of failing to appreciate distinctions in content between items in a given domain of interest. For us, this means that, at least in the initial screening phase, unrotated solutions are examined. One aspect of the structure of a cognitive map is its complexity: How easily are the responses to the focal items reduced to a lower-dimensional space? To put it another way, how much information is lost when the responses are projected into a given low-dimensional space? We define the complexity of a map by such information loss; a simple cognitive map is one in which little information is lost when the responses are projected into a low-dimensional latent space, while conversely a complex map is one in which relatively much information is lost. This leads to our final hypothesis: the greater the cognitive competence, the more complex the mental map, and therefore the greater the information loss when responses to survey questions are projected into a low-dimensional latent space.

Data and measures _____

8.1 Our analytic logic, which we will describe shortly, requires large samples, preferably conducted in numerous countries, which contain measures of cognitive competency. These requirements are met by the triennial Programme for International Student Assessment (PISA) of student literacy, sponsored by the Organisation for Economic Co-operation and Development (OECD). The initial assessment (PISA 2000) concentrated on reading achievement; the second assessment (PISA 2003) focused on mathematics achievement. The PISA data are both large and nationally representative of 15-year-old students in the participating countries. For the 2000 assessment, 31 countries chose to administer the optional cross-curricular competencies module that contained the items analysed in this chapter ($N = 149,526$). Forty countries (excluding Liechtenstein due to insufficient sample size for our purposes) with 275,833 students participated in the 2003 assessment.

Both of these data sets are analysed here for several reasons. First, in both years, students were asked to respond to a set of questions regarding their study habits, which provides a convenient common focal domain. However, the two data sets differed in the number of items (17 and 14 in 2000 and 2003, respectively), their wording (see Tables 8.1 and 8.2), and their context (general versus specifically mathematics study habits). These differences permit us to assess how robust the solutions are despite these differences in the measurement of the focal domain. Second, the response options differed between the two years. In 2000 the four response options were 'almost never', 'sometimes', 'often' and 'almost always'; while in 2003 a four-point Likert format was used ranging from 'strongly agree' to 'strongly disagree'. In our approach, we expect task simplification processes, manifested by item non-differentiation, to be involved regardless of the response format used. The different response formats permit us to assess the generality of the task simplification dynamic. Third, gender is implicated in both reading and mathematics achievement. If we analysed just the 2000 data, then cognitive competency might be conflated with gender since the top reading achievers would be disproportionately populated by girls, while the low reading achievers would be characterized by a heavy concentration of boys. The reverse gender conflation might occur if we analysed just the 2003 data, since disproportionately more boys are among the top mathematics achievers. Fourth, while it is clear that verbal skills are essential to competently complete survey questions, it is unclear whether other competencies, such as mathematical skills, might also be implicated. A comparison of the 2003 findings with those for 2000 will provide relevant information.

The review of the literature revealed that response style measures were susceptible to both the polarity and the skew of the items that comprise the domain of interest, which we call the *focal domain*. This resulted in the measures of response quality being confounded with substantive content. Additionally, the response styles are often highly intercorrelated within a given domain but not between domains. For these reasons, we follow the recommended practice of obtaining additional response quality measures from a set of independent items (Weijters, Schillewaert and Geuens, 2008), which we label the *supplementary domain*.

Focal domain: Study habits

The focal domain in this chapter consists of students' description of their study habits. In 2000 students were asked about their general study habits, whereas in

Table 8.1 Distribution of PISA 2000 focal domain study habit items (%)

When I study...	Almost never	Some-times	Often	Almost always
I try to memorize everything that might be covered	10	35	33	23
I start by figuring out exactly what I need to learn	7	27	38	27
I memorize as much as possible	13	33	33	20
I work as hard as possible	7	35	37	22
I try to relate new material to things I have learned in other subjects	13	42	32	13
I memorize all new material so that I can recite it	23	42	25	10
I keep working even if the material is difficult	8	37	37	17
I force myself to check to see if I remember what I have learned	9	33	35	23
I practice by saying the material to myself over and over	11	33	34	23
I figure out how the information might be useful in the real world	13	38	33	15
I try to figure out which concepts I still haven't understood	6	37	41	16
I try to do my best to acquire the knowledge and skills taught	4	31	44	21
I try to understand the material better by relating it to things I already know	7	35	40	19
I make sure that I remember the most important things	3	24	44	29
I figure out how the material fits in with what I have already learned	7	39	38	15
and I don't understand something I look for additional information to clarify this	11	39	34	17
I put forth my best effort	5	31	39	25

2003 they were asked specifically about how they study mathematics. Tables 8.1 and 8.2 provide the item wordings together with their distributions. Several aspects of the study habit items are worth noting. The first is that for 15 of the 17 PISA 2000 items, the percentage of 'almost always' exceeds that of 'almost never'. In only one instance ('I memorize all new material so that I can recite it') is the reverse true. Similarly, in 2003, on 11 of the 14 items more students strongly agreed than strongly disagreed with the statement; again, on only one item ('I go over some problems in Mathematics so often that I feel as if I could solve them in my sleep') was the opposite clearly the case. These patterns suggest that the study habit items are normatively desirable ones on balance. If so, then students' descriptions of their study habits are possibly conflated with impression management dynamics.

Second, without exception in either data set, the Pearson correlations among these items are positive – subscribing to any one of the study habits is associated

Table 8.2 Distribution of PISA 2003 focal domain study habit items (%)

There are different ways of studying Mathematics. To what extent do you agree with the following statements?	Strongly agree	Agree	Disagree	Strongly disagree
When I study for a Mathematics test, I try to work out what are the most important parts to learn	26	62	9	2
When I am solving Mathematics problems, I often think of new ways to get the answer	11	43	40	6
When I study Mathematics, I make myself check to see if I remember the work I have already done	17	59	21	3
When I study Mathematics, I try to figure out which concepts I still have not understood properly	22	65	11	2
I think how the Mathematics I have learnt can be used in everyday life	14	46	32	8
I go over some problems in Mathematics so often that I feel as if I could solve them in my sleep	9	27	48	16
When I study for Mathematics, I learn as much as I can off by heart	10	41	38	11
I try to understand new concepts in Mathematics by relating them to things I already know	13	56	26	5
In order to remember the method for solving a Mathematics problem, I go through examples again and again	16	54	26	5
When I cannot understand something in Mathematics, I always search for more information to clarify the problem	17	56	23	4
When I am solving a Mathematics problem, I often think about how the solution might be applied to other interesting questions	8	38	46	8
When I study Mathematics, I start by working out exactly what I need to learn	16	61	20	3
To learn Mathematics, I try to remember every step in a procedure	17	61	19	3
When learning Mathematics, I try to relate the work to things I have learnt in other subjects	9	40	43	8

with a tendency to subscribe to all of the others (mean $r = 0.35$ and 0.31 in 2000 and 2003, respectively). This feature raises a further data quality concern, since such a pattern is also consistent with a response set interpretation.

Our measure of task avoidance rests on a count of the number of study habit items to which the student failed to provide a substantive response. Since the number of study habit items differs between the two years, the measures are on different scales. To make them comparable, the measures were converted to a common percentage of item non-response scale.

An appropriate measure of task simplification is less obvious. Is there a statistic that captures all forms of task simplification and that is also applicable to all types of response formats? Such a statistic would have its highest value when a respondent gives an identical response to all items in the domain, regardless of which response that is. The other extreme would occur, theoretically, when a respondent uses every response option with equal frequency, resulting in a rectangular (or equiprobable) distribution. Linville, Salovey and Fischer (1986) developed the converse of such a measure, which they called the probability of differentiation, for their study of racial stereotyping: $P_D = 1 - \Sum p_i^2$, where P_D is the probability of differentiation, p_i is the proportion of items for which the ith response was given, and the sum is over the number of response options provided. The larger the value of P_D, the more differentiated the responses of an individual are. Note that their measure assumes only a categorical level of measurement. Our index of response differentiation (IRD) modifies their measure by adjusting it for its maximum value, which depends solely on the number of response categories. That is, we obtain the ratio of the observed response differentiation to the maximum possible response differentiation for a given number of response options. With four response options, for example, the maximum value of the probability of differentiation is 0.75. The IRD is our main measure of response differentiation.

The individual's standard deviation of responses across a given domain has sometimes been used as a measure of response differentiation, since it usually increases with increased response differentiation. While both the standard deviation and the IRD yield a score of zero whenever a respondent utilizes only one response alternative, the maximum value of these two measures occurs under quite different circumstances. The IRD obtains its maximum value when each response alternative is used equally often. In contrast, the standard deviation achieves its maximum when only the extreme end-point responses are chosen. Therefore, the standard deviation is conflated with ERS. Finally, the standard deviation requires metric measures. Nevertheless, to assess the robustness of our task simplification hypothesis, we use both the IRD and the individual's standard deviation of responses. We expect more consistent patterns using the IRD than the standard deviation.

Achievement scores on the standardized reading and mathematics tests constitute our measures of cognitive competence. The OECD standardized these tests to have an international mean of 500 with a standard deviation of 100. The primary purpose for the OECD was to provide measures of achievement that could be used to compare the performance of students from different countries. This resulted in unequal proportions of students performing at a given level of competence in different countries. Our focus is not on comparing student performance cross-nationally. Rather, it is first to compare students at different levels of performance within a given country, and then to see to what extent the task avoidance and task simplification patterns are replicated in other countries. To compare students solely with other students in the same country, we divided students into country-specific decile groups. An additional advantage of such a procedure is that it minimizes any country-specific cultural or methodological biases that might lurk in the achievement measures. A consequence of our procedure is that in all countries the cut-offs for the middle decile groups are relatively close to each other.

As indicated above, task simplification can occur at the response option level by favouring a subset of the options provided. Task simplification might also occur in a second way, namely by constructing simpler or less nuanced mental maps. There is no straightforward way of tapping the complexity of an individual's mental map. However, it is possible to construct a measure of the complexity of cognitive maps at a group level. We start with the assumption that the simpler a mental map, the higher the proportion of variance in the focal items that is explained by the first latent dimension. As mental maps become more differentiated, the second dimension becomes increasingly important. We use the ratio of the first to the second eigenvalue as our measure of the complexity of the mental maps. Our hypothesis is that the greater the cognitive competence, the smaller the eigenvalue ratio.

To test these hypotheses, the unit of comparison will be country decile groups. To put it another way, we control for both country and performance decile groups simultaneously. As a result, the number of 'cases' is 310 (10×31) and 400 (10×40) for 2000 and 2003, respectively.

Supplementary domain: Social integration

For our supplementary domain we selected a set of items that overcame one of the disadvantages of the study habit items, namely the absence of items with reverse polarity. An identical set of six polarity-balanced items on students' perception of

Table 8.3   Distribution of supplementary domain social integration into school items (%)

	Strongly disagree	Disagree	Agree	Strongly agree
PISA 2000				
1 I feel like an outsider (or left out of things)	54	36	7	2
2 I make friends easily	3	10	59	28
3 I feel like I belong	5	12	57	26
4 I feel awkward and out of place	44	43	10	3
5 Other students seem to like me	4	15	67	14
6 I feel lonely	50	40	8	2
PISA 2003				
1 I feel like an outsider (or left out of things)	48	44	5	2
2 I make friends easily	2	9	62	27
3 I feel like I belong	4	14	59	23
4 I feel awkward and out of place	41	49	8	2
5 Other students seem to like me	2	11	71	16
6 I feel lonely	54	38	6	2

their social integration into their school was available for both PISA data sets. Table 8.3 provides the wording and the distribution of these items. Note that about half the students in both data sets strongly disagreed with the negatively formulated items. In contrast, just over one-quarter strongly agreed with the positive polarity items. That is, the distribution of all items is skewed, and the direction of the skew is a function of the polarity of the items. For the supplementary domain, the two measures of item differentiation and task avoidance are calculated.

Both study habits and social integration into the school are relevant to all students and equally accessible, requiring no specialized knowledge, since the referent is the self. Hence, these items should provide a relatively strong test of the role of cognitive complexity in response quality. More specifically, differences in response quality are unlikely to be due to lack of knowledge about the topics being investigated, increasing the likelihood that any differences in data quality found associated with the achievement tests are due to cognitive competence and their effects on task avoidance and task simplification.

Response quality, task simplification, and complexity of cognitive maps _____

8.2 To exemplify our analytic approach, we first present findings from PISA 2000 for three countries: Chile, Denmark, and South Korea. These countries were chosen strategically to represent different continents, cultures and languages. Each row in Table 8.4 represents a case; together these three countries represent 30 cases, which are based on the responses of about 14,000 students. Within each country, the students were divided into decile groups based on the distribution of reading achievement scores in that country. In Chile, for example, 489 students (10%) scored less than 310, while at the opposite end, 10% had scores exceeding 532. Note that the upper bounds for each decile group are higher in Denmark than in Chile: the cut-offs for the bottom and top decile groups are 375 and 614, respectively. These higher cut-offs reflect the fact that Danish students typically perform better across the spectrum of reading achievement than their Chilean counterparts. In a further country contrast, the bottom decile groups of South Korean students performed better than the bottom decile groups of Danish students, but with increasing competence decile groups, the performance gap between Danish and South Korean students diminishes. That is, the South Korean school system appears to produce students who have relatively superior reading performance with relatively little dispersion in their performance. In other words, South Korean reading achievement is relatively high and egalitarian.

The third column contains our measure of task avoidance. For each student, the non-response proportion (out of 17 study habit items) was calculated and subsequently aggregated to the decile groups level. As an example, on average Chilean students in the lowest achievement decile groups failed to respond to

4.67% of the study habit items, while Chilean students in the next decile group failed to respond to just under 2% of the items. Note that for both Chile and Denmark, a clear declining trend in non-response is evident with increasing cognitive competence, with just trivial reversals in each country. For South Korea, the percentage of non-response is so low in all performance decile groups that no meaningful differences can be detected. Also note the substantial country differences in task avoidance. These large country differences in characteristics associated with performance decile groups are one of the reasons why country-specific decile group measures are necessary.

Our primary measure of response differentiation is the IRD. Two features stand out. First, as expected, in each country the IRD increases with achieve-

Table 8.4 Focal domain measures of response quality and eigenvalues for Chile, Denmark, and South Korea by reading achievement decile groups

Decile groups	Achievement upper bound	Percentage missing	IRD	Standard deviation	Eigenvalues				Eigenvalue ratio (λ_1/λ_2)
					λ_1	λ_2	λ_3	λ_4	
Chile (N = 4,889)									
1	310	4.67	0.65	0.70	7.42	1.02	0.86	0.78	7.24
2	350	1.99	0.68	0.72	6.86	1.31	0.98	0.87	5.23
3	379	2.15	0.69	0.72	6.99	1.32	0.93	0.91	5.29
4	400	1.28	0.69	0.73	7.00	1.45	0.95	0.83	4.81
5	422	1.15	0.71	0.77	6.31	1.73	0.98	0.89	3.64
6	443	1.03	0.71	0.76	6.25	2.03	1.00	0.91	3.07
7	465	1.04	0.72	0.79	5.77	2.08	1.10	0.95	2.78
8	494	1.16	0.73	0.81	5.69	2.34	1.00	0.96	2.43
9	532	0.24	0.73	0.85	5.66	2.53	1.05	0.98	2.23
10		0.18	0.76	0.90	5.32	2.72	1.16	1.01	1.96
Denmark (N = 4,235)									
1	375	7.01	0.61	0.64	7.68	1.04	0.93	0.84	7.36
2	422	3.41	0.67	0.64	6.64	1.14	1.08	0.84	5.84
3	454	2.39	0.68	0.66	6.57	1.14	0.96	0.87	5.77
4	480	1.52	0.71	0.68	6.60	1.18	0.97	0.86	5.59
5	504	1.30	0.69	0.67	6.57	1.15	1.07	0.83	5.73
6	527	0.90	0.71	0.69	6.14	1.23	1.08	0.97	5.00
7	550	0.65	0.71	0.69	6.52	1.22	0.99	0.96	5.35
8	576	0.56	0.72	0.70	6.30	1.23	1.18	1.02	5.14
9	614	0.67	0.73	0.72	6.11	1.22	1.15	1.03	4.99
10		0.43	0.75	0.74	5.83	1.41	1.18	1.05	4.14
South Korea (N = 4,982)									
1	427	0.35	0.65	0.68	7.34	1.21	0.87	0.83	6.07
2	464	0.29	0.71	0.75	6.56	1.58	1.01	0.86	4.16
3	487	0.21	0.72	0.76	6.70	1.55	1.00	0.93	4.32
4	506	0.57	0.73	0.76	5.91	1.78	1.12	0.94	3.32
5	523	0.41	0.75	0.77	6.03	1.84	1.09	0.91	3.27
6	541	0.11	0.75	0.76	5.93	1.82	1.15	0.96	3.26
7	560	0.12	0.76	0.78	5.51	2.01	1.13	0.98	2.75
8	580	0.10	0.75	0.75	5.63	1.83	1.17	0.96	3.08
9	607	0.08	0.76	0.77	5.81	2.01	1.06	0.95	2.88
10		0.11	0.76	0.79	5.81	2.16	1.13	0.89	2.69

ment decile groups, with only two reversals. Second, the numeric values of the IRD are remarkably similar across the three countries; its value for the lowest decile groups ranges between 0.61 and 0.65, and between 0.75 and 0.76 for the highest decile groups. Likewise, the difference in IRD between the lowest and highest decile groups is between 0.11 and 0.14 in the three countries. Our secondary measure of response differentiation is the individual's standard deviation of responses to the study habit items. The column labelled *Standard deviation* contains the mean of these individual standard deviations for each decile group. Similarly to what was found for the IRD, in each country the lowest standard deviation occurs in the bottom decile groups and the highest in the top decile groups, reflecting a general tendency for the standard deviation to increase with increasing cognitive competency. Unlike the IRD, however, the range in standard deviation between the top and bottom decile groups is decidedly different across the three countries. This range is twice as large for Chile $(0.90 - 0.70 = 0.20)$ as for Denmark $(0.74 - 0.64 = 0.10)$. This is the first empirical indication that the IRD may be superior to the standard deviation as a measure of response differentiation.

The next four columns give the first four eigenvalues from the unrotated solution. Although CatPCA would be the appropriate method to analyse these data, we chose PCA because the patterns can already be seen in the metric framework. In the remainder of the analyses we use CatPCA. A first issue concerns the number of factors that might be warranted. By the Kaiser eigenvalue criterion, the number of dimensions in the solutions varies between two and four, and this variation is a function of both country and decile groups. In Chile, two dimensions are extracted by this criterion for the bottom half of reading performers. For the next four decile groups, three factors are extracted, while in the top decile group a fourth factor has an eigenvalue greater than 1.0. For South Korea, a two-dimensional solution is sufficient for the bottom decile group, and a three-factor solution is adequate for the remaining ones. Contrast this with Denmark, where a four-dimensional solution is warranted by the Kaiser criterion for the top three decile groups. If we used the scree test instead, a one-dimensional solution would be sufficient for all decile groups for all three countries. More important than the number of dimensions that are necessary is the amount of information contained in each of the dimensions, as indicated by the relative magnitudes of the eigenvalues.

Starting with the first eigenvalue, notice that it tends to decrease with increasing cognitive competence for all three countries. In contrast, the second, third, and fourth eigenvalues tend to increase with increasing reading performance; again, this is true in all three countries. As a result of these trends, the ratio of the second to the first eigenvalue decreases with reading achievement decile groups; in Chile this ratio declines from a high of 7.24 in the bottom decile group to a low of 1.96 in the top decile group. The corresponding figures for Denmark are 7.36 and 4.14, while for South Korea they are 6.07 and 2.69. These ratios, we argue, capture the complexity of the mental maps as contained

Table 8.5   Mean response quality by cognitive competencies

Decile groups	Non-response Focal	Non-response Supple-mentary	IRD Focal	IRD Supple-mentary	Standard deviation Focal	Standard deviation Supple-mentary	Eigenvalues λ_1	Eigenvalues λ_2	Ratio λ_1/λ_2
PISA 2000									
1	11.22	7.18	0.641	0.702	0.440	0.619	7.599	1.298	6.071
2	5.81	3.69	0.662	0.726	0.446	0.644	6.930	1.423	5.101
3	4.13	2.58	0.674	0.739	0.451	0.653	6.709	1.447	4.805
4	3.09	2.14	0.685	0.743	0.459	0.654	6.579	1.507	4.544
5	2.47	1.92	0.697	0.745	0.466	0.660	6.310	1.620	4.111
6	1.95	1.41	0.701	0.749	0.470	0.662	6.373	1.610	4.209
7	1.57	1.30	0.709	0.747	0.477	0.659	6.138	1.742	3.773
8	1.46	1.19	0.713	0.750	0.481	0.662	6.188	1.769	3.751
9	1.16	1.21	0.722	0.748	0.491	0.654	5.917	1.884	3.244
10	1.04	0.95	0.730	0.751	0.502	0.655	5.805	2.054	3.010
η^2	0.624	0.592	0.681	0.598	0.616	0.280	0.258	0.263	0.600
PISA 2003									
1	11.27	15.73	0.578	0.667	0.399	0.615	6.602	1.265	6.029
2	5.00	9.42	0.612	0.705	0.408	0.625	6.111	1.380	4.811
3	3.38	7.54	0.628	0.719	0.415	0.630	5.709	1.528	4.269
4	2.58	6.36	0.643	0.729	0.422	0.637	5.337	1.555	3.810
5	1.86	5.51	0.650	0.732	0.424	0.638	4.808	1.819	3.031
6	1.55	5.11	0.659	0.737	0.429	0.641	4.988	1.566	3.456
7	1.22	4.60	0.666	0.740	0.431	0.642	4.632	1.680	2.992
8	1.04	4.39	0.672	0.742	0.435	0.643	4.392	1.793	2.700
9	0.88	4.11	0.680	0.744	0.441	0.643	4.325	1.860	2.610
10	0.55	3.60	0.695	0.745	0.456	0.642	4.106	1.902	2.416
η^2	0.594	0.634	0.738	0.547	0.563	0.197	0.395	0.157	0.434

in the responses of the students to the study habit items. Concretely, in Chile among the bottom tenth of reading achievers, the first dimension is over seven times as important (from a variance binding point of view) as the second factor. In contrast, among the top tenth of Chilean students, the first factor is only twice (1.96) as important as the second (i.e., the second factor contains about half as much information as the first one). To put it another way, among high-performing students, substantially more information is contained in the second (and subsequent dimensions) than is the case among low-performing students. This pattern holds in all three countries exemplified here. In short, despite the diversities in language, culture, and continental location of these three countries, the relationships of verbal competence with item non-response, response differentiation, and task simplification are virtually identical.

The calculations exemplified for these three countries were performed for the remaining 28 countries for the PISA 2000 data, but this time using CatPCA for all countries. Then analogous calculations were done for the relationships of response quality to achievement in mathematics, using the PISA 2003 data. Finally, the relationships of unit non-response and item differentiation to

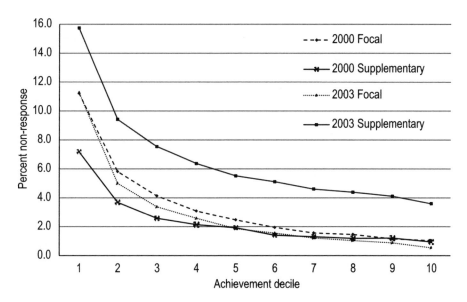

Figure 8.1 Percentage missing by achievement decile groups

cognitive competencies were calculated for the supplementary domain in both data sets. Table 8.5 presents the numerical results. The information contained in this table is based on aggregated cases (310 cases for PISA 2000 and 400 cases for PISA 2003, where each 'case' is a country decile group). To compare the various patterns for the aggregated data, we provide a series of graphs.

Starting with declining the task, Figure 8.1 shows a consistent relationship between achievement decile groups and percentage of item non-response. The form of this relationship is curvilinear, with the greatest drop in unit non-response occurring between the lowest two decile groups, with diminishing effects in subsequent decile groups. This form holds for both data sets (and therefore both verbal and numeric forms of cognitive competency) and for both focal and supplementary domains. The proportion of variance in unit non-response accounted for by achievement decile groups is remarkably similar, ranging from 59% to 63% (see η^2 in the first column, bottom row of both parts of Table 8.5).

Figure 8.2 documents several patterns regarding item response differentiation using the IRD. First, in both data sets and for both the focal and supplementary domain, there is a positive association between the IRD and achievement decile groups. This is in accordance with our second hypothesis. Second, the form of the relationship is approximately linear for the focal items in both data sets, while the relationship is curvilinear for the supplementary items – a difference that was not anticipated. Third, the quality of the data, at least with respect to the response differentiation criterion, appears to be better in PISA 2000 than in 2003. This is indicated by the fact

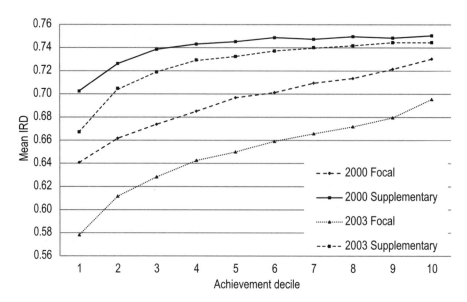

Figure 8.2   Item response differentiation by achievement decile groups

that the IRD is higher in 2000 for both domains than in 2003 for the respective domains. For the focal domain, one could argue that this may be due to the different items and response options provided in the two years. However, the same argument cannot be used for the supplementary domain, since identical items and response formats were used in both years. Finally, the explained variance is higher for the focal than the supplementary domain (68% versus 60% in 2000; 74% versus 55% in 2003). A likely reason is that the focal domain contains more than twice the number of items than the supplementary domain, which decreases the sampling fluctuation for the focal domain measure.

Keeping in mind that the standard deviation of a set of items has interchangeably been used as a measure of response differentiation and as a measure of ERS, the visually most striking aspect is the huge difference between the focal and supplementary standard deviations (see Figure 8.3). The standard deviation of the supplementary items is about half as large again as that of the focal items. What might account for this? The standard deviation requires metric data and is susceptible to the magnitude of the skew in the distribution. The items comprising the supplementary domain (social integration into the school) are substantially more skewed than those of the focal domain (compare Tables 8.2 and 8.3). This provides additional evidence that the standard deviation is not suitable as a measure of response differentiation in ordered categorical data. While the IRD was also higher for the supplementary items than the focal ones, the difference between the two was not as marked. Even more troubling perhaps is the difference in explained variance between the

ASSESSING THE QUALITY OF SURVEY DATA

two domains, which is at least twice as high in the focal domain as in the supplementary domain (62% versus 28% in 2000; 56% versus 20% in 2003). Such volatility in the magnitude of the relationship between cognitive competence and the standard deviation of items is a further indicator of its unsuitability for our purposes. While the IRD of the focal items also had a stronger relationship with achievement decile groups than did the supplementary items, the difference in strength was not nearly as dramatic. In one respect the standard deviation was similar to the IRD: the relationship of the standard deviation to the achievement decile groups appears to be more linear for the focal domain than for the supplementary domain.

As can be seen in Figure 8.4, there is a monotonically declining relationship (with a slight exception between the fifth and the sixth decile groups) between achievement decile groups and the ratio of the first to the second eigenvalue. This ratio drops from about 6.0 in the bottom decile group to half that or less in the top decile group. The implication is that the second dimension contains at least twice as much information among students in the top achievement decile group as it does among those in the bottom decile group.

Several patterns in our data are worth noting. Of fundamental importance is our finding that the higher the cognitive competence, the greater the complexity of the mental maps. One manifestation of this is the number of factors extracted with eigenvalues greater than one for the entire sample when physically controlling for literacy or numeracy skills. As Table 8.6 for the PISA 2000 data shows, these range from two factors for the bottom decile groups (where for the first decile group the second eigenvalue is just 1.000), and

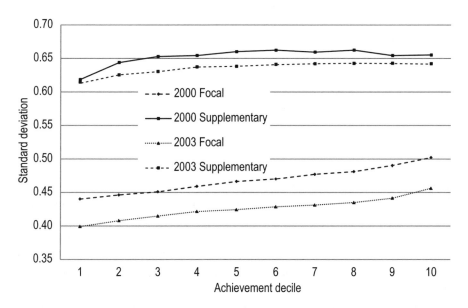

Figure 8.3 Item standard deviation by achievement decile groups

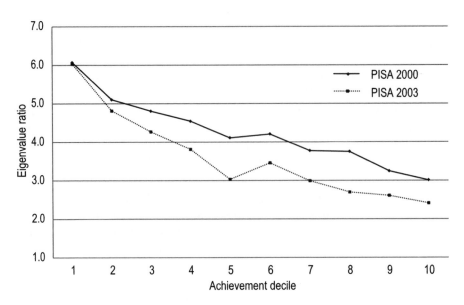

Figure 8.4   Focal domain eigenvalue ratios by achievement decile groups

Table 8.6   CatPCA eigenvalues exceeding 1.0 by reading achievement decile groups (PISA 2000)

Decile groups	λ_1	λ_2	λ_3	λ_4
1	7.66	1.00		
2	7.01	1.16		
3	6.75	1.21		
4	6.49	1.34	1.04	
5	6.35	1.42	1.09	
6	6.21	1.50	1.11	
7	5.99	1.61	1.17	
8	6.03	1.67	1.17	
9	5.73	1.82	1.20	1.03
10	5.56	1.98	1.25	1.06

three factors for the fourth to eighth decile groups, to four factors for the top two decile groups. In all solutions there is a pattern (with one exception) such that for any given factor, the eigenvalues decrease as one moves up the decile groups. These two attributes (the number of factors and the value of the associated eigenvalues) buttress our opposition to a reification of the number of dimensions contained in any domain. They point to the conclusion that the cognitive maps obtained of young people with high literacy skills appear to be more complex than those of their less skilled counterparts. In other words, one needs more dimensions to represent the mental map of high literacy

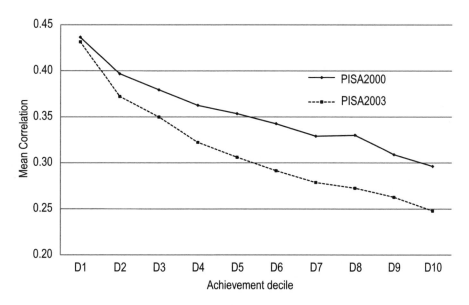

Figure 8.5 Mean Pearson correlation coefficients among focal domain items by achievement decile groups

achievers to the same level of adequacy as one would need to represent the mental map of low literacy achievers.

A second implication concerns the relationship between cognitive ability and response quality. A cursory reading of the literature on response quality would lead one to believe that there is a positive relationship between cognitive ability and response quality. In line with this, we documented that item non-response decreases with increasing cognitive competencies, as does non-differentiation between items. Both of these relationships are indicators of better response quality among those with greater cognitive achievement. However, consistency of responses as manifested by high inter-item correlations, producing high reliability coefficients, is usually the first definition of response quality that comes to mind. On that criterion, there is a negative association: the higher the cognitive ability, the lower the inter-item association. Figure 8.5 shows the mean correlation coefficients across the entire data set between items in the focal domain by achievement decile groups. For both data sets, a consistent decline in average inter-item correlations is documented. In other words, the responses of the cognitively least competent seem to be substantially more reliable than those of the more competent, regardless of whether mathematics or reading achievement is used as a measure of cognitive competence. The apparent contradiction is resolved by introducing the notion of reliable but invalid variance. In any event, our analyses reiterate the importance of recognizing that sometimes consistent responses do not mean high-quality responses.

Conclusion

8.3 The primary purpose of this chapter has been to systematically assess the cross-national applicability and fruitfulness of our conceptualization of response quality and its relationship to cognitive competencies. Our starting premise was that the dynamics involved in responding competently to questionnaires are similar to those involved in discharging any other verbal tasks. From this premise, we hypothesized that, when faced with a challenging task, humans everywhere can either decline it, or simplify it to make it more manageable. We argued that task simplification takes two forms, both of which reduce response quality. The first form is to simplify the task of which response option to choose. This is captured by the IRD (and less well by the standard deviation). The second form is to fail to appreciate distinctions in the content of the items of a given domain. Such failure to differentiate between the content of related items is reflected in the eigenvalue ratios. Our analyses documented consistently strong relationships of these three measures with cognitive competencies internationally, suggesting that our approach has merit.

Several features of our analytic logic are perhaps worth reiterating. First, we successfully replicated all of the results on a data set in which the number of items in the focal domain, their wording, and the response options differed. This provides some confidence that our approach may be robust across at least some study architecture features. Second, we obtained the same patterns using mathematics achievement rather than reading achievement as a measure of cognitive competency. While we cannot conclude that mathematical skills are necessary for obtaining quality responses to questionnaire items (since it is known that reading and mathematics achievement are strongly related), we can conclude that our findings are not specific to a particular measure of cognitive competency. Third, we were able to document that the IRD is not nearly as volatile as the standard deviation in its relationship to cognitive competency. Specifically, the IRD appeared to be less affected than the standard deviation by skew and polarity of the items and to be more stably and strongly related to cognitive competency.

At the same time, several limitations should be noted. First, most countries participating in the PISA studies are members of the OECD, and therefore are relatively industrialized. No countries in Africa and only two in Asia – South Korea and Japan – are represented. This severely restricts our ability to assess the extent to which our approach is cross-nationally applicable. Second, in all participating countries, only 15-year-old students were assessed in the context of their school. The patterns we documented may not be generalizable to respondents of other ages and other contexts. On the other hand, the advantage of having only 15-year-olds is that there are no confounding age effects. Third, the only readily available measure of task simplification required us to perform our analyses at an aggregate country achievement decile group level. While the relationships documented at this level are strong (accounting for half to nearly three quarters of the variance in the relationships among our focal domain measures), at the individual level they are likely to be quite modest.

Our analytic logic also has several implications for survey research generally. The first concerns the dimensionality of a set of items. For PCA, two criteria have been recommended to assess how many dimensions are represented in any set of items on a focal domain: the Kaiser criterion that the eigenvalues are greater than 1.0; and the scree test which defines the number of necessary dimensions as the number occurring before the 'elbow' when the number of dimensions are plotted against the (ordered) eigenvalues. While criteria such as these are sometimes useful, they unfortunately contribute to an implicit reification of the number of dimensions characterizing a given phenomenon. Thus, there are debates about how many distinct 'learning styles' there really are, with OECD concluding that three basic learning strategies exist in all of the countries that participated in PISA 2003. This conclusion was supported by CFA which, in their judgement, provided acceptable fit. The evidence we have provided in this chapter undermines the fruitfulness of defining a distinct number of learning strategies that is applicable cross-nationally – or even within a single country. That is, the number of relatively distinct learning strategies depends on the cognitive competence of the respondents.

A further implication of our analysis concerns strategies for cross-national research. The three-country statistics (Table 8.4) revealed large cross-national differences in the magnitude of the variables of interest, such as the item non-response rate. These country-level differences can mask the magnitude of the relationships being investigated. For example, within each of the three countries there was a consistent negative relationship between reading achievement decile groups and item non-response. However, the non-response at the *highest* achievement level in one country (0.43 in Denmark) exceeded the non-response rate at the *lowest* achievement level of another country (0.35 in South Korea). The implication is that all measures should be made relative to the country mean. This implies, of course, that all analyses should first be done at the country level and then be repeated for all countries that are to be compared. The association between variables is then assessed after subtracting the country mean from each of the variables whose associations are being assessed.

Finally, our findings have some relevance for the debate about whether standardized achievement tests impede genuine learning by focusing on the test. Our findings show that students who perform well on standardized achievement tests also provide responses to survey questions of above average quality. This implies that achievement tests have some validity as measures of cognitive competence: students who do well in these standardized tests perform well in other verbal tasks.

9

Conclusion

We started this book with the observation that it is easy to compute quality coefficients, such as the percentage of non-response and measures of reliability such as Cronbach's alpha, but enormously difficult to assess the quality of data. The chapters inbetween uncovered a large variety of threats to the integrity of survey data, ranging from systematic data entry errors to outright falsification of complete interviews on the part of research institutes and their staff, not to mention the numerous sources of error introduced through respondents' limited interest and cognitive ability. The sheer variety of possible errors and the frequency of their occurrence in the data sets we examined came as somewhat of a surprise, since we analysed well-known data sets that formed the evidence for a huge number of scholarly publications in leading international journals. The numerous problems we uncovered in these respected, high-quality survey projects underscores the importance of thorough data screening procedures. It is also precisely because of the great variety of sources of error that there is no simple omnibus screening procedure. In the process of screening the data sets used in this book, we often felt like data detectives whose job it was to establish whether a 'crime' had been committed, what the nature of the crime was, and who the perpetrators were.

As mentioned, for our data screening applications we relied primarily on well-known, publicly available data sets such as the ISSP, WVS and ESS. We chose to focus on such data for two reasons. First, since the data are publicly available, our calculations can be independently verified, refuted, or extended by other researchers. Second, these ongoing survey projects benefit from the active participation of survey research experts from numerous countries and as a result, the data obtained are likely to be of above average quality. Analysing data that are known to be of relatively high quality was important to us since one of our objectives was to argue that data quality should never be assumed and that therefore all data sets need to be screened for their quality before undertaking substantive analyses. The fact that we found various deficiencies in the quality of the data was not intended to impugn the integrity of these valuable survey research projects, but rather to reinforce the conclusion that all data are dirty.

In the course of writing this book, we became convinced that several common practices on the part of research analysts are perhaps as much of a deterrent to sound analysis as is the quality of the data with which they are working. These include:

- cavalier use of statistical techniques that impose untested assumptions;
- favouring measures of reliability over assessments of validity;
- using scaling techniques to create empirical measures rather than to understand the underlying cognitive maps;
- premature rotation of factor-analytic solutions;
- undue reliance on fit statistics and tests of statistical significance in empirically based concept-formation practices;
- objectification of the number of dimensions underlying a given domain of interest.

We are not the first to draw attention to many of these practices. However, their continued use prompts us to reiterate them. Perhaps the most easily rectified practice is the use of statistical techniques that impose untested assumptions. The analyses we conducted for this book show that even the assumption that Likert responses represent an ordered categorical level of measurement is sometimes not justified, never mind the assumption that such data are metric. Nevertheless, some analysts continue to use difference of means tests, compute Pearson correlation coefficients, and conduct PCA on such data. A preliminary analysis using CatPCA would ascertain whether the assumption of ordered categorical measures is justified (through the absence of tied quantifications) and the optimal quantifications produced could be used for further analysis. Likewise, the assumption of multivariate normality and the absence of outliers are simply assumed. Plotting the object scores produced by MCA or CatPCA would quickly display the distribution of respondents in this latent space, including any outliers and their positions. In other words, the severity of the violation of various assumptions can be assessed, and in this way a decision can be made as to whether the violations are too egregious for the purposes at hand.

Many researchers generally believe that the higher the reliability of a measure, the better is its quality. While this is true, *ceteris paribus*, the fact is that all things are not equal, as Campbell and Fiske's (1959) multi-trait, multi-method analyses revealed. In particular, high reliability is often due to common method variance, producing artefactually high associations between measures of a concept obtained through a common method. Indeed, our analyses on the relationship between cognitive competence and response quality (Chapter 8) indicated that respondents for whom the reliability of responses were highest were precisely the ones whose data quality was arguably the worst. To put it bluntly, high reliability can be an indicator of poor data quality. This is so whenever the high reliability is a method-induced artefact.

Factor-analytic techniques, regardless of whether they are exploratory or con-firmatory, are typically conducted with one purpose in mind: to create the best empirically based interval-like measures of theoretical concepts. We have no argument with this practice *per se*. Our concern is that this goal is usually ful-filled by the simple expedient of tossing out any items that do not load highly and cleanly on a given dimension. We have argued in this book that good survey analysis requires one to examine carefully the location in the latent space of all responses for all items of a given domain.

Closely connected to using traditional scaling techniques is the absence of a focus on the unrotated solutions. It is understandable why researchers concen-trate on the rotated solution, since those solutions usually increase the explained variances by the second and subsequent factors, increase an item's factor load-ing on a given factor and decrease its loading on other factors. This increases the reliability of the measures reflecting a given factor, both of which are considered desirable properties of empirical measures of concepts. However, potential dan-gers lurk behind these practices. One danger is that the rotated solution capital-izes on non-substantive features of the items being used. Specifically, rotation increases the likelihood that distributional rather than substantive differences are the basis for the item loadings. This is especially apparent when items of mixed polarity are subjected to factor analysis. Often the rotated solution reflects the polarity of the items rather than the similarity of the content of the items (Chapter 5). It must be kept in mind that most domains are normatively regulated. The statistical consequence of this is that such domains have a pro-nounced skew rather than being normally distributed. This feature means that positively formulated items will be skewed in a given direction, while negatively formulated items will be skewed in the opposite direction. When items of mixed polarity are rotated, the typical result is that all items of a common polarity form one factor while opposite-polarity items form a second factor. This feature has often resulted in analysts concluding that two unipolar con-cepts are necessary rather than a single bipolar concept. Paying closer attention to the unrotated solution, it would frequently have become apparent that the highest loadings for most, if not all of the items, are on the first dimension, which would suggest that a bipolar concept might be a more appropriate and parsimonious conceptualization.

Analysts often conclude that two unimodal concepts are necessary, since fit measures would invariably have rejected the acceptability of a single bimodal concept in favour of two unimodal ones. Nevertheless, this results in the awk-ward theoretical conclusion that agreement with a positively formulated item contributes to an increase in the value of the underlying (positive) latent con-cept, but disagreement with that item does not contribute to the diminution of the positive factor; likewise, agreement with a negatively formulated item con-tributes to the value of the underlying (negative) unipolar factor but disagree-ment with such an item has no effect on the value of the positive factor. This led to a proliferation of concepts such as intrinsic job satisfiers versus extrinsic job dissatisfiers (Herzberg, 1974), sources of positive self-esteem and sources of negative self-esteem (see Mirowsky and Ross, 1991: 217, for a solid critique of the traditional factor-analytic approaches that lead to nonsensical conclusions such as 'the resources for achieving success are useless for avoiding failure'). However, as methodologists made increasing advances in their ability to model substantive factors simultaneously with method-induced ones, it became apparent that single bipolar factors with common methods factors often fit as well as models postulating separate substantive factors. The lesson to be learned from these exercises is that fit statistics may be helpful in determining appropriate modelling of data structures, but they must never be allowed to be sovereign if the goal is to produce sensitive, theoretically informed analyses.

A final practice that we would discourage is the search for the 'true' number of factors underlying any domain of interest and whether the number of factors and their meaning are the same for different groups or countries or cultures. The number of dimensions for any domain is not determined by the domain (objective bias) but by the amount of information that analysts are willing to ignore in their construction of the most parsimonious model that nevertheless captures a sufficient amount of the variation in the domain of interest. In our opinion, it is fruitless to debate how many distinct learning styles exist, for example, and whether they are universally the same. Instead, the focus needs to be on how much information is lost when only a limited number of dimensions are retained for consideration. Thus, in Chapter 8 we were able to show that the first dimension accounts for decreasing amounts of variation with increasing cognitive competency, while the second dimension accounts for increasing amounts. This pattern holds for most countries and is much more stable than is the number of factors extracted and which items have their highest loadings on which factors.

Some researchers appear to cling to an overly realist understanding of research. Kankaraš and Moors (2009: 558), for instance, consider measurement equivalence to be established 'when measurements measure the same latent traits across all groups, nations or cultures'. We would rephrase this to say that measures can be treated as equivalent *when identical latent structural and measurement models can be applied to the observed responses with a fit that is considered acceptable for the purposes at hand and with a minimum of untested assumptions or ad hoc adjustments*. The problem is that typically an acceptable fit is accomplished in one of two ways: by deleting items that behave poorly, or by permitting theoretically unexplained links, such as in partial homogeneity models or unique error covariances in structural equation modelling. Such procedures essentially discard the puzzles that need to be explained and resolved.

We have also come to the conclusion that the search for an exhaustive set of response styles and subsequent attempts to control for the response styles identified is not likely to be a fruitful avenue for a variety of reasons. First, and perhaps most importantly, the review of the empirical literature revealed that currently identified response styles are extremely difficult to disentangle from substantive variation while simultaneously being highly correlated with each other (Baumgartner and Steenkamp, 2001). Second, no convincing arguments have been made for the theoretical meanings of some of the response styles, such as disacquiescence. Third, recent research has identified still more distinct combinations of response preferences than previously documented. One of these is a tendency to disproportionately choose both the extreme end-points and the mid-point of a given response scale. This is an apparently contradictory response style since it simultaneously includes two response styles that have always been considered to be polar opposites: mid-point responding and extreme response style. Rather than focus on a proliferation of possible response styles and their possible causes, we have come to the conclusion that it is more fruitful to think of all possible combinations of response preferences as manifestations of a task simplification dynamic. In their attempt to comply with the research demands of providing acceptable responses, respondents simplify the cognitive demands by favouring a subset of the possible response options; some respondents may choose the first, middle, and end options, others may favour responses near the middle, while still others may find it easiest to choose between the relatively clear end-points. In our analyses we adapted a measure of response differentiation (which we called the index of response differentiation – IRD) which captures all tendencies to disproportionately favour certain response options or combinations of responses. We were able to show that this index was consistently and strongly related to respondents' cognitive competence across many different countries and across several different response formats and item domains.

Readers may well ask whether dirty data can be repaired, and if so, how and under what conditions. The answer is not altogether encouraging, since some forms of compromised data may not be salvageable. The problem with poor-quality data is not so much that they contain errors, but rather that these errors may lead the analyst to false conclusions. So the emphasis needs to be more on how to minimize the likelihood of erroneous conclusions. We can offer a number of suggestions for improving data quality and minimizing wrong conclusions. First, during the course of the research, the procedures we used for identifying suspect interviews coming from a subset of interviewers can be implemented on an ongoing basis. Interviewers whose interviews conform to suspect patterns can then be monitored more closely. Where the field work has already been completed, it should be standard practice that a code for the interviewer is entered into each respondent's record. By doing this, future researchers can use our techniques to identify suspect interviewers.

Second, the procedures we used to detect duplicate cases can be applied to any data set that contains a sufficient number of items to permit one to conclude that cases with precisely the same value on the (nonsensical) latent space derived from those items probably represent falsified cases – that is, cases that were manufactured through a simple expedient such as cut and paste. Again, the substantive analyses can be rerun, temporarily deleting those cases that have a high probability of being duplicates.

Third, recent methodological advances make the detection and control of all manner of response propensities increasingly possible without making unwarranted assumptions regarding level of measurement and normality of distributions. Even simple techniques, such as routinely including the IRD score as a control variable for task simplification differences, should minimize the confusion between genuine substantive relationships and method-induced relationships. This is especially important in cross-national comparative studies.

Our approach to quality research gives equal attention to errors arising from respondent characteristics, study architecture characteristics, institutional and interviewer behaviours, and analyst practices. We are not averse to attributing to analysts and interviewers the same dynamics as we attribute to respondents. We assumed, for example, that both respondents and interviewers have access to cultural scripts and each of them use such knowledge for their own ends: respondents to get through the interview quickly and satisfactorily; interviewers to also get through the interview quickly, thereby maximizing their own benefits. Interviewers magnify associations between weakly related events based on their lay theories of what is associated with what, and it is this feature that we used to detect faked interviews. In the same manner, respondents may well create illusory correlations by parroting cultural knowledge rather than reflecting on how to express their personal opinions.

Our book has focused almost exclusively on data quality. Hence, readers could be forgiven if they were to conclude that we consider poor data quality to constitute the sole threat to the integrity of survey-based findings. We actually do not; a major source of erroneous findings, in our opinion, can often be traced to faulty researcher practices, some of which were outlined above. Careful attention to detail is not to be confused with a focus on the trivial. As the saying goes, the devil is in the detail. Rerunning analyses making a different set of plausible assumptions may ultimately be more important than washing the data.

References

AAPOR (2003) 'Interviewer falsification in survey research: Current best methods for prevention, detection and repair of its effects'. Available at www.aapor.org/pdfs/falsification.pdf.

Alessandri, Guido, Michele Vecchione, Corrado Fagnani, Peter M. Bentler, Claudio Barbaranelli, Emmanuela Medda, Lorenza Nistico, Maria A. Stazi and Gian V. Caprara (2010) 'Much more than model fitting? Evidence for the heritability of method effect associated with positively worded items of the Life Orientation Test Revised'. *Structural Equation Modeling: A Multidisiciplinary Journal* 17: 642–653.

Alwin, Duane F. (1997) 'Feeling thermometers versus 7-point scales: Which are better?' *Sociological Methods & Research* 25: 318–340.

Andrews, Frank M. (1984) 'Construct validity and error components of survey measures: A structural modeling approach'. *Public Opinion Quarterly* 48: 409–442.

Arce-Ferrer, Alvaro J. (2006) 'An investigation into the factors influencing extreme-response style: Improving meaning of translated and culturally adapted rating scales'. *Educational and Psychological Measurement* 66: 374–392.

Bachman, Gerald G. and Patrick M. O'Malley (1984) 'Yea-saying, nay-saying, and going to extremes: Black–white differences in response styles'. *Public Opinion Quarterly* 48: 491–509.

Balch, George I. (1974) 'Multiple indicators in survey research: The concept "sense of political efficacy"'. *Political Methodology* 1: 1–43.

Barnette, J. Jackson (2000) 'Effects of stem and Likert response option reversals on survey internal consistency: If you feel the need, there is a better alternative to using negatively worded items'. *Educational and Psychological Measurement* 60: 361–370.

Bass, Bernard M. (1956) 'Development and evaluation of a scale for measuring social acquiescence'. *Journal of Abnormal and Social Psychology* 53: 296–299.

Baumgartner, Hans and Jan-Benedict E. M. Steenkamp (2001) 'Response styles in marketing research: A cross-national investigation'. *Journal of Marketing Research* 38: 143–156.

Belli, Robert F., A. Regula Herzog and John Van Hoewyk (1999) 'Scale simplification of expectations for survival: Cognitive ability and the quality of survey responses'. *Cognitive Technology* 4: 29–38.

Benzécri, J.-P. et al. (1973) *L'Analyse des Données.* Volume 2: *L'Analyse de Correspondence.* Paris: Dunod.

Berinsky, Adam J. (2002) 'Political context and the survey response: The dynamics of racial policy opinion'. *Journal of Politics* 64: 567–584.

Bernstein, Robert, Anita Chadha and Robert Montjoy (2001) 'Overreporting voting: Why it happens and why it matters ' *Public Opinion Quarterly* 65: 22–44.

Billiet, Jaak B. and Eldad Davidov (2008) 'Testing the stability of an acquiescence style factor behind two interrelated substantive variables in a panel design'. *Sociological Methods & Research* 36: 542–562.

Billiet, Jaak B. and McKee J. McClendon (2000) 'Modeling acquiescence in measurement models for two balanced sets of items'. *Structural Equation Modeling: A Multidisiciplinary Journal* 7: 608–628.

Bishop, George and Andrew Smith (2001) 'Response-order effects and the early Gallup split-ballots'. *Public Opinion Quarterly* 65: 479–505.

Blais, André, Neil Nevitte, Elisabeth Gidengil and Richard Nadeau (2000) 'Do people have feelings toward leaders about whom they say they know nothing?' *Public Opinion Quarterly* 64: 452–463.

Blasius, Jörg, Paul Eilers and John Gower (2009) 'Better biplots'. *Computational Statistics and Data Analysis* 53: 3145–3158.

Blasius, Jörg and Jürgen Friedrichs (2007) 'Internal heterogeneity of a deprived urban area and its impact on residents'. *Housing Studies* 22: 753–780.

Blasius, Jörg Jürgen Friedrichs, and Jennifer Klöckner (2008) *Doppelt benachteiligt? Leben in einem deutsch-türkischen Viertel*. Wiesbaden: VS-Verlag.

Blasius, Jörg and John C. Gower (2005) 'Multivariate prediction with nonlinear principal components analysis: Application'. *Quality and Quantity* 39: 373–390.

Blasius, Jörg and Michael Greenacre (2006) 'Multiple correspondence analysis and related methods in practice'. In Michael Greenacre and Jörg Blasius (eds), *Multiple Correspondence Analysis and Related Methods*, pp. 3–40. Boca Raton, FL: Chapman & Hall/CRC.

Blasius, Jörg and Victor Thiessen (2001a) 'Methodological artifacts in measures of political efficacy and trust: A multiple correspondence analysis'. *Political Analysis* 9: 1–20.

Blasius, Jörg and Victor Thiessen (2001b) 'The use of neutral responses in survey questions: An application of multiple correspondence analysis'. *Journal of Official Statistics* 17: 351–367.

Blasius, Jörg and Victor Thiessen (2006a) 'Assessing data quality and construct comparability in cross-national surveys'. *European Sociological Review* 22: 229–242.

Blasius, Jörg and Victor Thiessen (2006b) 'A three-step approach to assessing the behavior of survey items in cross-national research'. In Michael Greenacre and Jörg Blasius (eds), *Multiple Correspondence Analysis and Related Methods*, pp. 433–454. Boca Raton, FL: Chapman and Hall/CRC.

Blasius, Jörg and Victor Thiessen (2009) 'Facts and artifacts in cross-national research: The case of political efficacy and trust'. In Max Haller, Roger Jowell, and Tom Smith (eds), *Charting the Globe. The International Social Survey Programme 1984–2009*. London: Routledge.

Box, George E. P. (1987) 'Science and statistics'. *Journal of the American Statistical Association* 71: 791–799.

Brewin, Chris R. and David A. Shapiro (1984) 'Beyond locus of control: Attribution of responsibility for positive and negative outcomes'. *British Journal of Psychology* 75: 43–49.

Cambré, Bart, Jerry Welkenhuysen-Gybels and Jaak Billiet (2002) 'Is it content or is it style? An evaluation of two competitive measurement models applied to a balanced set of ethnocentrism items'. *International Journal of Comparative Sociology* 43: 1–20.

Campbell, Donald T. and Donald W. Fiske (1959) 'Convergent and discriminant validation by the multi-trait-multimethod matrix'. *Psychological Bulletin* 56: 81–105.

Carr, Leslie G. (1971) 'The Srole items and acquiescence'. *American Sociological Review* 36: 287–293.

Ceci, Steven J. (1991) 'How much does schooling influence general intelligence and its cognitive components? A reassessment of the evidence'. *Developmental Psychology* 27: 703–722.

Converse, Jean M. (1976) 'Predicting no opinion in the polls'. *Public Opinion Quarterly* 40(4): 515–530.

Converse, Philip (1964) 'The nature of belief systems in mass publics'. In David Apter (ed.), *Ideology and Discontent*. New York: Free Press.

Cote, Joseph A. and Ronald Buckley (1987) 'Estimating trait, method, and error variance: Generalizing across 70 construct validation studies'. *Journal of Marketing Research* 24: 315–318.

Couch, Arthur and Kenneth Keniston (1960) 'Yeasayers and naysayers: Agreeing response set as a personality variable'. *Journal of Abnormal and Social Psychology* 60: 151–174.

Credé, Marcus (2010) 'Random responding as a threat to the validity of effect size estimates in correlational research'. *Educational and Psychological Measurement* 70(4): 596–612.

Crespi, Leo P. (1945) 'The cheater problem in polling'. *Public Opinion Quarterly* 9: 431–445.

Cronbach, Lee J. (1950) 'Further evidence on response sets and test design'. *Educational and Psychological Measurement* 10: 3–31.

Dayton, Elizabeth, Chunliu Zhan, Judith Sangl, Charles Darby and Ernest Moy (2006) 'Racial and ethnic differences in patient assessments of interactions with providers: Disparities or measurement biases?' *American Journal of Medical Quality* 21: 109–114.

De Leeuw Jan. (2006) 'Nonlinear principal component analysis and related techniques'. In Michael Greenacre and Jörg Blasius (eds), *Multiple Correspondence Analysis and Related Techniques*, pp. 107–133. Boca Raton, FL: Chapman & Hall/CRC.

DiStefano, Christine and Robert W. Motl (2006) 'Further investigating method effects associated with negatively worded items on self-report surveys'. *Structural Equation Modeling: A Multidisiciplinary Journal* 13: 440–464.

DiStefano, Christine, and Robert W. Motl (2009) 'Personality correlates of method effects due to negatively worded items on the Rosenberg Self-Esteem scale'. *Personality and Individual Differences* 46: 309–313.

Edwards, Allen L. (1957) *Techniques of Attitude Scale Construction*. New York: Appleton.

Elliott, Marc N., Amelia M. Haviland, David E. Kanouse, Katrin Hambarsoomian and Ron D. Hays (2009) 'Adjusting for subgroup differences in extreme response tendency in ratings of health care: Impact on disparity estimates'. *Health Services Research* 44: 542–561.

Faulkenberry, G. David and Robert Mason (1978) 'Characteristics of nonopinion and no opinion response groups'. *Public Opinion Quarterly* 42(4): 533–543.

Ferber, Robert (1966) 'Item nonresponse in a consumer survey'. *Public Opinion Quarterly* 30: 399–415.

Finkel, Steven E. (1985) 'Reciprocal effects of participation and political efficacy'. *American Journal of Political Science* 29: 891–913.

Fowler, Floyd J. Jr (2002) *Survey Research Methods*. Thousand Oaks, CA: Sage.

Francis, Joe and Lawrence Busch (1975) 'What we don't know about "I don't knows"'. *Public Opinion Quarterly* 39: 207–218.

Friedrichs, Jürgen and Jörg Blasius (2000) *Leben in benachteiligten Wohngebieten.* Opladen: Leske + Budrich.

Friedrichs, Jürgen and Jörg Blasius (2003) 'Social norms in distressed neighborhoods. Testing the Wilson hypothesis'. *Housing Studies* 18: 807–826.

Gifi, Albert (1990) *Nonlinear Multivariate Analysis.* New York: Wiley.

Goffman, Erving (1959) *The Presentation of Self in Everyday Life.* Garden City, NY: Doubleday Anchor.

Gove, Walter R. and Michael R. Geerken (1977) 'Response bias in surveys of mental health: An empirical investigation'. *American Journal of Sociology* 82: 1289–1317.

Gower, John C. and David J. Hand (1996) *Biplots.* London: Chapman & Hall.

Green, Donald P. (1988) 'On the dimensionality of public sentiment toward partisan and ideological groups'. *American Journal of Political Science* 32: 758–780.

Greenacre, Michael (1984) *Theory and Applications of Correspondence Analysis.* London: Academic Press.

Greenacre, Michael (1988) 'Correspondence analysis of multivariate categorical data by weighted least squares'. *Biometrika* 75: 457–467.

Greenacre, Michael (2007) *Correspondence Analysis in Practice.* Boca Raton, FL: Chapman & Hall/CRC.

Greenacre, Michael and Oleg Nenadić (2006) 'Computation of multiple correspondence analysis, with code in R'. In Michael Greenacre and Jörg Blasius (eds), *Multiple Correspondence Analysis and Related Methods,* pp. 523–551. Boca Raton, FL: Chapman & Hall/CRC.

Greenacre, Michael and Raphael Pardo (2006a) 'Multiple correspondence analysis of subsets of response categories'. In Michael Greenacre and Jörg Blasius (eds), *Multiple Correspondence Analysis and Related Methods,* pp. 197–217. Boca Raton, FL: Chapman & Hall/CRC.

Greenacre, Michael and Raphael Pardo (2006b) 'Subset correspondence analysis: Visualization of selected response categories in a questionnaire survey'. *Sociological Methods and Research* 35: 193–218.

Greenleaf, Eric A. (1992a) 'Improving rating scale measures by detecting and correcting bias components in some response styles'. *Journal of Marketing Research* 29: 176–188.

Greenleaf, Eric A. (1992b) 'Measuring extreme response style'. *Public Opinion Quarterly* 56: 328–351.

Griesler, Pamela C., Denise B. Kandel, Christine Schaffran, Mei-chen Hu and Mark Davis (2008) 'Adolescents' inconsistency in self-reported smoking: A comparison of reports in school and in household settings'. *Public Opinion Quarterly* 72: 260–290.

Groves, Robert M., Stanley Presser and Sarah Dipko (2004) 'The role of topic interest in survey participation decisions'. *Public Opinion Quarterly* 68: 2–31.

Hayashi, Chikio (1954) 'Multidimensional quantification – with the applications to the analysis of social phenomena'. *Annals of the Institute of Statistical Mathematics* 5: 231–245.

Hayes, Bernadette C. and Clive S. Bean (1993) 'Political efficacy: A comparative study of the United States, West Germany, Great Britain and Australia'. *European Journal of Political Research* 23: 261–280.

Heerwegh, Dirk and Geert Loosveldt (2011) 'Assessing mode effects in a national crime victimization survey using structural equation models: Social desirability bias and acquiescence'. *Journal of Official Statistics* 27:49–63.

Heiser, Willem J. and Jacqueline J. Meulman (1994) 'Homogeneity analysis: Exploring the distribution of variables and their nonlinear relationships'. In Michael J. Greenacre and Jörg Blasius (eds), *Correspondence Analysis in the Social Sciences*, pp. 179–209. London: Academic Press.

Herzberg, Frederick (1974) *Work and the Nature of Man*. London: Crosby Lockwood Staples.

Holbrook, Allyson L., Young Ik Cho and Timothy Johnson (2006) 'The impact of question and respondent characteristics on comprehension and mapping difficulties'. *Public Opinion Quarterly* 70: 565–595.

Holbrook, Allyson L., Jon A. Krosnick, David Moore and Roger Tourangeau (2007) 'Response order effects in dichtomous categorical questions presented orally: The impact of question and respondent attributes'. *Public Opinion Quarterly* 71: 325–348.

Hui, C. Harry, and Harry C. Triandis (1989) 'Effects of culture and response format on extreme response style'. *Journal of Cross-Cultural Psychology* 20: 296–309.

Javaras, Kristin N. and Brian D. Ripley (2007) 'An 'unfolding' latent variable model for Likert attitude data: Drawing inferences adjusted for response style'. *Journal of the American Statistical Association* 102: 454–463.

Judd, Charles M., Jon A. Krosnick and Michael A. Milburn (1981) 'Political involvement and attitude structure in the general public'. *Amercian Sociological Review* 46: 660–669.

Kankaraš, Miloš and Guy Moors (2009) 'Measurement equivalence in solidarity attitudes in Europe: Insights from a multiple-group latent-class factor approach'. *International Sociology* 24: 557–579.

Kreuter, Frauke, Stanley Presser and Roger Tourangeau (2008) 'Social desirability bias in CATI, IVR, and web surveys: The effects of mode and question sensitivity'. *Public Opinion Quarterly* 72: 847–865.

Kroh, Martin (2007) 'Measuring left-right political orientation: The choice of response format'. *Public Opinion Quarterly* 71: 204–220.

Krosnick, Jon A. (1991) 'Response strategies for coping with the cognitive demands of attitude measures in surveys'. *Applied Cognitive Psychology* 5: 213–236.

Krosnick, Jon A. (1999) 'Survey research'. *Annual Review of Psychology* 50: 337–367.

Krosnick, Jon A. and Duane F. Alwin (1987) 'An evaluation of a cognitive theory of response-order effects in survey measurement'. *Public Opinion Quarterly* 51: 201–219.

Krosnick, Jon A., Allyson L. Holbrook, Matthew K. Berent, Richard T. Carson, W. Michael Hanemann, Raymond J. Kopp, Robert C. Mitchell, Stanley Presser, Paul A. Ruud, V. Kerry Smith, Wendy R. Moody, Melanie C. Green and Michael Conaway (2002) 'The impact of "no opinion" response options on data quality: Non-attitude reduction or an invitation to satisfice?' *Public Opinion Quarterly* 66: 371–403.

Krysan, Maria (1998) 'Privacy and the expression of white racial attitudes: A comparison across three contexts'. *Public Opinion Quarterly* 62: 506–544.

Kuncel, Nathan R. and Auke Tellegen (2009) 'A conceptual and empirical reexamination of the measurement of the social desirability of items: Implications for detecting desirable response style and scale development'. *Personnel Psychology* 62: 201–228.

Le Roux, Brigitte and Henry Rouanet (2004) *Geometric Data Analysis*. Amsterdam: North-Holland.

Lebart, Ludovic, Alain Morineau and Ken Warwick (1984) *Multivariate Descriptive Analysis. Correspondence Analysis and Related Techniques for Large Matrices*. New York: Wiley.

Lenski, Gerhard E. and John C. Leggett (1960) 'Caste, class, and deference in the research interview'. *American Journal of Sociology* 65: 463–467.

Linville, Patricia W., Peter. Salovey and Gregory. W. Fischer (1986) 'Stereotyping and perceived distribution of social characteristics: An application to ingroup-outgroup perception'. In John F. Dovidio and Samuel. L. Gaertner (eds), *Prejudice, Discrimination, and Racism*, pp. 165–208. New York: Academic Press.

Malhotra, Neil, Jon A. Krosnick and Randall K. Thomas (2009) 'Optimal design of branching questions to measure bipolar constructs'. *Public Opinion Quarterly* 73: 304–324.

Marsh, Herbert W. (1986) 'Negative item bias in ratings scales for preadolescent children: A cognitive-developmental phenomenon'. *Developmental Psychology* 22: 37–49.

McClendon, McKee J. (1991) 'Acquiescence: Tests of the cognitive limitations and question ambiguity hypotheses'. *Journal of Official Statistics* 7: 153–166.

McHorney, Colleen A. and John A. Fleishman (2006) 'Assessing and understanding measurement equivalence in health outcome measures: Issues for further quantitative and qualitative inquiry'. *Medical Care* 44: S205–S210.

Mirowsky, John and Catherine E. Ross (1991) 'Eliminating defense and agreement bias from measures of the sense of control: A 2 × 2 index'. *Social Psychology Quarterly* 54: 127–145.

Mondak, Jeffrey J. (1999) 'Reconsidering the measurement of political knowledge'. *Political Analysis* 8: 57–82.

Moors, Guy (2004) 'Facts and artefacts in the comparison of attitudes among ethnic minorities. A multigroup latent class structure model with adjustment for response style behavior'. *European Sociological Review* 20: 303–320.

Murayama, Kou, Mingming Zhou and John C. Nesbit (2009) 'A cross-cultural examination of the psychometric properties of responses to the achievement goal questionnaire'. *Educational and Psychological Measurement* 69: 266–286.

Nederhof, Anton J. (1985) 'Methods of coping with social desirability bias: A review'. *European Journal of Social Psychology* 15: 263–280.

Nenadić, Oleg and Michael Greenacre (2007) 'Correspondence analysis in R, with two- and three-dimensional graphics: the ca package'. *Journal of Statistical Software* 20. http://www.jstatsoft.org/v20/i03/

Nishisato, Shizuhiko (1980) *Analysis of Categorical Data: Dual Scaling and its Applications*. Toronto: University of Toronto Press.

Nishisato, Shizuhiko (2007) *Multidimensional Nonlinear Descriptive Analysis*. Boca Raton, FL: Chapman & Hall/CRC.

Oskamp, Stuart (1977) *Attitudes and Opinions*. Englewood Cliffs, NJ: Prentice Hall.

Parry, Geraint, Georg Moyser and Neil Day (1992) *Political Participation and Democracy in Britain*. Cambridge: Cambridge University Press.

Payne, Stanley L. (1951) *The Art of Asking Questions*. Princeton, NJ: Princeton University Press.

Podsakoff, Philip M., Scott B. MacKenzie, Jeong-Yeon Lee and Nathan P. Podsakoff (2003) 'Common method biases in behavioral research: A critical review of the literature and recommended remedies'. *Journal of Applied Psychology* 88: 879–903.

Porras, Javier and Ned English (2004) 'Data-driven approaches to identifying interviewer data falsification: The case of health surveys'. Paper presented at the American Association for Public Opinion Research, 59th Annual Conference, 13–16 May,

Phoenix, AZ. http://www.amstat.org/sections/SRMS/proceedings/y2004/files/Jsm2004-000879.pdf

Reips, Ulf-Dietrich, and Frederick Funke (2008) 'Interval-level measurement with visual analogue scales in Internet-based research: VAS Generator'. *Behavior Research Methods* 40: 699–704.

Ross, Catherine E. and John Mirowsky (1984) 'Socially-desirable response and acquiescence in a cross-cultural survey'. *Journal of Health and Social Behavior* 25: 189–197.

Ross, Catherine E., John Mirowsky and Shana Pribesh (2001) 'Powerlessness and the amplification of threat: Neighborhood disadvantage, disorder, and mistrust'. *American Sociological Review* 66: 568–591.

Rouanet, Henry (2006) 'The geometric analysis of structured individuals × variables tables'. In Michael Greenacre and Jörg Blasius (eds), *Multiple Correspondence Analysis and Related Methods*, pp. 137–159. Boca Raton, FL: Chapman & Hall/CRC.

Sampson, Robert J. and W. Byron Groves (1989) 'Community structure and crime: Testing social disorganization theory'. *American Journal of Sociology* 94: 774–802.

Sampson, Robert J., Jeffrey D. Morenoff and Thomas Gannon-Rowley (2002) 'Assessing neighborhood effects: Social processes and new directions in research'. *Annual Review of Sociology* 28: 443–478.

Sampson, Robert J., Stephen W. Raudenbush and Fellen Earls (1997) 'Neighborhoods and violent crime: A multilevel study of collective efficacy'. *Science* 277: 918–924.

Saris, Willem E., Melanie Revilla, Jon A. Krosnick and Eric M. Shaeffer (2010) 'Comparing questions with agree/disagree response options to questions with item-specific response options'. *Survey Research Methods* 4: 61–79.

Schäfer, Christian, Jörg-Peter Schräpler, Klaus-Robert Müller and Gert G. Wagner (2005) 'Automatic identification of faked and fraudulent interviews in the German SOEP'. *Schmollers Jahrbuch* 125: 183–193.

Schmitt, Neal and Daniel M. Stults (1985) 'Factors defined by negatively keyed items: The result of careless respondents?' *Applied Psychological Measurement* 9: 367–373.

Schriesheim, Chester A., Regina J. Eisenbach and Kenneth D. Hill (1991) 'The effect of negation and polar opposite item reversals on questionnaire reliability and validity: An experimental investigation'. *Educational and Psychological Measurement* 51: 67–78.

Sigelman, Lee and Richard G. Niemi (2001) 'Innumeracy about minority populations: African Americans and Whites compared'. *Public Opinion Quarterly* 65: 86–94.

Silver, Brian, Barbara Anderson and Paul Abramson (1986) 'Who overreports voting?' *American Political Science Review* 80: 613–624.

Simon, Herbert A. (1957) *Models of Man.* New York: Wiley.

Smith Jr., Everett V., Melissa B. Wakely, Renée E. L. De Kruif and Carl W. Swartz (2003) 'Optimizing rating scales for self-efficacy (and other) research'. *Educational and Psychological Measurement* 63: 369–391.

Smith, Peter B. (2004) 'Acquiescent response bias as an aspect of cultural communication style'. *Journal of Cross-Cultural Psychology* 35: 50–61.

Spector, Paul E., Paul T. Van Katwyk, Michael T. Brannick and Peter Y. Chen (1997) 'When two factors don't reflect two constructs: How item characteristics can produce artifactual factors'. *Journal of Management* 23: 659–677.

Steenkamp, Jan-Benedict E. M. and Steven M. Burgess (2002) 'Optimum stimulation level and exploratory consumer behavior in an emerging consumer market'. *International Journal of Research in Marketing* 19: 131–150.

Steinmetz, Holger, Peter Schmidt and Shalom H. Schwartz (2009) 'Testing measurement invariance using multigroup CFA: Differences between educational groups in human values measurement'. *Quality & Quantity* 43: 599–616.

Sturgis, Patrick, Nick Allum and Patten Smith (2008) 'An experiment on the measurement of political knowledge in surveys'. *Public Opinion Quarterly* 85: 90–102.

Subar, Amy F., Regina G. Ziegler, Frances E. Thompson, Christine Cole Johnson, Joel L. Weissfeld, Douglas Reding, Katherine H. Kavounis and Richard B. Hayes (2001) 'Is shorter always better? Relative importance of questionnaire length and cognitive ease on response rates and data quality for two dietary questionnaires'. *American Journal of Epidemiology* 153: 404–409.

Thiessen, Victor (2010) 'Disentangling content from style: The importance of cognitive ability in youth's survey responses'. Unpublished manuscript.

Thiessen, Victor and Jörg Blasius (1998) 'Using multiple correspondence analysis to distinguish between substantive and non-substantive responses'. In Jörg Blasius and Michael Greenacre (eds), *Visualization of Categorical Data*, pp. 239–252. San Diego, CA: Academic Press.

Thiessen, Victor and Jörg Blasius (2008) 'Mathematics achievement and mathematics learning strategies: Cognitive competencies and construct differentiation'. *International Journal of Educational Research* 47: 362–371.

Tourangeau, Roger and Kenneth A. Rasinski (1988) 'Cognitive processes underlying context effects in attitude measurement'. *Psychological Bulletin* 103: 299–314.

Tourangeau, Roger, Lance J. Rips and Kenneth A. Rasinski (2000) *The Psychology of Survey Response*. New York: Cambridge University Press.

Turner, Charles F, James N. Gribble, Alia A. Al-Tayyib and James R. Chromny (2002) 'Falsification in epidemiologic surveys: Detection and remediation'. Technical Papers on Health and Behavior Measurement (Report #53). Available at http://dragon.soc.qc.cuny.edu/Staff/turner/TechPDFs/53_Falsify.pdf

Van de Vijver, Fons J. R. and Ype H. Poortinga (1997) 'Towards an integrated analysis of bias in cross-cultural assessment'. *European Journal of Psychological Assessment* 13: 29–37.

Van Rijckevorsel, Jan (1987) *The Application of Fuzzy Coding and Horseshoes in Multiple Correspondence Analysis*. Leiden: DSWO Press.

Van Rosmalen, Joost, Hester Van Herk and Patrick J. F. Groenen (2010) 'Identifying response styles: A latent-class bilinear multinomial logit model'. *Journal of Marketing Research* 47: 157–172.

Van Schuur, Wijbrandt H. and Henk A. L. Kiers (1994) 'Why factor analysis often is the incorrect model for analyzing bipolar concepts, and what model to use instead'. *Applied Psychological Measurement* 18: 97–110.

Watkins, David and Steven Cheung (1995) 'Culture, gender, and response bias: An analysis of responses to the Self-Description Questionnaire'. *Journal of Cross-Cultural Psychology* 26: 490–504.

Watson, Dorothy (1992) 'Correcting for acquiescent response bias in the absence of a balanced scale: An application to class consciousness'. *Sociological Methods & Research* 21: 52–88.

Weech-Maldonado, Robert, Marc N. Elliott, Adetokunbo Oluwole and Ron D. Hays (2008) 'Survey response style and differential use of CAHPS rating scales by Hispanics'. *Medical Care* 46: 963–968.

Weijters, Bert, Maggie Geuens and Niels Schillenwaert (2010) 'The stability of individual response styles'. *Psychological Methods* 15: 96–110.

Weijters, Bert, Niels Schillewaert and Maggie Geuens (2008) 'Assessing response styles across modes of data collection'. *Journal of the Academy of Marketing Science* 36: 409–422.

Wilkinson, A. Earl (1970) 'Relationship between measures of intellectual functioning and extreme response style'. *Journal of Social Psychology* 81: 271–272.

Wolfe, Rory and David Firth (2002) 'Modelling subjective use of an ordinal response scale in a many period crossover experiment'. *Applied Statistics* 51: 245–255.

Wong, Nancy, Aric Rindfleisch and James E. Burroughs (2003) 'Do reverse-worded items confound measures in cross-cultural consumer research? The case of the Material Values Scale'. *Journal of Consumer Research* 30: 72–91.

Index